A GUIDE TO SANDWICH GLASS

BLOWN TABLEWARE, PRESSED CUP PLATES AND SALTS

RAYMOND E. BARLOW
JOAN E. KAISER

PHOTOGRAPHS BY
  FORWARD'S COLOR PRODUCTIONS, INC.
  LEN LORETTE
  HUGO G. POISSON

EDITED BY LLOYD C. NICKERSON

BARLOW-KAISER PUBLISHING COMPANY, INC.

OTHER BOOKS BY RAYMOND E. BARLOW AND JOAN E. KAISER

The Glass Industry in Sandwich Volume 1
The Glass Industry in Sandwich Volume 2
The Glass Industry in Sandwich Volume 3
The Glass Industry in Sandwich Volume 4
A Guide to Sandwich Glass Pressed Tableware
A Guide to Sandwich Glass Whale Oil Lamps and Accessories
A Guide to Sandwich Glass Kerosene Lamps and Accessories
A Guide to Sandwich Glass Vases, Colognes and Stoppers
A Guide to Sandwich Glass Witch Balls, Containers and Toys
A Guide to Sandwich Glass Candlesticks, Late Blown and Threaded Ware
Barlow-Kaiser Sandwich Glass Price Guide

A GUIDE TO SANDWICH GLASS
BLOWN TABLEWARE, PRESSED CUP PLATES AND SALTS
First Edition

Copyright © 1993 by Raymond E. Barlow and Joan E. Kaiser

All correspondence and inquiries should be directed to

Barlow-Kaiser Publishing Company, Inc.
P.O. Box 265
Windham, NH 03087

in conjunction with

Schiffer Publishing Ltd.
77 Lower Valley Road, Rt. 372
Atglen, PA 19310

This book may be purchased from the publisher.

Try your bookstore first.

First Printing

Library of Congress Catalog Number 93-84876
International Standard Book Number 0-88740-553-3

Front cover: Photo 1334b Shell and Ribbing decanter, c. 1830. *Courtesy of The Bennington Museum, Bennington, Vermont.*
Back cover: Photo 1268 Beehive sugar bowl, c. 1830. Photo 1331 Mustard casters, c. 1828. Photo 1406 Sunburst (Star Bottom) cup plate, c. 1845. Photo 1457 Shell salt, c. 1845.

INTRODUCTION

A book that will guide you when you are in the process of buying, selling or appraising Sandwich glass is the most important tool you can own. This book is one of a series of guide books that describes in detail every type of glass that was produced in Sandwich, Massachusetts. All of its photos are taken from those that appear in Volume 1 of *The Glass Industry in Sandwich*, a larger book by the same authors. The identification numbers are the same as those in the larger edition, which allows easy cross-reference. (Guide books with photos from Volumes 2, 3 and 4 are available.)

The photos from the large edition, Volume 1, have been divided into two smaller guides. This guide contains the complete chapters on free-blown and blown molded tableware, pressed cup plates, and open and shaker salts. Another guide contains the chapter on pressed tableware, which includes the Lacy glass so closely associated with the term *Sandwich glass*.

The extensive categorization and illustration of Sandwich glass will make this guide valuable for field use. The prices in this guide reflect the market at the time of publication.

WHAT IS SANDWICH GLASS?

It is simple to define Sandwich glass. It was all glass that was produced within Sandwich, Massachusetts, a town on Cape Cod that was founded in 1637.

Glass production came to Sandwich in 1825, when Deming Jarves built and operated an enterprise that became world famous. He called it the Sandwich Glass Manufactory. It was incorporated as the Boston and Sandwich Glass Company in 1826. During the sixty-three years it was active, the factory produced an average of 100,000 pounds of glass per week. Yet this production was only *part* of the glass that should be attributed to Sandwich factories.

In 1859, the Cape Cod Glass Works was established and began to manufacture glass. For ten years, this second factory produced 75,000 pounds of finished glassware each week in competition with the Boston and Sandwich Glass Company. When this company closed, production once again started up in 1883 under the name of the Vasa Murrhina Art Glass Company. Because of manufacturing difficulties, very little of their spangle and spatter glass reached the market. However, the pieces that can be documented should be given Sandwich attribution.

There were several later attempts to manufacture glass in Sandwich after the closing of the Boston and Sandwich Glass Company factory in 1888. In that year, a group of glassworkers built a small glass works and called themselves the Sandwich Co-operative Glass Company. This venture lasted only three years, but its products are recognized as Sandwich glass.

Still another company, the Electrical Glass Corporation, started production in 1890, followed by the Boston and Sandwich Glass Company II, the Boston and Sandwich Glass Company III, and the Sandwich Glass Company. The Alton Manufacturing Company was the last to produce glass on this site. Its most notable product resembled Tiffany glass and was called Trevaise. Like its predecessors, the Alton Manufacturing Company was short-lived, and, in 1908, glass was no longer manufactured in Sandwich. *But the glass made by all of these small companies is recognized as Sandwich glass because of its geographical source.*

There were several other companies in Sandwich that worked on glass but did not make it. They cut it, etched it, engraved it, decorated it, and assembled it. The glass that they worked on, called *blanks*, was brought to Sandwich from factories in Pennsylvania. Regardless of what was done to the surface of this Pennsylvania product, *it cannot be called Sandwich glass*. Only glass that has been shaped while hot can be attributed to a particular factory.

This book deals only with the glass that was manufactured in Sandwich and is therefore entitled to be called Sandwich glass.

INVENTORY OF SANDWICH GLASS

No.	Description	Condition	Date Purchased	Amount	Date Sold	Amount

FREE-BLOWN AND BLOWN MOLDED TABLEWARE

1825–1908

Of all inventions attributed to Man by the early 1800's, only one took a combination of opaque substances and creatively changed them into a transparent product called *glass*. When fashioned into a container, it held everything but acid. When cut into window panes, it let light in while keeping water and wind out. When cut and polished into telescope lenses, it allowed astronomers to scan the skies. Used in eyeglasses, people could read who otherwise would have remained un-read and untaught. If its practical uses were not enough, it also provided beauty of color and form. Using sand and other common ingredients to stabilize and strengthen it and give it color and smoothness, Man had truly wrought a miracle with glass.

In order to mass produce this "miracle" in a quality accept-able to the public, in the 1800's a glass factory owner had to locate a sand pit capable of producing pure quartz sand. Large mines were found along the Maurice River in New Jersey and in the Berkshire Mountains of western Massachusetts. (See Chapter 10 in Volume 2 for the history and operation of the glass sand industry in western Massachusetts.) The sand had to be washed of all impurities, dried to a pouring consistency and transported to the mixing room of the glass house that would put it to use. Other dry raw materials were mixed with the sand resulting in a mixture called a *batch*. At Sandwich, most batches were for a high quality glass that was obtained by adding a quantity of metallic red lead that was made from oxygenated pig lead ground under water, then dried to a very fine powder. A basic formula suitable for a furnace fired by wood, as the Boston and Sandwich Glass Company furnaces were during its infancy, was published in *The Cabinet Cyclopedia; Useful Arts* by Reverend Dionysius Lardner printed in Philadelphia, Pennsylvania, in 1832.

White sand	100 parts
Red lead	50 to 60
Pearl-ash	30 to 40
Oxide of arsenic	0–75 to 1

According to Lardner, a different mixture was used in a furnace fired by coal; the proportion of red lead was increased, resulting in a finished product that was softer, a little less durable but more brilliant.

White sand	100 parts
Red lead	80 to 85
Pearl-ash	35 to 40
Nitre	2 to 3
Oxide of manganese	0–6

The colorless, transparent end product was called *flint glass*, because, in years preceding the use of metallic lead, colorless glass was made from pulverized flint, a very hard subspecies of quartz that when struck by steel produces a spark. Flint glass was called *crystal* in some countries, a term carried over to the present day, especially in relation to cut glass. When colored glass was needed, similar formulas were used, adding to each batch the ingredient or ingredients necessary to turn the glass to the desired color while in the process of melting. Even though red lead was also a key ingredient in formulas for colored glass, it was the transparent, colorless glass that was referred to as *flint glass* in glass company catalogs and price lists. (Editor's note: To add to the confusion of glass collectors, the transparent, colorless *flint glass* was also termed *white glass*, while glass that was opaque white was known as *enamel*.) To a six hundred pound batch, the following materials were added to obtain certain colors as listed by English glassmaker Apsley Pellatt in his book *Curiosities of Glass Making*, 1849.

Soft white enamel—24 lbs. arsenic, 6 lbs. antimony
Hard white enamel—200 lbs. putty (tin and lead)
Blue transparent—2 lbs. oxide of cobalt
Azure blue—6 lbs. oxide of copper
Ruby red—4 oz. oxide of gold
Amethyst or purple—20 lbs. oxide of manganese
Common orange—12 lbs. iron ore, 4 lbs. manganese
Emerald green—12 lbs. copper scales, 12 lbs. iron ore
Gold topaz—3 lbs. oxide of uranium

Of course, glassmakers had their favorite formulas that worked for them under their factory's special conditions. Each glass factory employed people skilled in chemistry who im-proved and refined the formulas over the years. When the authors were digging at the site of the Boston and Sandwich Glass Company, it was interesting to unearth an unbelievable number of deliberate variations of a single color. For example,

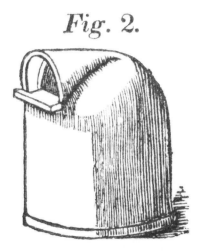

Clay furnace pot in which flint glass was melted. This "*Fig. 2.*" and the following illustrations were taken from Reverend Dionysius Lardner's *The Cabinet Cyclopedia; Useful Arts* published in Philadelphia, Pennsylvania, in 1832.

Blowpipe illustrated as "*Fig. 3.*" by Lardner and described as a "hollow iron rod or tube".

Glass blower elongating bubble of glass on end of blowpipe.

Pontil rod described by Lardner as a "punt, or pontil".

there were over fifty transparent and opaque shades of blue obtained by varying the amount of cobalt added to the batch to obtain the color and varying the amount of other minerals to obtain degrees of opacity. The wide variation held true for all colors manufactured in Sandwich although the color range in blue was by far the most extensive. The fact is that blue was the cheapest to produce.

In the glass factory mixing room, each batch was made ready by constant turning of the sand after the other ingredients in the formula were added. At this time, *cullet*, which was recycled glass made from a like formula, could be incorporated into the mixture. Cullet was obtained from several sources. Much of it came from the factory itself as waste glass that was separated from articles that were hand tooled. As much as two-thirds of the glass used to blow shallow dishes and wine glasses was waste, sheared from their upper portions when rims were formed. This glass was dropped into a cauldron of hot water that shattered it into smaller pieces. The pieces were milled to an even texture and stored in bins until needed in the mixing room. Cullet was also purchased directly from other factories and from middlemen.[1] Cullet was a necessary commodity that brought 3 cents a pound on the open market. It was included at that price in glass company inventories.[2]

When the mixing was completed, the batch was transported to the furnace room to be shoveled into clay pots that hung around the inside perimeter of the furnace. According to Deming Jarves in his book *Reminiscences of Glass-making*, his earliest Sandwich furnace held eight hundred pounds of glass in each of eight pots. After the pots were filled, the opening in each was temporarily bricked up. Gradually over an eighteen to twenty hour period, the massive fire built below the pots liquefied the sand mixture. Then the bricks were removed from the opening of each pot. The surface of the melted glass, now glowing orange from the heat, was skimmed to remove impurities called *gall*. The molten glass was ready to be shaped into a usable article.

An eight-pot furnace furnished glass for four *shops*, as each group of glassmakers was known. A *gatherer*, usually a young man not yet skilled in the art of shaping an article, approached the molten glass with a blowpipe, a hollow iron rod about five feet long. One end was dipped into the glass and turned several times to gather a small gob of glass. When a large gather was needed, the rod was exposed to the air to cool the gob slightly, then inserted into the pot again so that a larger portion would adhere. Upon removal from the pot, the gatherer carried the blowpipe to the head glass blower, who continually rotated the blowpipe to keep the gather from sagging and dropping to the floor. The head glass blower was called a *gaffer*. He held the blowpipe with the glass end down to lengthen the gob beyond the end of the blowpipe, and used his skill to blow the gob into a primitive bubble. This was the first step in making a free-blown or blown molded article and was the only step required for the manufacture of witch balls and cover balls as pictured in Chapter 8 of Volume 3.

Meanwhile, a *servitor*, a glassmaker who served the gaffer, had picked up a *punt*, also termed a *pontil rod*. This rod was approximately the same shape as a blowpipe, but was smaller and lighter and had no hole through it. The servitor inserted it into the pot of hot glass, pulling out a small amount of glass on its very end. Quickly moving to the working area of the gaffer, he placed the hot glass-covered end of the pontil rod against the reheated surface of the blown bubble opposite the blow-pipe. (To keep the glass at a flexible working consistency during these stages of manufacture, the gaffer or servitor inserted the partially made article into a *glory hole*, a small hole built into the furnace for the purpose of reheating.) The two hot surfaces united, securing the bubble onto the pontil rod. The gaffer tapped the blowpipe to break it free of the bubble. He could now hold the bubble by the pontil rod as he sat in his chair to shape the article.

The chair had arms on which the gaffer supported the pontil rod as he continued to rotate it back and forth and a flat working surface called a *marver* on which the bubble could be rolled to smooth its surface, so named because in earlier days a slab of marble had been used for this purpose. (Marble was superseded by a flat iron plate, yet the term remained in use.) The blown bubble was shaped into its final form by the use of an assortment of simple tools such as a *procello*, metal spring tongs with which the bubble was opened up, drawn out or pinched, and a *battledore*, a wooden paddle used to flatten. When the gaffer was satisfied with the size and form of his product and the rim was sheared and folded if required, the article was cracked free of the pontil rod leaving a rough scar on the bottom that we call a *pontil mark*. A *sticker-up* or *taker-in* boy was called to carry the item on a pronged stick to an annealing oven.

The annealing of glass was as important a process as the blowing of it. The article's progress through the tunnel of an annealing oven, or *leer*, was watched closely. The leer was heated by wood and a constant temperature maintained that took stress out of the glass yet did not cause overheating and a resultant sag. The glass entered the leer by being placed on iron pans which were drawn through the tunnel by a system of chains. Its temperature decreased as it reached the far end, where the articles were removed from the pans by a taker-in boy. From this area, finished articles were sent to the packing room. Unfinished articles were sent to the cutting shop to have pontil scars smoothed and designs cut, or to the engraving and decorating departments.

Working alongside the gaffers who were adept at completely making glass articles by free blowing and hand tooling were gaffers in nearby shops who were skilled in blowing glass into patterned molds. Writers and collectors have struggled for years to find a proper title for this method of glassmaking. Deming Jarves described it as "blown molded glass or that which was blown into hinged iron molds". The term *blown molded* appears in the Sandwich Glass Manufactory sloar book in which an accounting of the items produced by each shop was recorded.[3] Glass blowers' molds ranged in complexity from one-piece, open dip molds into which possibly only the lower third of a glass bubble was dropped, to two-, three- and four-section hinged molds with closed-in necks. A hinged mold had handles by which an apprentice opened it. The opened hinged mold was placed on the floor with the apprentice squatting beside it to close it around an elongated bubble inserted by the gaffer standing overhead. The gaffer blew into

Annealing oven, or leer, through which finished glass was drawn to cool it evenly and remove stress. This "*Fig. 9.*" and the preceding illustrations were taken from Reverend Dionysius Lardner's *The Cabinet Cyclopedia; Useful Arts* published in 1832.

Glassworker in his chair holding a blowpipe in his left hand as he rotated it to maintain the form of the glass elongated bubble. His assistant held a pontil rod with a disk of glass that will become a foot. When the two glass units attach, the glassworker will use the tool in his right hand to crack the elongated bubble away from the blowpipe.

With the blowpipe detached from the now-open elongated bubble, the glassworker held the pontil rod in his left hand and rotated it as he shaped the glass into its required configuration by means of a procello held in his right hand.

Procello, a hand tool resembling tongs used to expand and contract glass into its final form.

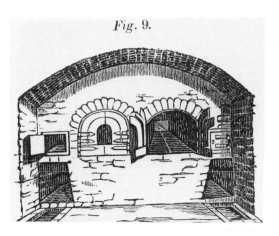

the blowpipe and with air power forced the glass against the mold conforming it to its shape. When the gaffer was satisfied that his bubble of glass filled the mold completely and a cooling period of fifty or sixty seconds had elapsed, his helper opened the mold and the article still attached to the blowpipe was removed. The gaffer then took his place at his chair and marver, his servitor helped him transfer the molded glass from the blowpipe to the pontil rod and the finish work continued as before.

In order to facilitate the mass production of an enormous inventory line of glassware, factory employees utilized unpatterned hinged molds that served as pre-formers. This eliminated a few of the time-consuming steps of expanding and pinching the bubble as well as insuring that like items would be reasonably consistent in form and capacity. Authors Barlow and Kaiser emphasize that pre-formed articles were so completely hand-tooled after removal from the iron or wood preformers that no sign of soft mold seams remained. It is therefore impossible at times to determine when a pre-former was used. It is certain, however, that all patterned and unpatterned molds and all unpatterned pre-formers used at glass factories in Sandwich were full-size molds, meaning that the fully expanded bubble pressing against the mold was the full size of the completed article. *Glassware that was blown into part-size molds and expanded by the blowpipe after removal, thereby muting their patterns, was not manufactured by any glass factory in Sandwich.* Neither was it the policy of Sandwich factories to enhance the beauty of mass produced blown glass by applying excess decoration in the form of lily pads, threading and rigaree. (However, decorative threading and rigaree became part of production in later years.) The goal of Deming Jarves was to refine each step in the manufacturing process to eliminate waste of motion and materials. His glass companies produced quickly-made utilitarian items for the masses that could be easily packed and shipped for worldwide distribution. We doubt whether the few intricately-contrived glass money boxes with applied rigaree and free-formed peafowl were meant to stray far from the Sandwich area.

If you visit a small glass house today, you will observe that the methods by which blown glass is formed have changed but little with time. Although a modern furnace maintains the melted batch at an even temperature and electric eyes open the pots and glory holes, very few changes have taken place in the design of the blowpipe, pontil rod and hinged molds. Full-size patterned metal molds are still in use. Unpatterned wooden molds are used as pre-formers that send out a puff of white smoke when hot glass touches them. The wooden molds must be replaced every six months because of scorching.

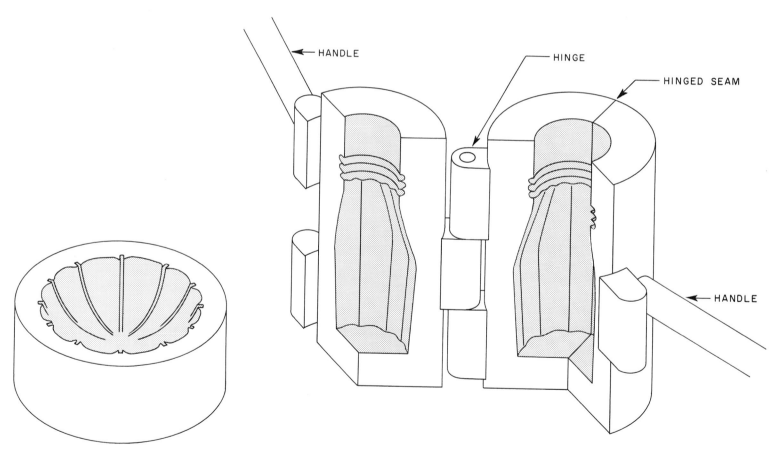

Fig. 9   Molds in which glass was blown to give it form and pattern. On the left is a shallow one-piece dip mold. A bubble of glass on a blower's pipe settled into the mold as lung pressure forced the glass to conform to the pattern. A mold such as this was used to make the Flute lamp font in photo 2006. It left no seam marks on the finished object. On the right is a three-section hinged mold with one section opened to reveal the form of a ribbed mustard caster. The two closed sections were also hinged. The two handles allowed a servitor or apprentice to close the mold around an elongated bubble of glass and open it after the bubble was inflated to conform to the pattern. Two- and four-section hinged molds were also used, depending on the simplicity or complexity of the form and/or pattern. Soft vertical marks from the mold seams are on the finished object, sometimes pronounced when a worn mold no longer closed properly.

Because there has been no change in the methods of blowing glass into form, the ability to make reproductions is constantly present. The collector must be ever alert to this fact. When you see what appears to be an old style of glass suddenly cropping up in several antiques shows, flea markets and shops, be aware that there is in the glass industry at all times the desire to make reproductions. Although most placed on the market are originally presented to the public as reproductions, there is always the unscrupulous individual who feeds "repros" into the antiques pipeline as genuine.

A case in point came to light in 1973 when Dwight P. Lanmon, Robert H. Brill and George J. Reilly wrote an article in the *Journal of Glass Studies* entitled "Some Blown 'Three-Mold' Suspicions Confirmed". Information contained in the report was released to the general public in the January 1983 issue of *The Magazine ANTIQUES*. Under the title "Unmasking an American glass fraud", Mr. Lanmon, Director of The Corning Museum of Glass in Corning, New York, related the experience of George S. McKearin and his daughter Helen McKearin, a tale unmatched in the history of collecting American glass. George and Helen McKearin were the authors of the widely-accepted book *American Glass*, which was published in 1941 and is still in print fifty years later as *The Glass Industry in Sandwich* goes to press. In 1934, the McKearins were convinced by what appeared to be unquestionable documentation that a collection of clear and colored blown molded patterned glass belonging to George Mutzer, a glassmaker who had worked in Philadelphia, Pennsylvania, was genuinely old. Mutzer's father Gottlieb and his grandfather Frederick had also worked glass. Mutzer had sworn in a notarized affidavit that his grandfather had made the glass offered to the McKearins. Because the McKearins had seen identically patterned glass in the Boston area, they attributed the Mutzer pieces to the Boston and Sandwich Glass Company even though the Mutzer name could not be connected to the Sandwich glass industry. The McKearins purchased George Mutzer's "family" glass. At least nine of the pieces were pictured in *American Glass* and at least six in their subsequent book *Two Hundred Years of American Blown Glass*.

The classification system established by George and Helen McKearin for the identification of blown molded patterns that appears in *American Glass* is widely used by collectors. Line drawings illustrate one article in each of the patterns that had been seen by them in their many years of dealing in and writing about antique glass. The McKearins separated all of the patterns into five groups designated by Roman numerals I to V. Each Roman numeral is preceded by a "G", which simply stands for "group".

GI   Bands of vertical, diagonal and twisted ribbing.

GII   Bands of vertical and diagonal ribbing combined with diamond diapering and other minor elements such as herringbone. A few of the patterns imitate English and Irish cut designs of the period.

GIII   Bands of vertical, diagonal and twisted ribbing combined with diamond diapering, sunbursts and other minor elements such as herringbone. Sunbursts also have their equivalent in English cut patterns.

GIV   Pointed and rounded arches, originally called *flutes*, and other minor fern-like elements.

GV   Pronounced rounded ribbing and arched ribbing combined with bold elements such as plumes, stars, rosettes, guilloche and peacock tail. These flamboyant patterns were termed *Baroque*.

As categorized in *American Glass*, the following were made by the Sandwich Glass Manufactory and/or the Boston and Sandwich Glass Company.

GI-   3 (Type 1, 2), 6, 7 (Type 1, 2, 3, 4), 9, 10, 11, 12, 13, 14, 24, 29.
GII-   1, 5, 11, 12, 13, 16, 18, 21, 22, 33, 37.
GIII- 2 (Type 1, 2), 3, 4, 5, 6, 7, 8, 9, 12, 13, 14, 15, 16, 17, 18, 19, 20, 21, 22, 23, 24, 25, 26, 27.
GIV- 2, 3, 6, 7.
GV-   1, 2, 3, 4, 6, 8, 9, 10, 12, 13, 14, 17, 18.

Returning to the problem of the Mutzer reproductions, Mr. Lanmon identified them as follows.

American Glass
Plate 103, Nos. 7, 8 GIII-5
Plate 110, No. 8 GII-18
Plate 125, Nos. 1–5 GIII-5
Plate 127, No. 6 GIII-5
Two Hundred Years of American Blown Glass
Plate 9, No. 3 GII-18
Plate 10, No. 2 GIII-5
Plate 10, No. 3 GIII-6
Plate 19, No. 2 GIII-5
Plate 68, No. 5 GIII-6
Plate 87, No. 5 GIII-5

The Mutzer pieces were acquired by The Corning Museum of Glass, where, based on their unusual colors and forms, personnel continued to doubt authenticity. Research by Dwight Lanmon and his associates, including chemical analysis, concluded that the Mutzer and other related pieces that had come onto the antiques market had been manufactured no earlier than the mid-1920's. An interview with Philip Glick, the Clayton, New Jersey, dealer who had originally brought the Mutzer pieces to the McKearins' attention, revealed that the dealer believed they were reproductions made in Philadelphia, possibly at the Gillinder factory that employed both Gottlieb and George Mutzer. It is evident that the Mutzer family was responsible for the eventual placement of fakes in the collections of advanced glass scholars and several major museums.

A similar group of reproductions in blown molded geometric patterns that can fool the unwary was made by the Clevenger brothers of Clayton, New Jersey. The three brothers descended from a long line of glassmakers but fell on hard times during World War I. According to Adeline Pepper in her book *The Glass Gaffers of New Jersey*, they made a practice beginning in 1926 of collaborating with a Clayton antiques dealer and determining which pieces of antique glass could be sold in the antiques market if they were reproduced. The antiques dealer not only agreed to sell the product, but financed the building of the Clevenger glass furnace in operation by 1927. New molds were made by a Milville, New Jersey, mold maker. Although the Clevengers and their dealer/agent advertised "Finest Reproductions of Pressed and Blown Glass", American glass scholar and author Ruth Webb Lee publicly called attention to the Clevenger line. The brothers and their dealer friend parted company in the 1930's and the Clevengers' new adviser was none other than Philip Glick, the

Clayton dealer who had called the Mutzer pieces to the attention of the McKearins! Documentation proves that reproduction of pieces in the GIII-5 pattern were still being made in 1950.

The two groups of reproductions are only a small part of the reproductions available now. From time to time, other glass factories have copied blown molded patterns, sometimes at the request of major museums to sell in their gift shops. Some are excellent in molded form, but are in colors that for the most part were not used at the Sandwich Glass Manufactory and Boston and Sandwich Glass Company during the years when this style of tableware was in production. Whether reproduced by the Mutzers, Clevengers or other glass works throughout the Twentieth Century, they can be identified as reproductions if you look for certain telltale signs: The impressions made by the molds are well defined; there is little or no wear from extended use. Hand work that must be done after articles are removed from molds is poorly executed. Rims of pitchers have no graceful curves but are sheared horizontally and have a quickly formed spout that is too small. Generally speaking, handles are not adequate for the weight of the pitcher and its contents; the pitchers are not intended for hard use at the hands of a family or in a public eating place as were Nineteenth Century creams and jugs. Reproductions are made strictly as show pieces. The lines of "repros" are static because the articles were annealed in new leers with good temperature control; thus they do not show the sagging and irregularities characteristic of early 1800's manufacture.

By the late 1830's, the method of forcing hot glass into a mold with a metal plunger improved dramatically. A larger percentage of Sandwich production was accomplished by a mechanical pressing machine instead of lung power and a blowpipe. But it is a mistake to believe that the blowing of glass was curtailed. Throughout the 1840's and 1850's, shops that had been blowing glass continued to do so, making heavy blanks for cut colognes, lamp shades and globes and tableware. As the demand for less breakable pressed glass increased, new furnaces were built and new shops were hired, manned by people experienced in the skill of pressing. The production of blown molded glass and press molded glass continued simultaneously.

The acceptance of kerosene as fuel for lighting devices created a demand for new styles of glass lamps and chimneys in the 1850's. When the Cape Cod Glass Works began to produce in 1859 (see Chapter 3 in Volume 3), it took the manpower of both factories to satisfy the lamp market. Although the mass market was depressed during and after the years of the Civil War, the need for lamp glassware carried the industry through those difficult times. Glassworkers returning from battle faced a backlog of orders for lamp bases and fonts. It was an ideal working requirement for the men in Sandwich. Shops skilled in the mechanics of pressing into molds pressed lamp bases and shops that blew into molds made fonts. (See Volume 2, which is devoted to lamps and accessories.) Both manufacturing techniques continued in harmony until an unstable market and the death of Deming Jarves caused the closing of the Cape Cod Glass Company in 1869 (see Chapter 4 in Volume 3). In the late 1860's, a top management decision was made at the Boston and Sandwich Glass Company when competition from Pennsylvania houses forced the reduction of pressed glass production of tableware in favor of a highly refined method of manufacturing blown molded unpatterned tableware inex-

pensively.

The newly developed glass blowing system was the result of ongoing improvements to the molds in which the glass was blown. Manufacturing experts such as the Boston and Sandwich Glass Company's head machinist Hiram Dillaway and the Mount Washington Glass Company's Samuel R. Bowie devised ways by which the elongated glass bubble after having been blown into the mold was mechanically rotated inside the mold while still in a molten condition to eliminate marks that had been left by seams between the hinged sections of the old style molds in which the bubble remained stationary. On February 22, 1870, Hiram Dillaway was issued patent No. 100,127 by the United States Patent Office for such a mold made of graphite. As stated by Dillaway, the manufacture of a graphite mold was an invention that had been patented in the United States as No. 91,946 by Jean Baptiste Lhote of Paris, France, on June 29, 1869. Lhote assigned his patent to Sewall Henry Fessenden of Boston, Massachusetts, who succeeded Deming Jarves as agent of the Boston and Sandwich Glass Company.[4] Dillaway, free to adapt molds made of graphite to his own specifications, designed a graphite mold in which the inner surface touched the blown bubble of glass in only four places by sections that had spaces between them. "It will readily be seen that when the bottle is blown in the mold and is rotated, its surface will be brought to the requisite circular form at all points, though the glass is not wholly surrounded by the molding surface."

Beyond eliminating mold marks, the new types of molds were perfected to allow the gaffer to produce exactly the same item, duplicated time after time, without the hand tooling that caused variations one to another. Because there was less stretching and pulling, the surface had a brilliant finish. To the industry as a whole, the tableware blown during the later years was known as *bubble glass* and the last twenty years of Boston and Sandwich Glass Company production was devoted to this method. A newspaper clipping found by the authors in a scrapbook belonging to the family of Henry Francis Spurr, superintendent of the factory, with the dateline "Sandwich, Mass., Oct. 2, 1882" stated, "In the blowing department there are twelve shops—forty-four men". This was shortly after a time when it is known that the company employed a total of only seventy-five hands. (Spurr's years in Sandwich are recorded in Chapters 1 and 2 of Volume 4.) The resultant ware without pattern was decorated, engraved and etched with a variety of attractive designs. (In addition to the photos in this volume, see Chapters 11 and 15 in Volume 4.) Many of the late blown pieces were embellished by the application of claw feet, reeded handles and decorative prunts as photographed by the Boston and Sandwich Glass Company for a catalog believed to have been printed in 1874 and available to collectors as a reprint. Unadorned by engraving or etching, the ware served as blanks for the manufacture of Overshot (Frosted Ware as shown in Chapter 6 in Volume 4) and Threaded Glass (see Chapter 13 in Volume 4).

All flint glass companies worked closely with pewterers, tinsmiths and brass founders who supplied metal trimmings for glass objects. The opening of one such supplier was announced in the *Old Colony Memorial*, a Plymouth, Massachusetts, newspaper, on November 3, 1827.

Taunton, October 24. A manufactory of Britannia Ware, operated by steam, and owned by Messrs. Babbitt, Cross-

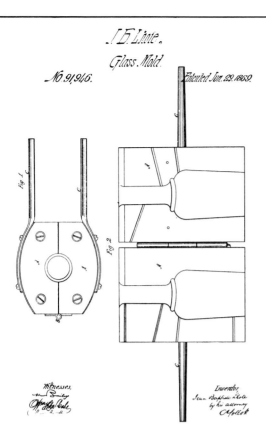

J.B. Lhote,
Glass Mold.

No. 91,946.

Patented Jun. 29. 1869.

Fig. 1

Fig. 2

Witnesses,

Inventor,
Jean Baptiste Lhote
by his attorney
C. Pollok

Jean Baptiste Lhote's patent No. 91,946 for an improvement in molds for glass made from graphite, dated June 29, 1869. Lhote assigned it to Sewall Henry Fessenden, agent of the Boston and Sandwich Glass Company.

United States Patent Office.

JEAN BAPTISTE LHOTE, OF PARIS, FRANCE, ASSIGNOR TO SEWELL HENRY FESSENDEN, OF BOSTON, MASSACHUSETTS.

Letters Patent No. 91,946, dated June 29, 1869.

IMPROVEMENT IN MOULDS FOR GLASS FROM GAS-CARBON OR GRAPHITE.

The Schedule referred to in these Letters Patent and making part of the same.

To whom it may concern:

Be it known that I, JEAN BAPTISTE LHOTE, of Paris, France, have invented certain new and useful Improvements in the Manufacture of Moulds for Moulding Glass or like Material; and I hereby declare the following to be a full, clear, and exact description of the same, reference being had to the accompanying drawings.

My invention consists in manufacturing the body of moulds for moulding glass, or like material, from the material which is formed in the interior of gas-retorts, and which is called "graphite," or "carbon," or "corrosion."

This material may be employed either in its natural state, or it may be agglomerated.

When I employ it in the state of agglomeration, I pulverize it, and I boil it for about half an hour, more or less, in neat's-foot oil and ammonia, say twenty-eight ounces of neat's-foot oil and seven ounces of ammonia; or the graphite, after being pulverized, may be agglomerated by an agglutinant, such as molasses, for example, say one part of molasses to three parts of powdered graphite.

I place this paste in a cast-iron tube, opening on a hinge and well luted. I submit it to a heat of 1,470° to 1,830° Fahrenheit, for about eight hours, more or less.

I then withdraw it from the fire, allow it to cool, remove the luting, open the tube, and take out the agglomerated graphite.

I do not limit myself to the preparation above described, for I can employ any binding-material which will agglomerate the graphite to form the mould.

When I employ the graphite in its natural state, as it comes from the retort, I dispense with the pulverization and agglomeration. I cut and work it so as to obtain the mould directly in its mass, the form of which mould will vary according to the article to be blown therein.

When moulds are required to blow articles of large size, I join, or connect, by screws or otherwise, several pieces of the graphite, so as to obtain a mass sufficiently large to form the mould.

In the annexed drawings—

Figure 1 represents in plan a graphite mould.

Figure 2 shows the mould open.

The mould is in two parts A A, which open on a hinge, B.

A strong piece of sheet-metal may be passed round the two parts of the mould; but this metal may be dispensed with, and the inner ends of the two arms, or handles, C C, for opening and closing the mould, may be secured by screwing directly to the graphite.

The interior configuration of the mould may be made to correspond with the form of any object desired to be moulded.

To prevent oxidation and rust, the sheet-metal before named and the arms C C may be galvanized; and having now described the nature of my invention, and the manner in which the same is or may be carried into effect,

What I claim, and desire to secure by Letters Patent, is—

1. Manufacturing the moulds, as hereinbefore described, from the graphite, or material which is formed in the interior of gas-retorts.

2. Manufacturing the moulds by pulverizing the graphite, and then agglomerating it by a binding-material, as hereinbefore described.

3. Manufacturing the moulds by cutting and working the graphite, in its natural state, into the required form, as hereinbefore described, without pulverizing and agglomerating it.

4. Manufacturing the moulds, especially when required to be of large size, by joining or connecting several pieces of the graphite, as hereinbefore described.

5. As a new manufacture, moulds made of the graphite, or material which is formed in the interior of gas-retorts, either in its natural state or agglomerated, substantially as specified.

In testimony whereof, I have signed my name to this specification before two subscribing witnesses.

J. B. LHOTE.

Witnesses:
RICE W. HARRIS,
C. LAFOND.

United States Patent Office.

HIRAM DILLAWAY, OF SANDWICH, MASSACHUSETTS.

Letters Patent No. 100,127, dated February 22, 1870.

IMPROVED MOLD FOR FORMING BLOWN GLASSWARE.

The Schedule referred to in these Letters Patent and making part of the same.

To all whom it may concern:

Be it known that I, HIRAM DILLAWAY, of Sandwich, in the county of Barnstable, and State of Massachusetts, have invented an Improved Mold for Forming Blown Glass Bottles and other Glassware; and I do hereby declare that the following, taken in connection with the drawings which accompany and form part of this specification, is a description of my invention, sufficient to enable those skilled in the art to practice it.

This invention relates particularly to the construction of glass molds, in which the molding surfaces are formed of "graphite," "gas carbon," or "corrosion" of gas retorts, as shown in the United States Patent No. 91,946, though the invention is also applicable, to greater or lesser extent, to common metal and wood, and to stone-glass molds.

Ordinarily, glass molds, for forming round bottles and other blown ware, circular in section, are made with hinged jaws or members, the interior surfaces of which, when the mold is shut, form a matrix, fitting to the whole circular surface of the bottle or other article in process of formation.

In my invention, instead of making the mold of two or more jaws, which, when closed together, form a matrix, I construct the mold of several pieces, leaving between each two adjacent molding faces an open space. These separate pieces I prefer to make of gas-retort carbon or "corrosion," and I fasten each directly to the inner surface of one or the other of the open-and-shut jaws, or to suitable stocks fastened to the jaws.

My invention consists, primarily, in a glass mold for forming blown-round bottles and similar ware, having its molding surfaces composed of separate pieces, placed at intervals in the jaws, or so that their molding surfaces do not join.

The invention also consists in making a mold of pieces of gas carbon or gas-retort graphite, each of which pieces is separate from the others, all being united to the jaws to form the mold.

The invention further consists in making a mold with pieces, each of which is removably attached to the jaws, so that the same jaws may be used for reception of dies for the formation of an indefinite number of molds, instead of requiring a separate number of molds for each, and also so that small pieces of graphite or other material, otherwise useless, may be used in making up the mold.

The drawings represent a mold embodying my improvements.

A shows a plan of the mold.

B, a section on the line x x.

C, a horizontal section on the line y y.

a a denote two jaws, hinged at one end, as seen at b, and having handles c at their other end, for opening and shutting the mold.

Within or to the inner surfaces of the jaws a are

of which, in radial planes through the most inwardly parts thereof, are concentric at all parts in the same horizontal plane with the axial line of the mold when the jaws are closed.

The blocks do not abut when the mold is closed, but are made narrow at their molding faces, and these faces may be curved or circular in cross-section, to correspond with the circular form, in corresponding section, of the bottle or other articles formed or shaped in the mold, or they may be straight in cross-sectional planes, as seen at A, or may even be made angular at their molding edges, edges, or surfaces.

For the number of pieces thus arranged I prefer four, but two or any other greater number may be used.

It will readily be seen that when the bottle is blown in the mold and is rotated, its surface will be brought to the requisite circular form at all points, though the glass is not wholly surrounded by the molding surfaces.

The molding pieces may be made of metal or wood, as in common molds, or of steatite or other stone, but I prefer to make them of the material previously mentioned, namely, gas-retort carbon, or gas "corrosion," cutting each piece of this material to the proper shape, as shown in the drawings, and fixing it directly to the inner surface of the jaw, by screws e, as shown at D, or making it dovetailing in cross-section, and securing it in a dovetailing mortise or recess, in a stock, f, as shown at A, B, and C.

By making the mold with open spaces, I am enabled to make use of thin or narrow pieces of material, like graphite, large and perfect pieces of which cannot easily be obtained; and whatever material be used, there is much less molding surface to be turned or planed down than when the mold is made with a continuous surface.

I claim a mold, for forming or shaping bottles and other blown glassware, circular in section, having its molding surface formed on the inner faces or edges of pieces or blocks, with open spaces between them, substantially as described.

Also, forming each jaw of a mold of a series of pieces of gas-retort carbon, or gas corrosion, having spaces between them, each of which pieces forms one of the faces of the mold, substantially as shown and described.

Also, in combination with the jaws a a, the molding-blocks or pieces, removably attached thereto, substantially as described.

Also, in combination with the jaws and molding-blocks or pieces, the stocks f, for receiving the blocks, substantially as shown and described.

HIRAM DILLAWAY.

Witnesses:
JOSEPH L. ROGERS,

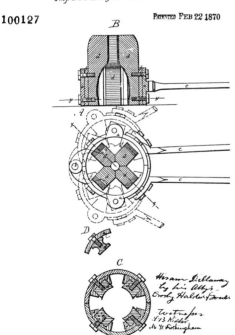

Hiram Dillaway.
Imp'd Mould for Glass-ware.

100127

PATENTED FEB 22 1870

B

Hiram Dillaway
by his Att'ys
Crosby Halstead & Gould

Witnesses
A. B. Kidder
Jn. H. Frothingham

Machinist Hiram Dillaway's patent No. 100,127 for an improved graphite mold for forming blown glassware, dated February 22, 1870. Glass blown into the mold touched the inside surface in only four places and was rotated to eliminate seam marks.

Applications to the United States Patent Office were accompanied by a working model of the invention. This is a wooden model of machinist Hiram Dillaway's patent No. 100,127 for a graphite mold. Dillaway was from a Boston family of commercial mold makers. He became head of the machine shop at the Boston and Sandwich Glass Company and worked under Deming Jarves at the Cape Cod Glass Company and the Mount Washington Glass Works as well. *Courtesy, Sandwich Glass Museum, Sandwich Historical Society*

man & Co. has been in operation in part, for a few weeks in this village.....This is, we believe, the second or third establishment for the manufacture of this kind of ware in the country; and is the first manufactory of any kind which has been attempted to be operated by steam in this vicinity.

Invoices of the Taunton Britannia Manufacturing Company dated April 17 and May 11, 1832, show the sale of four-, five- and six-bottle caster frames to the Boston and Sandwich Glass Company. Sandwich glass casters are found in stands signed Israel Trask, a pewterer in Beverly, Massachusetts, and pewterer Roswell Gleason, whose business connection with the glass company is documented by papers dated September 1, 1839, preserved at the Sandwich Glass Museum, Sandwich Historical Society. A report as part of the United States Census signed by Deming Jarves on March 26, 1832, states that $35,000 annually was paid out for plated Britannia, brass, copper and tin trimmings to glass. "The material is foreign, but the articles are all made here."[5] This situation was often reversed; glass was sold from the Sandwich factory before metalwork was in place to be combined with the necessary furnishings by other wholesalers and retailers in distant locations. During years of use, breakage caused newer glass casters to be replaced in older frames and older glass casters to be transferred to newer stands. Thus it becomes impossible to decide with authority that all pieces of a complete caster set when purchased in the antiques market are original to each other.

When referring to the McKearin classification system as you study the photos, it should be remembered by collectors of Sandwich glass that the blown molded patterns recorded represent the products of all flint glass houses operating in the United States. *The Glass Industry in Sandwich* pictures only patterns that have been documented as Sandwich without question. Since the McKearin classification was adopted, more patterns have been identified as undeniably American and some of them Sandwich. Because of the nature of the

McKearins' numbering system, new patterns cannot be incorporated into it. This is a fault of any classification system, whether it be McKearin for blown molded glass, Lee-Rose for cup plates or Neal for Lacy salts. It is a judgment call at best, and our comment should not be taken as an affront to the dedicated scholars who preceded us.

THESE SIMPLE HINTS WILL HELP YOU IDENTIFY SANDWICH FREE-BLOWN AND BLOWN MOLDED TABLEWARE

When glass has been blown into a patterned mold, its inner surface conforms to the pattern on its outer surface and mold marks are generally smooth.

All patterned molds used at Sandwich were full size. Articles that were expanded after they were removed from part-size molds are not Sandwich.

Tableware blown into patterned molds during the early years was not embellished with applied lily pads, rigaree, chains or threading that would inhibit packing and shipping for worldwide distribution. Sandwich glass was made for hard use in the home and in public eating establishments on land and at sea.

All Sandwich sunburst patterns have a lower band of vertical ribbing or herringbone. On some reproductions, sunbursts are at the bottom.

Blown molded geometric patterns in dark colors that occur naturally because of impurities in the glass sand were produced in bottle factories. Decanters and inkwells in dark amber, olive green, brown and black were not made in Sandwich.

Look carefully for the monogram, or "logo", on reproductions that were made for museum gift shops; it is sometimes well hidden within the pattern. Examine for the place where a "logo" may have been removed. Be aware, however, that glass houses manufacturing reproductions for museums have been known to replace a mold section with one that had no monogram so they can feed new glass into the antiques market at the expense of the museum that paid for the mold.

Suspect pieces that do not follow the lines of known antique forms.

Beware of pieces in unusual colors that were not mass produced in the early 1800's.

Study the reprint of the Boston and Sandwich Glass Company catalog from the 1870's.

NOTES TO CHAPTER 7

1. On November 9, 1827, Deming Jarves wrote to William Stutson, "Will endeavor to get you cullet."
2. A document from the Falmouth Glass Company in Falmouth, Massachusetts, marked "materials on hand" is preserved at the Sandwich Glass Museum, Sandwich Historical Society. Dated January 25, 1851, it listed "1800 pounds bought cullet" and "2000 pounds made cullet" both at 3 cents a pound. (A brief history of the Falmouth works can be found in note 8 on page 35 of Volume 2.) A monthly statement of P. M. Lund in account with the Union Glass Company in Somerville, Massachusetts, dated March 30, 1867, shows Mr. Lund, who purchased merchandise from the Union works, credited with 2077 pounds of cullet at 3 cents a pound.
3. Beginning July 30, 1825, John Snowden's shop made "103 blown molded no ring decanters" and "73 5" blown molded dishes".
4. An interesting sidelight is that Jean Baptiste Lhote's letters patent was witnessed by Rice W. Harris. According to Boston and Sandwich Glass Company records, the Board of Directors read several letters from Rice W. Harris of London at their March 1866 meeting. Harris was a member of a family that operated English glass houses and may have been the same Rice Harris that was paid $5000 to teach Sandwich workers how to make opal glass, according to an undated note in company files.
5. *Documents Relative to the Manufactures in the United States Collected and Transmitted to the House of Representatives by the Secretary of the Treasury.*

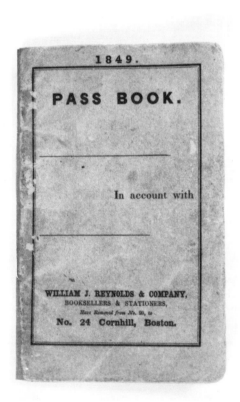

Benjamin Haines was a gaffer in charge of Shop No. 2 when the Sandwich Glass Manufactory began production in July 1825. In later years, he used as his notebook a blank 1849 passbook. In it he sketched a variety of articles and noted specifications for their manufacture. Several of the items correspond with like items produced by his shop as documented in the factory sloar book. With grateful appreciation to the Sandwich Glass Museum, we print Haines' notebook in its entirety and suggest that you refer to it when you study the photos that follow. *Courtesy, Sandwich Glass Museum, Sandwich Historical Society*

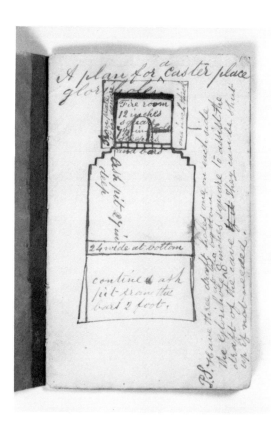

The first three pages of Benjamin Haines' notebook show plans for "a caster place glorihole". Haines' faint numbers are on the right corner of each right page as was the custom during his time. *Courtesy, Sandwich Glass Museum, Sandwich Historical Society*

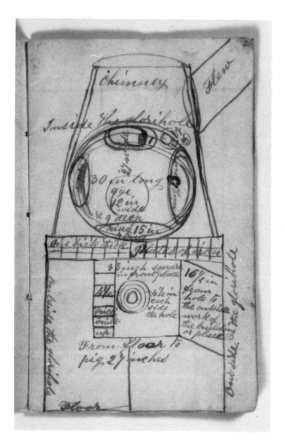

Page 2 shows a cross section of the inside of the glory hole, which was a separate furnace in which glass articles were reheated as necessary for hand tooling. *Courtesy, Sandwich Glass Museum, Sandwich Historical Society*

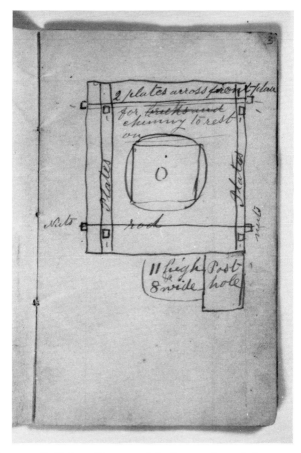

On page 3, Haines illustrated the iron rods and plates on which the glory hole chimney rested. Metal work such as this was manufactured by the Manomet Iron Company in North Sandwich (see pages 162–165 in Volume 3). *Courtesy, Sandwich Glass Museum, Sandwich Historical Society*

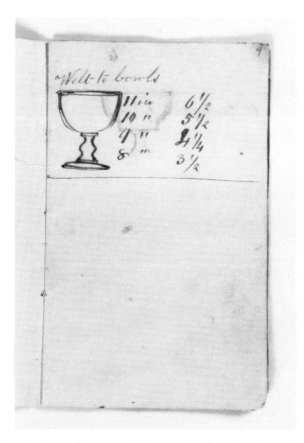

Page 4 shows the rounded form of a deep bowl attached to a high foot. Note that the word "compote" was not in glass terminology. *Courtesy, Sandwich Glass Museum, Sandwich Historical Society*

Opposite page 5, Haines illustrated an ogee nappie with specifications for its making. Abbreviated "O. G." by Haines, *ogee* is an architectural description of concave and convex. *Courtesy, Sandwich Glass Museum, Sandwich Historical Society*

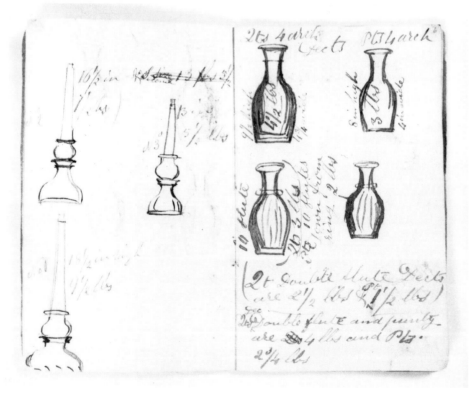

Decanters with arches, flutes and punties are illustrated on page 6. The authors are not able to ascertain the purpose of the footed pedestals shown opposite in three sizes. Some items in this notebook may very well be on tables at antiques shows unrecognized as Sandwich. *Courtesy, Sandwich Glass Museum, Sandwich Historical Society*

Page 7 shows a lamp font on a nondescript base and a jug of one-quart capacity. On the opposite page, note descriptions "Grecian Border" and "flute and hooped". *Courtesy, Sandwich Glass Museum, Sandwich Historical Society*

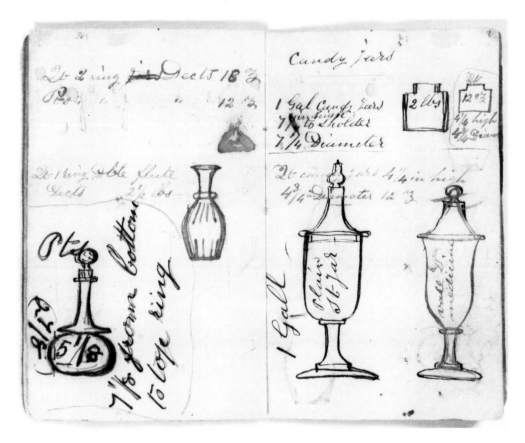

The candy jars on page 8 are erroneously called "apothecary jars", but they held candies, sweetmeats and small cakes in confectionery stores. *Courtesy, Sandwich Glass Museum, Sandwich Historical Society*

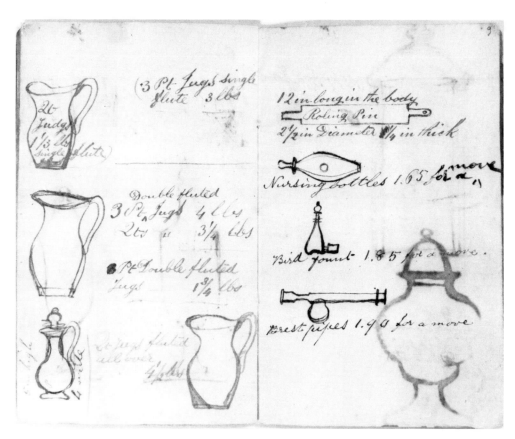

Page 9 shows the variety of household articles that were made by flint glass companies. It was not necessary to make them from the very best flint glass batches, but from batches of lesser quality that utilized a percentage of cullet. *Courtesy, Sandwich Glass Museum, Sandwich Historical Society*

Page 10 shows four candy jars and five covers. Haines' attention to dimensions shows that their form was finalized by hand tooling and measured by simple instruments to conform to factory standards. It is anatomically logical that the knopped stem above the foot was called a *leg*. *Courtesy, Sandwich Glass Museum, Sandwich Historical Society*

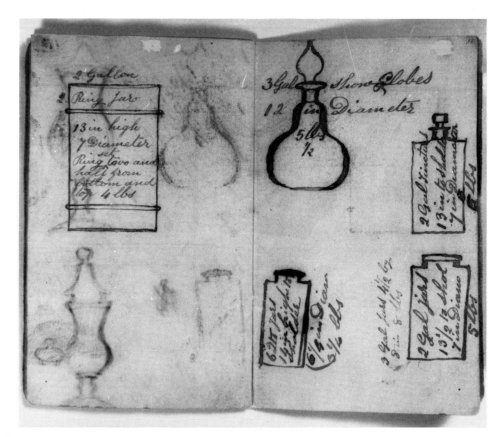

Page 11 illustrates articles used by apothecaries. In an era when many people could not read trade signs, a show globe filled with colored water indicated that drugs for medicinal purposes were sold on the premises. The stoppered bottle held tincture, a medicinal substance in alcohol. The ring jar shown opposite had two rings applied around its body after it was blown. Occasionally the rings were blue. *Courtesy, Sandwich Glass Museum, Sandwich Historical Society*

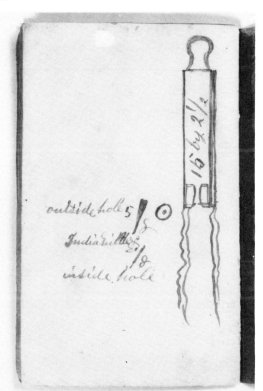

The last page of Benjamin Haines' workbook presents a challenge to collectors. The authors believe what was meant by an "India fitting" was a brass tube with two inscribed rings, as shown in the drawing, that was usually used as the fitting to hold a candle or peg lamp in an India shade, a type of hanging hurricane shade similar to that shown on a Three-Dolphin standard in photos 2144–2146, 4049 and 4050. *Courtesy, Sandwich Glass Museum, Sandwich Historical Society*

"Fig. 1. FLINT-GLASS MANUFACTORY" as illustrated in the ninth edition of *Encyclopedia Britannica* published in 1878.

1253 BLOWN TOY DECANTER WITH HAND-FORMED RIBBED BALL STOPPER

(a) Decanter 3" H. x 1½" Dia.
(b) Stopper 1⅛" H. x ½" Dia.
(c) Combined size 3½" H. x 1½" Dia. 1825–1830

This piece is the same size as the toy decanter shown in photo 3315. The stopper indicates early vintage. Toys for children were a major production line, so it is not unusual to find ones that were made throughout the period of glassmaking in Sandwich. These little blown decanters without stoppers can often be found at antique bottle shows for less than $5. When identified as Sandwich glass and fitted with an appropriate stopper, value escalates into the hundreds of dollars.

1254 BLOWN CRUET WITH HAND-FORMED TAM-O'-SHANTER STOPPER

(a) Cruet 5⅛" H. x 2⅜" Dia.
(b) Stopper 1⅛" H. x ⅞" Dia.
(c) Combined size 5⅝" H. x 2⅜" Dia. 1825–1830

Cruets were used on the table for vinegar and oil. This cruet was blown and tooled into shape, the bottom reworked to set flat on the table. The neck was reheated and hand tooled to form the lip on which rests a stopper. Collectors refer to stoppers made by combining a ball finial with a disk as "tam-o'-shanter stoppers". However, sloar book records list them simply as cruet stoppers. Unpatterned blown cruets are more difficult to find than their blown molded counterparts, which were molded in several patterns to make them highly saleable. A study of stoppers that were dug from the site of the Boston and Sandwich Glass Company can be found in Chapter 6 of Volume 3. A similar dark blue cruet and stopper was reproduced by the Metropolitan Museum of Art. It appears in a 1988 catalog.

1255 BLOWN BOTTLE WITH SLIDE STOPPER

(a) Bottle 9¾" H. x 4" Dia.
(b) Slide stopper 2½" H. from finial to lip 1830–1870

This bottle was purchased in Sandwich in 1947 with the slide stopper in place. The bottle is so plain that no one can be sure of its origin without documentation. However, many fragments that match the neck and bottom were dug from the site of the Boston and Sandwich Glass Company. The slide stopper matches those dug from the site as shown in photo 3224, making the authors one step closer to determining that this plain bottle was made in Sandwich. It is likely that a thinly blown bottle such as is shown here, with no bar lip to absorb the pressure of the cork, had another type of stopper at the time it was made.

1256 BLOWN MOLDED BAR DECANTERS WITH CUT FLUTES
(a) Ring 10¾" H. x 4½" Dia.
(b) No ring 11" H. x 4½" Dia. 1840–1860
Early records show that decanters with plain necks were called *no ring decanters*. Both types were made at Sandwich. The ring on the shoulder of decanter A was used to strengthen the weakest part of the decanter. The heavy rim was called a *bar lip*. Bar lip decanters were never fitted with glass stoppers. They had metal "slide stops", most of which had glass or clay marbles to cover the opening as shown in photos 1255 and 3222–3224. Note how the color shades from light to dark. As the gaffer drew out the neck, the glass thinned until it became almost clear. If he thought that the decanter was weak in that area, he applied the ring. The flutes were cut after the decanter was annealed. *Courtesy of The Toledo Museum of Art (Acc. No. 65.111 A&B)*

1257 BLOWN BUTTON STEM WINE
7½" H. x 2¾" Dia. at rim 1828
In the spring of 1828, Deming Jarves made plans to construct a second glass furnace at the Boston and Sandwich Glass Company. In anticipation of expansion, he hired gaffer Edward Haines, a young brother of Benjamin Haines who had been working in Manchester, England. His arrival in the United States was noted by Jarves in his June 10, 1828, correspondence to William Stutson. "As young Haynes (sic) has arrived, he can have a chair of Kerne's (sic) next week." Haines family legend states that this stemmed wine with its many buttons was made by Edward as a demonstration piece while Jarves watched. Haines applied button after button to prove his experience until Jarves said, "That's enough. Put a bowl on it!" This whimsical piece certainly was not produced for the mass market—yet note how closely Nicholas Lutz paralleled this effort when in 1889 he built up the stem of the Threaded champagne shown in photo 3415. *Courtesy, Sandwich Glass Museum, Sandwich Historical Society*

1258 BLOWN EMERALD SHAPE CLARET
4¾" H. x 2⅞" Dia. 1865–1869
This very popular form was listed by the Boston and Sandwich Glass Company as an emerald shape claret in its 1874 catalog. James Danforth Lloyd, color expert at both the Boston and Sandwich Glass Company and the Cape Cod Glass Company, experimented with this purple color when he was at the Cape Cod works. He brought this claret home to study and decided that it was too drab a color to be a good seller, so it remained in his family's private collection. His descendants maintain that this claret is the only piece ever made in this color. Note the button-like wafer that separates the stem from the base. This was eliminated in later production. The emerald shape was made by the thousands in an array of other colors throughout the remaining years of the Boston and Sandwich Glass Company.

1259 BLOWN EMERALD SHAPE CLARETS

(a) 4½" H.
(b) 4⅝" H. 1870–1876

These clarets are also documented as having family ties to Sandwich glass-workers. The color would be considered opaque if the glass had been pressed into a mold to make a thick-walled vessel, but the pieces shown here were blown so thin that they assumed a fragile, translucent, eggshell appearance. They were also made in translucent green and translucent white. Note the slight variation in form between the two clarets. These differences would not prevent the clarets from being part of a matched set at the time of production and should not be a deterrent today. Refinements of manufacturing techniques, such as George Lafayette Fessenden's patent that follows, aided gaffers in creating blown holloware more alike in form and height.

G. L. FESSENDEN.
MANUFACTURE OF GLASS BOWLS, TUMBLERS, &c.
No. 184,604.   Patented Nov. 21, 1876.

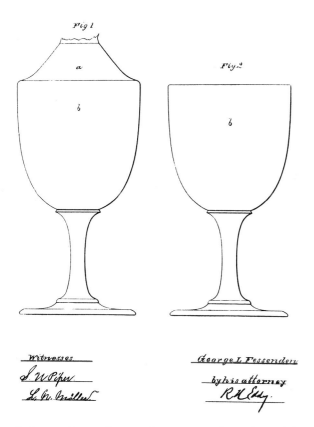

George Lafayette Fessenden was factory superintendent of the Boston and Sandwich Glass Company when he was granted patent No. 184,604 on November 21, 1876. Fessenden sought to reduce labor expense by blowing vessels into a mold, removing them from the mold, then annealing them before the upper portion of the bowl was cracked off and fire polished. A mold designed to delineate the rim where the cracking occurred insured the ware was even in height. Fessenden's years with the Sandwich company are recorded on pages 24–44 of Volume 3.

1260 BLOWN EMERALD SHAPE CLARETS

4½" H. x 2¼" Dia. 1876–1887

The refined form of this matched pair indicates manufacture at a time when mass production of Late Blown Ware was well under way. The thinness of late "bubble glass" made the color very faint except where the glass was thicker. The Boston and Sandwich Glass Company manufactured this type of glass in quantity in both clear and color. The clarets still exist in large numbers unrecognized by collectors as a Sandwich product. They can be found in transparent shades of red, canary, amber, blue and green. Colored bowls were also combined with clear stems and feet. Look for all of these variations with etched and engraved designs that can be authenticated by studying the designs in this series of books and in the 1874 Boston and Sandwich Glass Company catalog reprint.

UNITED STATES PATENT OFFICE.

GEORGE L. FESSENDEN, OF SANDWICH, MASSACHUSETTS.

IMPROVEMENT IN MANUFACTURE OF GLASS BOWLS, TUMBLERS, &c.

Specification forming part of Letters Patent No. **184,604**, dated November 21, 1876; application filed October 2, 1876.

To all whom it may concern:

Be it known that I, GEORGE L. FESSENDEN, of Sandwich, in the county of Barnstable and State of Massachusetts, have invented a new and useful Improvement in the Manufacture of Glass Bowls, Tumblers, or other articles of like character; and do hereby declare the same to be fully described in the following specification, and represented in the accompanying drawings, of which—

Figure 1 denotes an elevation of a goblet with its bowl blown in a mold. Fig. 2 is a side view of the goblet as finished.

My invention relates to the manufacture of bowls of glass, especially those of tumblers, goblets, wine glasses, and various other articles of like character.

In carrying out the invention, I first blow the bowl in a mold by the well-known process of glass blowing in a mold, in which case the bowl will be closed at the top, except there will be a blow-hole in the upper part of it, such closing of the bowl being as shown at *a* in Fig. 1.

After the bowl has been so blown it (with or without a foot fixed to it) is to be put into an annealing-furnace and there be annealed, and, after it may have been cooled, the top or superfluous part *a* is to be cut or cracked off from the rest, or part *b*, by a hot iron or other suitable means.

Such having been done, the bowl or part *b* is next to be plunged into the mouth of a glass-melting pot, while in a heated state, or into the flame of a "glory-hole," and there be submitted to a heat, such as will fuse and round the cut or cracked edge and fire-polish it, and the outer and inner surfaces of the bowl.

By this process tumblers or bowls may be made at much less expense, and in a better manner, and, with a finer finish, than by the old process, involving the opening, shearing off, and finishing of the bowl by hand, with the aid of tools. By my process, the molding of the bowl, and subsequently cutting or cracking off the superfluous part, and otherwise treating the whole as described, causes each bowl of a set or series to be of like size, which is a matter of much importance.

I claim—

1. My improvement in the art of making a glass bowl or article of glass having a bowl, such consisting in blowing the bowl in a mold, and next annealing such bowl, and, when cool, cutting or cracking off the cap or superfluous part, and finally submitting the rest (whether with or without a foot) to heat by means as described, so as to fuse the upper edge and round it, and fire-polish it, and also fire-polish the inner and outer surfaces of the article, all essentially as set forth.

2. As an improved article of manufacture, a glass bowl or article of glass, having a bowl made by the process described.

GEORGE L. FESSENDEN.

Witnesses:
C. H. LAPHAM,
C. H. CHAPOINT.

1261 BLOWN MOLDED TOOTHPICK DECORATED WITH MOSS ROSE
2¼" H. x 1⅝" Dia. 1895–1908

This unpatterned opal toothpick was blown molded by one of the small companies that attempted to continue the glassmaking industry at the Boston and Sandwich Glass Company site. The moss rose and painted ring on the rim match those of a vase belonging to descendants of decorators Mary and Ellen F. (Nell) Kelleher, sisters still listed as decorators in the *Bourne, Falmouth and Sandwich Directory* for 1900. When interviewed by the authors, long-time resident Lydia (Lila) Howland Peters remembered seeing Nell working at the "big factory". Discarded undecorated toothpicks were found in the factory yard. The moss rose was a favorite design often painted on opal plaques and dome shades at the turn of the century. Inexpensive novelty items were produced by the Boston and Sandwich Glass Company II (1895–1904), Boston and Sandwich Glass Company III (1904–1905) and the Sandwich Glass Company (1906–1907). A last feeble attempt at glassmaking was made by the Alton Manufacturing Company (1907–1909). The history of these companies is related in Chapter 4 of Volume 4.

1262 BLOWN SALVER
1⅜" H. x 9½" Dia. 1825–1870

"Of all of the articles of glass manufacture, none command a greater degree of attention than the article called the salver, and no other develops so pleasing and surprising effects in its processes. When seen for the first time, the change from a shapeless mass, the force with which it flies open at the end of the process, changing in an instant into a perfect article, all combine to astonish and delight the beholder." So wrote Deming Jarves in an article for the December 1852 issue of the *Journal of Mining and Manufacture* which was later included in his book *Reminiscences of Glass-making*. Today this piece would be called a "cake plate", but at the time of production it had other uses as well. When provided with a high foot rather than the low foot shown here, several with diminishing diameters were stacked to make a pyramid usually topped with a sweetmeat container. The pyramid held a variety of dessert confections and jellies from which a diner chose. The pyramid preceded the epergne (see Chapter 15 in Volume 4). When used singly, matching cake covers could be purchased as shown in the Cape Cod Glass Company's *List of Glass Ware* reprinted on page 110 of Volume 3. Both rims of this salver were folded under for strength, but the direction of the fold was left to the discretion of the gaffer.

1263 BLOWN BOWL ON HIGH FOOT
5½" H. x 4½" Dia. 1828–1835

The simple lines of early blown pieces can be seen in this footed bowl attributed to Charles Washington Lapham. Born October 25, 1809, Lapham would have been only fifteen years old when he was asked to gather the first piece of glass when the Sandwich Glass Manufactory opened on July 4, 1825. This was a common piece of tableware typically made in three units: a bowl with its rim folded out to give it strength, a button stem for a standard, and a circular foot. Footed bowls such as this were mass produced by all flint glass factories, so they cannot be attributed to a specific glass works without reliable documentation. *Courtesy, Sandwich Glass Museum, Sandwich Historical Society*

1264 BLOWN NAPPIE WITH PRESSED BASE
4⅝" H. x 6½" Dia., 2¾" Sq. base 1830–1845

This pressed square base with extended round corners was also used on lamps and candlesticks. It was pressed in a mold that was purchased from a commercial mold maker who supplied a number of glass factories with his product, so this base can be found on pieces made in the East and Midwest. The blown nappies varied in size. They were easy to make by simply blowing a glass bubble. The pressed base was attached to the side of the bubble that was opposite the blowpipe by means of the wafer that is visible in the photo. The blowpipe was broken away from the bubble and the bubble was reheated. When it was sufficiently hot, the glass was stretched into the desired nappie form that was reworked to form the rim. Reheated for the last time, the nappie was adjusted to stand straight. A slight twisting often took place which does not deter from value. Often one of a pair of footed nappies is twisted and one is not. They are still considered to be a matching pair.

1265 BLOWN SUGAR BOWL ON FOOT

(a) Bowl 4½" H. x 4⅛" Dia.
(b) Cover 2⅜" H. x 4⅜" Dia.
(c) Combined size 6½" H. x 4⅜" Dia. 1830–1835

This beautiful opaque silver blue sugar bowl belonged to Lillian Haines Tangney. Mrs. Tangney was the daughter of gaffer Edward Haines and the niece of Benjamin Haines. Family tradition attributes this piece to Benjamin, who was said to have made it about 1830. It is interesting to note, however, how closely it follows the lines of a sugar bowl that Jarves illustrated in orders accompanying his June 10, 1828, letter in which he informed Stutson of the arrival of Edward Haines from England. The foot of the bowl is a separate solid unit that was applied. The mark beneath the foot left by the pontil rod was polished in the cutting shop, a process termed *puntying*. The solid knob finial on cover B was also applied. It, too, has a polished pontil mark that is visible in the photo. A Sandwich glass article such as this is exceptionally rare and to find one is a challenge. With irrefutable documentation, expect to pay at least three times its price guide value. *Courtesy, Sandwich Glass Museum, Sandwich Historical Society*

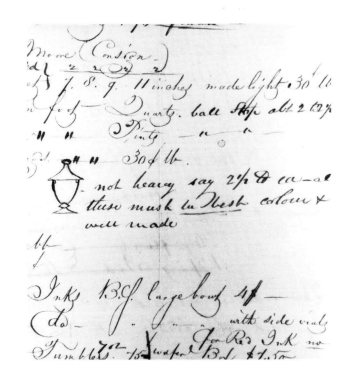

New York consignee Thomas D. Moore ordered "2 doz. Sugars on feet". Jarves included the order with instructions for their making in a June 10, 1828, letter to Stutson. "Not heavy, say 2½ lb. ea. All these must be *best* colour & well made". Except for the knop below the bowl, Jarves' drawing closely resembles the Haines sugar bowl above, which certainly is a "best" color. *Courtesy, Sandwich Glass Museum, Sandwich Historical Society*

1266 BLOWN JAM POT ON FOOT

(a) Pot 4" H. x 4½" Dia.
(b) Cover 2¾" H. x 4⅛" Dia.
(c) Combined size 6½" H. x 4½" Dia. 1830–1835

This jam pot is from the family collection of Charles Washington Lapham and, according to tradition, was made by him. Lapham was in his teens when he gathered the first piece of glass on opening day of the Sandwich Glass Manufactory in 1825. The well-formed dome of the cover made it possible to leave a spoon in the jam when the cover was in place. The cover, which has a folded, or *welted*, rim, rests inside the galleried rim of the pot. Its finial is the flat button form that was commonly used in its time but is seldom encountered and therefore seldom recognized today. Also common was the applied foot that appears to be too small in diameter to support the pot and its contents. The foot and button finial are the same as shown previously on the Haines sugar bowl. The combination of small foot and flat finial on the two well-documented Haines and Lapham pieces together with Jarves' drawing provide the collector with another valuable clue to the attribution of blown pieces to Sandwich. It is possible for today's glass blowers to duplicate these items, but new glass is rich in color, has high reflectivity and shows no signs of use. *Courtesy, Sandwich Glass Museum, Sandwich Historical Society*

1267 BLOWN SUGAR BOWL ON HIGH FOOT

(a) Bowl 5½" H. x 4⅞" Dia.
(b) Cover 4" H. x 4⅞" Dia.
(c) Combined size 8⅞" H. x 4⅞" Dia. 1828–1835
These early sugar bowls were made to take hard use. They had no handles, no rigaree, no pattern, no design. A shop was assigned the responsibility of making just the footed bowl. At another time, perhaps the next day or the next week, the same shop made the covers. Several types of covers might be made to fit the bowls. Some were steeple-shaped to allow a spoon to remain in the bowl, purchased by families who were accustomed to this practice. If family members used individual spoons for their sugar, a low cover sufficed. Sugar was a sticky yellow substance that caked up—not the white refined product of today. Covers were necessary on almost all food to protect it from flies, which were attracted from a considerable distance. When containers that held everyday staples were not in use, they were immediately removed from the table and placed in the safe (erroneously called "pie safe"). Bowl A was made in three parts that were combined while hot: the bowl, the knopped stem (interestingly called *leg* in Benjamin Haines' notebook), and the thick foot. The cover is flanged to fit inside the bowl. None of the rims were folded. The berry prunt on top of the uniquely-shaped finial is chipped. *The Bennington Museum, Bennington, Vermont*

1268 BLOWN BEEHIVE SUGAR BOWL

7½" H. x 5½" Dia. 1828–1835
Study the Beehive forms carefully. They illustrate one of the finest early manufacturing techniques perfected at Sandwich. It is possible that all blown Beehive pieces attributed to the Boston and Sandwich Glass Company were fashioned by William E. Kern, who first paid a poll tax to the Town of Sandwich in 1829. This sugar bowl belongs to the family of glass company machinist Hiram Dillaway and his son-in-law, color expert James D. Lloyd. The horizontal rings that vary in width were made by rotating the blown pieces against a pointed tool. Blown ringed pieces were made at other factories. A blue salt with very narrow rings is pictured by Adeline Pepper in her book *The Glass Gaffers of New Jersey*. In later years, a similar Ring pattern was made by blowing glass into a patterned mold. The later molded pieces are often mistakenly called "Beehive", but they are not scarce and should not command exorbitant prices (see Ring lamp font in photo 2278). When determining age and method of construction, look along the sides of the article for a vertical line where the sections of the mold were hinged together. If there are mold marks, the pieces were made at a later time. The finial on this very early cover was applied. After annealing, the finial was cut into facets.

1269 BLOWN BEEHIVE SUGAR BOWL OR JAM POT

(a) Bowl 5½" H. x 4½" Dia.
(b) Cover 3¾" H. x 3⅛" Dia.
(c) Combined size 8½" H. x 4½" Dia. 1829
This piece was made by William Kern for his sister Catherine on the occasion of her marriage to factory worker Frederick Eaton on December 27, 1829. It is the authors' opinion that Kern designed the steeple-shaped cover to allow a spoon to remain in the bowl when the cover was on. The inside of the cover has an opening that protrudes to the finial. Although a relatively large amount of glass was used in making this footed covered piece, the capacity of the bowl does not seem to equal the capacity of a matching cream. It is therefore possible that it may have held jam. Note the following photo. It shows the breakpoint between the rings where the cover meets the bowl, difficult to see when the cover is in place. *Courtesy, Sandwich Glass Museum, Sandwich Historical Society*

1270 UNITS OF ABOVE SUGAR BOWL OR JAM POT

Whether used for sugar or jam, care must be taken not to overfill the bowl. The cover has a deep rim that extends low into the bowl when the cover is in place. If the bowl is too full, the contents would stick to the cover and soil linens when the cover is placed on the table. Note the distance that a spoon handle should penetrate into the cover. The Nineteenth Century household was plagued with flies, making a cover a necessity rather than a luxury.

1271 BLOWN BEEHIVE CREAM

5" H. x 3¼" Dia. 1828–1835

The body of this cream was plain when first blown. A separate foot held by a pontil rod was fastened to the body. When the two units adhered, the ringed Beehive pattern was tooled by spinning the pontil rod and applying pressure with a hand tool. After the desired effect was obtained, the piece was reheated. The rim was sheared and the spout formed. A hollow handle was attached by first applying the side of its upper end to the body and then forming the tail at its lower end. When purchasing items of this quality, examine the body at the points where both ends of the handle were attached. Then check the handle itself where it is thinnest just above the crimps in the tail. Cracks often occur at these three points. Do not be persuaded into believing that any crack is a manufacturing flaw. *Courtesy, Sandwich Glass Museum, Sandwich Historical Society*

1272 BLOWN BEEHIVE CREAM OR SMALL JUG

6⅜" H. x 4" Dia. 1828–1835

The smallest pitcher in a given line of ware was a *cream*. Larger pitchers were called *jugs*, which ranged in size from slightly larger than a cream to capacious pieces for milk and water. Today it is difficult to determine the intended use of the flamboyantly executed piece in this photo. Compare the horizontal rings with the rings on the preceding cream. The same method of construction took place, but the rings are pronounced because more pressure was applied to give the piece added depth and clarity. A solid handle was applied after the body and foot were completed. When the spout was drawn out, the gaffer failed to give it depth, making it difficult to control the pour. This is a common complaint with early pitchers. For practical use, the large diameter foot may have made this piece unwieldy. *Courtesy, Sandwich Glass Museum, Sandwich Historical Society*

1273 BLOWN MOLDED PANELED CRUET WITH BLOWN TAM-O'-SHANTER STOPPER

(a) Cruet 6" H. x 2¾" Dia.

(b) Stopper 2" H. x 1⅛" Dia.

(c) Combined size 6⅞" H. x 2¾" Dia. 1835–1850

According to Webster's 1847 dictionary, a *cruet* was "a vial or small glass bottle, for holding vinegar, oil, &c." Some were made to be placed in stands. Others, such as this one, were designed to stand free on the table. This well-executed, twelve-sided cruet has a plain bottom. The neck ring was molded in one piece with the cruet, not applied later. The spots in the body are "pot stones" formed by a phenomenon that happened when the glass was melting. Alumina, an oxide of aluminum present in the clay from which the pot was made, separated from the inner wall of the pot. It combined with certain elements in the glass and solidified. Because the opaque stones expand and contract at a different rate than the glass itself, small fractures are often found around them. Inspect glass carefully for these defects when purchasing because value is greatly reduced. Even a small fracture will enlarge with time and may eventually destroy the piece. Note that the stopper was blown rather than hand-formed. As long as the stopper matches in color, either hand-formed or blown should be accepted as original. *Courtesy, Sandwich Glass Museum, Sandwich Historical Society*

1274 BLOWN MOLDED OCTAGONAL CASTERS

(a) Cruet 5⅞" H. x 2⅛" Dia.

    Wooden pattern for hexagonal stopper 2⅛" H. x 1⅛" Dia.

(b) Wooden pattern for caster 6⅝" H. x 2" Dia.

(c) Pepper 5⅝" H. x 2¼" Dia. 1835–1845

The solid wooden pattern in the center is a product of the first step in creating a metal mold in which cruet A and pepper C could have been blown. The wooden pattern for the hexagonal stopper, inserted into the cruet, served the same purpose. The patterns were made at the commercial mold maker's establishment. The mold maker sent one to each glass factory that ordered the matching mold. The patterns were stored at the glass factory and returned to the mold maker when a replacement mold was required. As you can see, both casters could have come from the same mold. To make the cruet A, the basic caster was removed from the mold and hand tooled to form a lip with two spouts from which to pour oil or vinegar. To make pepper C, the upper portion was simply sheared into a plain rim to accept a metal shaker cap. To make a matching mustard, the neck was expanded or a different mold with a wide diameter neck was purchased from the mold maker. Casters with their lower portion stepped in did not rest on their bottoms but were supported by metal rings as shown on the stand in photo 1284 or inserted into holes of a solid metal frame. For an example of the latter, see the toy version of octagonal casters in photo 3355. Both sizes were made in quantity by Sandwich and other factories.

1275 BLOWN MOLDED TWISTED CRUET WITH BLOWN TAM-O'-SHANTER STOPPER

McKearin GI-3 Type 1

(a) Cruet 5⅜" H. x 2½" Dia.

(b) Stopper 2⅛" H. x 1⅛" Dia.

(c) Combined size 6⅜" H. x 2½" Dia. 1825–1835

Twisted cruets were listed in the Sandwich Glass Manufactory sloar book in 1825 as early as the week of July 30. Repeated entries prove they were well received by the public. They are a form that was manufactured by other glass works prior to 1825, blown in molds purchased from commercial mold makers. The twists, or fine diagonal ribs to the left, were made from a pattern that was inscribed in the mold. The vertical mold seam can be seen in the photo on the right side of the cruet. Similar cruets were made in other molds that had one ring and no ring on the shoulder. This example has concentric rings on the bottom. The rim was tooled into a flat lip on which to rest a loosely fitting stopper. This stopper form is presently called "tam-o'-shanter", although they were listed as *cruet stoppers* in Sandwich Glass Manufactory and Boston and Sandwich Glass Company documents. Despite the fact that stoppers were often made on different days, they are usually well matched to the cruets in color. *Courtesy, Sandwich Glass Museum, Sandwich Historical Society*

1276 BLOWN MOLDED TWISTED CRUET
McKearin GI-3 Type 2
5¾" H. x 2½" Dia. 1825–1835
Deming Jarves' June 10, 1828, letter to William Stutson included an order from J. H. and H. L. Webb for "25 doz. twisted Cruets Blue White". (Editor's note: *White* denoted transparent, colorless glass.) This twisted cruet, now minus its stopper, is in the family collection of Annie Nye, a Boston and Sandwich Glass Company decorator who worked during the later years. The fine ribs that twisted to the left are molded into the piece. Mold marks extend vertically, well defined near the bottom, but faded on the reworked portion of the neck. Cruet bottles in various patterns are often called "toilet bottles". However, toiletries had a high alcohol content that demanded tight stoppers to prevent evaporation, whereas cruet stoppers fitted loosely and were interchangeable. They were not sent to the cutting shop to be machine fit to a particular bottle. This piece can be found in clear, blue and rarely amethyst. A light yellow-green twisted cruet with a matching tam-o'-shanter stopper is known.

1277 BLOWN MOLDED RIBBED TOY TUMBLER
McKearin GI-6
1⅞" H. x 1¾" Dia. 1830–1835
The pattern of shallow vertical ribs is the simplest of the blown molded patterns. The upper end of each rib in the GI-6 pattern forms a distinct arch. However, reworking and reheating the tumbler muted the pattern. Small tumblers such as this can be found at antiques shows and flea markets mixed in with Twentieth Century "whiskey tasters". They are easily identified as having been made during the early part of the Nineteenth Century, but attribution to the Boston and Sandwich Glass Company alone is impossible unless solid documentation accompanies the piece. *Courtesy, Sandwich Glass Museum, Sandwich Historical Society*

1278 BLOWN MOLDED RIBBED CASTERS
McKearin GI-7 Type 2
(a) Vinegar with hand-formed Waffle stopper 4⅝" H. x 1⅝" Dia.
    Stopper 1⅞" H. x 1" W.
    Combined size 5½" H. x 1⅝" Dia.
(b) Mustard fragment 3¼" H. x 1⅝" Dia. 1825–1830
Both bottles were made in molds that had twenty vertical ribs and unpatterned bases. The lip of vinegar A was formed by first folding the rim in and then flaring it. The hand-formed Waffle stopper sets low into the neck, but fits well and may be original. Mustard B was found at the factory site. Its lip was formed by shearing away the glass through the center line of the horizontal ring above the vertical ribs that is so clearly visible on the vinegar. The portion of the ring remaining was flared out to form a lip that was not folded. Despite this manufacturing difference, the bottles would be considered as matching when used in a caster set.

1279 BLOWN MOLDED RIBBED CRUETS WITH HAND-FORMED TAM-O'-SHANTER STOPPER

McKearin GI-7 Type 2
5¾" H. x 2½" Dia. 1825–1835

Here is an example of a pattern with vertical ribs that stop below a single horizontal ring. Collectors consider the rings to be a variation in pattern, but they served a purpose in their day by allowing the user to maintain a firm grip on a potentially oily surface. Cruet A is lying on its side to show how the ribs continue to the pontil mark. Other cruets have plain bottoms. All of the varieties in these photos were dug at the site of the Sandwich Glass Manufactory, which became the Boston and Sandwich Glass Company in 1826. This cruet with its tam-o'-shanter stopper was reproduced for the Sandwich Glass Museum by the Pairpoint Glass Company in Sagamore, Massachusetts. It is pictured in their 1990 gift catalog with a matching cream.

1280 BLOWN MOLDED RIBBED CRUETS WITH HAND-FORMED TAM-O'-SHANTER STOPPER

(a) Clear *McKearin GI-7 Type 3*
Cruet 5⅞" H. x 2¾" Dia.
Stopper 1½" H. x 1" Dia.
Combined size 6⅜" H. x 2¾" Dia.
(b) Blue *McKearin GI-7 Type 4*
Cruet 5¾" H. x 2½" Dia.
Stopper 2" H. x 1" Dia.
Combined size 7¼" H. x 2½" Dia. 1825–1835

Deming Jarves established a very old industry in a new location. Blown molded patterns such as these were previously used and would continue to be used in numerous flint glass and bottle glass factories. From records, we can establish with some authority when a pattern was first used in Sandwich. Fragments dug at the factory site verify production. But it is difficult to determine when production ceased because little-used patterns that were out of favor with buyers were kept on hand for special orders. Ribbed patterns of one form or another were used throughout Sandwich's glassmaking years. Note the variations in cruets alone. Cruet A has one molded horizontal ring with vertical ribs extended above it. Cruet B has two horizontal rings with ribs between and above them. Ribs that extend much beyond the upper ring are often blurred by reheating to form the lip. Note the pontil rod scar on the bottom of cruet C.

1281 BLOWN MOLDED RIBBED CASTERS

McKearin GI

(a) Mustard with blown molded acorn stopper
3⅝" H. x 2" Dia.
Stopper/cover 2" H. x 1⅞" Dia.
Combined size 4⅝" H. x 2" Dia.
(b) Cruet with hand-formed tam-o'-shanter stopper 4¼" H. x 2" Dia.
Stopper 3¾" H. x 1" Dia.
Combined size 5" H. x 2" Dia.
(c) Pepper 5" H. x 2" Dia. 1828–1835

Dictionaries and documents from the 1820's that were studied by the authors differentiate between *caster*, defined as a vial or phial for the table, and *bottle*, which held liquor. In later years, the term *caster bottle* or *castor bottle* was used. Regardless of the number of holes in a caster frame, the consumer had three choices of caster forms from which to choose. Any combination that was needed was correct. Extra casters were bought that could be interchanged depending on the meal being served. Note that the diameter increases halfway up each caster. At this point, the casters hung free when inserted into the rings of a caster stand. The mustard, cruet and pepper were each blown into a mold that had round shoulders and thirteen wide, rounded ribs. If you find the same pattern without the change in diameter at the center, the casters were usually used in stands that do not rotate.

1282 BLOWN MOLDED FLAT-RIBBED PEPPER CASTERS

McKearin GI-9, GI-14
(a) 4¾" H. x 1⅞" Dia.
(b) 4¾" H. x 2" Dia. 1828–1835

Here are two forms of the same pattern pepper. Pepper A can be used only in a stationary frame, while pepper B can also be used in a revolving frame. Each has ten flat ribs that begin at the bottom and end at three horizontal rings around the neck. The ribs are divided by a V-groove. The peppers match in diameter from the bottom to halfway up the side. The ribs on pepper A continue uninterrupted to the neck to make a clean-lined piece. The ribs on pepper B were cut deeper into the mold to form a ledge by which the pepper could be suspended from the holes of a revolving stand. (The V-grooves continue uninterrupted.) Other than the change in diameter, the peppers are alike. Both have brass caps that push onto plain rims.

1283 BLOWN MOLDED FLAT-RIBBED PEPPER CASTER

McKearin GI-9, GI-14
4⅜" H. x 2" Dia. 1828–1835

Articles that overheated in the annealing leer to a temperature that distorted their shape were thrown away. When dug from the glass works site years later, they are excellent proof that a certain form and pattern were manufactured there. Note the sag of the horizontal rings at the neck. Heat rises, so it was always the top of an item that melted first in the leer. The bottom is in perfect condition. Discoloration that can be seen throughout the pepper is from years of being buried in the ground. Unlike the previous peppers, this one has a horizontal ring around the bottom. Note the curved configuration from the ringed bottom to the midpoint ledge that supported the pepper in a stand. The upper half again curves gently toward the neck. A similar caster with straight sides was also made at the Boston and Sandwich Glass Company. It also has ten flat ribs and horizontal rings at the bottom and neck.

1284 BLOWN MOLDED FLAT-RIBBED CASTERS IN FIVE-HOLE STAND

McKearin GI-9, GI-14
(a) Cruets with pressed flaring hexagonal stopper 4⅜" H. x 2" Dia.
 Stopper 2¼" H. x 1" Dia.
 Combined size 5⅞" H. x 2" Dia.
(b) Tall mustard with pressed cover 4⅛" H. x 1⅞" Dia.
 Cover 1⅜" H. x 1⅝" Dia.
 Combined size 5¼" H. x 1⅞" Dia.
(c) Short mustard with pressed cover 3¾" H. x 2" Dia.
 Cover 1⅜" H. x 1⅝" Dia.
 Combined size 4⅞" H. x 2" Dia.
(d) Pepper 5" H. x 2" Dia. 1828–1835

All of the casters turn freely in this five-hole stand. There are five small rings into which the cruet stoppers are placed when the cruets are passed around the table. Revolving stands remained in style long after blown molded casters were made. The pepper and two cruets match in form and pattern. The mustards match in pattern but vary in form. The mustard on the left has a shorter shoulder, two horizontal rings, an elongated neck and a flat lip on which to rest a cover. The mustard on the right has three horizontal rings and a galleried rim. Both mustard casters have the same pressed cover with a slot to accept the handle of a wooden mustard stick. Each cover has twenty round ribs ending as scallops at the rim and a nipple finial. Mustards were also used for relish, horseradish, honey and jelly. Vinegars held soy sauce. The entire caster set, or at least the casters containing condiments that should be protected from flies, were stored in a food safe between meals.

1285 WOODEN PATTERN FOR BLOWN MOLDED FLAT-RIBBED CASTER

McKearin GI

1828–1835

Wooden patterns of numerous blown molded and pressed glass patterns seldom enter the antiques market. When they do, they are a welcome addition to a glass collection especially when a matching glass piece is located. The wooden pattern served as a tool for the mold maker. They were stored at the glass factory and, when a new or replacement mold was needed, they were taken out of inventory and sent to the mold maker. After the mold was completed, the mold and the wooden pattern were sent to the glass factory. The flat ribs are wider than depicted previously. A likely factory name may have been *Panel and Groove* or *Flute and Groove*. See the similar pressed pattern on the base of a Tulip vase in photo 3024. *Courtesy of Richard A. Bourne Co., Inc.*

1286 BLOWN MOLDED RIBBED PEPPER CASTER

McKearin GI-24

4¼" H. x 1¾" Dia. 1825–1835

Cylindrical pepper casters such as this were carried to the table in caster frames. Matching salt shakers were not used because salt caked up and was too coarse to pass through the perforated metal cap. Depending on the needs of the household, a caster frame may have held several pepper casters that contained different types of pepper. This is a pleasing pattern of horizontal rings around the bottom, a band of diagonal ribbing to the right, four horizontal rings, a band of vertical ribbing, a muted horizontal ring surrounding the shoulder and a band of vertical ribbing extending toward the neck. The rim was welted to the inside to strengthen it. Its perforated metal cap was never in place because the caster was discarded at the factory. The following photo shows why.

1287 SECOND VIEW OF ABOVE PEPPER CASTER

Here is the other side of the pepper shown previously. It was dug from the Boston and Sandwich Glass Company site, where it had been discarded because four pieces of cullet did not melt properly. They were not seen when the hot glass was gathered from the pot, so they became incorporated into the side of the pepper. The disfigurement showed only as the glass cooled. The chunks interrupted the pattern, rendering the article unsaleable even as a second. So it was thrown away, dumped as fill at the factory site to be resurrected by author Barlow. Items with this type of manufacturing defect are sought by collectors, who are willing to pay more for one-of-a-kind examples.

1288 BLOWN MOLDED FLUTED AND HOOPED DECANTER

McKearin GI-29

5½" H. x 3" Dia. 1825–1835

Lists of glassware to be made for specific wholesalers and consignees were sent to Sandwich from Jarves' Boston office. They are intriguing because they contribute detail missing from the sloar book. For example, on June 10, 1828, Jarves sent Stutson an order to be sent to J. H. and H. L. Webb for dozens of "flint, fluted and hooped" ship tumblers, straight-sided wines, lemonades (tumblers with applied handles), jelly glasses (for dessert jellies), quart and pint decanters and champagnes. That description fits the pattern of the small decanter in this photo, the wide vertical ribs being "flutes" and the horizontal rings being "hoops". It is a pattern that lends itself to the holloware forms itemized in the Webb order. This piece is not complete. It should have a stopper. Any of several Sandwich stopper patterns would be acceptable, but the color must match. (See Chapter 6 in Volume 3 for a study of Sandwich stoppers.) Fragments of this pattern were dug at the site of the Boston and Sandwich Glass Company. Several forms of tableware in this pattern were manufactured at the Saratoga Mountain Glass Works and the Mount Vernon Glass Works, both in New York. The pattern was adapted to a "cut Flute and Hoop" design photographed on page 23, row 1 of the 1870's Boston and Sandwich Glass Company catalog. *Courtesy, Sandwich Glass Museum, Sandwich Historical Society*

1289 BLOWN MOLDED DIAMOND DIAPER PATTY-PAN

McKearin GII-1
¾" H. x 4¼" Dia. 1825–1835

Glass company records during the early 1800's listed dishes by form rather than use, so we may never know the exact purpose for which this shallow piece with flat sides was intended. The rayed center is highly crowned, bulged by the pressure of attaching a pontil rod. The flat diamond diapered sides slope upward just enough to prevent us from calling it a plate, but it could hold a small dessert such as a patty or a ratafia cake. The scar in the center is from cracking the pan from a pontil rod that held it while the rim was expanded and folded. Most dishes that held food had rims folded out and under so that their contents did not permeate the fold. The direction of the fold cannot determine origin. This pattern of rather large diamonds is not usually recognized on blown Sandwich pieces. It is generally associated with the New England Glass Company, but fragments dug from the Sandwich site prove it was also manufactured at the Boston and Sandwich Glass Company. Each diamond is faceted, a mold making technique common to pressed glass.

1290 BLOWN MOLDED DIAMOND DIAPER PATTY-PAN

McKearin GIII-1, Lee-Rose 3
¾" H. x 4" Dia. 1825–1835

The classification system established by George and Helen McKearin for the identification of blown molded geometric patterns as published in their book *American Glass* does not take into consideration the various ways by which diamonds were molded. At first glance, this "bottle green" plate-like pan resembles the one shown previously, but close inspection reveals that it was blown into a different dip mold. Each diamond has a dimpled center. Dimpled diamonds and faceted diamonds were both made in Sandwich as well as in other factories. Note the irregularity on the rim at the upper right. When the gaffer folded the rim around the pan to the beginning point, excess glass had accumulated. It was turned back into a pleat, giving the article individual identification. The piece in this photo is from the collection of Albert C. Marble and was included in Ruth Webb Lee and James H. Rose's *American Glass Cup Plates*. The suggestion that all small blown plates were cup plates is tentative at best, as authors Lee and Rose also note. The high kick-up in the center resulted in an uneven surface on which to rest a tea cup. *Albert C. Marble Cup Plate Collection, Worcester Historical Museum, Worcester, Massachusetts*

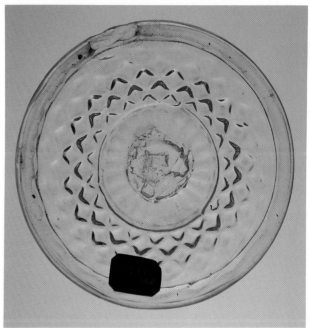

1291 BLOWN MOLDED DIAMOND DIAPER CRUET CASTER WITH HAND-FORMED WAFFLE STOPPER

McKearin GII-11
(a) Cruet 5" H. x 1⅞" Dia.
(b) Replaced stopper 1⅞" H. x 1⅛" W. 1825–1830

A *caster*, later also spelled *castor*, was defined by Noah Webster in 1847 as "a small phial or vessel for the table; as, a set of *casters*". The term *casters* was defined as "A stand with bottles for oil, vinegar, &c." Three forms were used in caster stands—a mustard, a pepper and a cruet. This cruet was made very early in Sandwich glass history. It has eight horizontal rings above a plain bottom. A band of diamond diapering bellies out, above which are five horizontal rings. When drawing up the glass to make the neck, the rings widened and were almost obliterated. You may find this caster with its lip welted up and in, as is this one, or out and under. This operation was at the discretion of the gaffer. Extra effort was expended to form a spout, although the bottle was also made with a plain lip. The hand-formed Waffle stopper is a replacement that sets too high in the neck, but its form is one of several correct for the cruet. It was pressed by the use of two patterned dies, one on each side of a pair of pincers. Diagonal lines were on one of the dies and, at right angles, diagonal lines were on the other die. The crossing parallel lines produced the waffle effect. Some glass companies referred to cruets as *vinegars*.

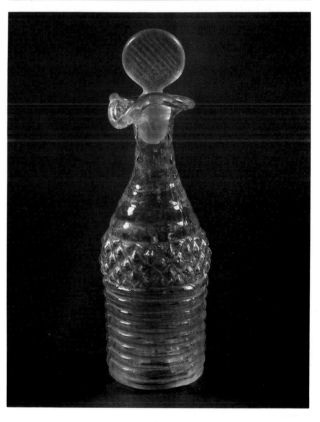

1292 BLOWN MOLDED DIAMOND DIAPER TOY TUMBLER

McKearin GII-16

1⅛" H. x 1⅝" Dia. 1825–1830

Colored blown molded Sandwich glass is rare and toys are doubly so. Small tableware pieces matching their adult-size counterparts in form and pattern were manufactured from the opening days of the Sandwich Glass Manufactory in 1825 to the dying years of the industry in the 1890's. The manufacture of glass toys was important because there was a ready market for tiny items that could be made from small pools of good glass near the bottom of the clay pots in which glass was melted. Assortments of toy items were wholesaled to retailers who sold them individually as playthings. See Chapter 10 in Volume 3 for more information about Sandwich toys. *The Bennington Museum, Bennington, Vermont*

1293 BLOWN MOLDED DIAMOND DIAPER

McKearin GII-16

(a) Toy tumbler 1¾" H. x 1⅝" Dia.

(b) Toy hat salt 1¾" H. x 2" Dia. 1825–1830

The pattern on these toys is a variant of the pattern classified as GII-16 by George and Helen McKearin in their book *American Glass*. The variant shown here does not have pronounced horizontal rings to separate the bands of vertical ribs and diamond diapering. The upper third of both pieces is unpatterned. Tumbler A is often referred to as a "whiskey taster", a Twentieth Century term that should not be used for Nineteenth Century toys. Glass company records listed *tumblers* for adult use and *toy tumblers* for children. There is no question in the authors' minds that many forms were made exclusively for children to use in play or at the table. Hat salt B is less than 2" high and was referred to as a *toy hat salt* in Sandwich Glass Manufactory and Boston and Sandwich Glass Company sloar books. Although alike in pattern, the bottom of the tumbler is plain and the bottom of the salt has concentric circles. The tumbler is discolored from blue glass that was on the end of a pontil rod that held it when the rim was sheared. *Courtesy, Sandwich Glass Museum, Sandwich Historical Society*

1294 BLOWN MOLDED DIAMOND DIAPER NAPPIE

McKearin GII-16

1⅛" H. x 5¼" Dia. 1825–1835

It is often said that shallow bowls, called *nappies*, were made by reworking glass blown in decanter molds. In the opinion of the authors, to rework a pattern that at one time was cylindrical would completely destroy it. We believe that molds in which shallow pans and nappies were made were designed for that purpose only. Note how perfectly the ribs surround the center. Not until the nappie turns upward does the pattern of diamonds become muted. By the time the rim was turned outward, the pattern completely disappeared. The base pattern of eleven concave dots is one of many found on New England Glass Company and Sandwich blown molded pieces. It may be the pattern referred to as "planet bottom" in New England Glass Company invoices. The single ring enclosed by the dots serves a twofold purpose. It adds to the pattern while minimizing the scar left by a pontil rod. *The Bennington Museum, Bennington, Vermont*

1295 BLOWN MOLDED DIAMOND DIAPER SLOP BOWL ON FOOT

McKearin GII-16

3⅝" H. x 5¼" Dia. 1825–1835

Although this bowl found other uses, it was originally intended to receive waste such as tea leaves that had settled to the bottom of teacups. Tea leaves if left in the cup rendered a second filling of tea bitter. In later years, as shown in photos 4289 and 4290, tea leaves were captured in a perforated, covered spoon that was stirred into a cup of hot water to the desired strength of tea. Then the leaves were dumped into the slop bowl. Bowls such as these saw double duty as wine washers, even though they do not have specially formed lips on which to rest stems of wine glasses. One that carries a diamond pattern appears in an 1818 English print entitled *Fox Hunting: The Toast* pictured on page 56 of *Glass of the British Military 1755–1820* by Olive R. Jones and E. Ann Smith. A wine glass upended in the bowl leaves no doubt about its use. The slop bowl in our photo has a ring of diamonds on the bottom, to which was applied an unpatterned low foot. *The Bennington Museum, Bennington, Vermont*

1296 BLOWN MOLDED COVER FOR SUGAR BOWL

McKearin GII-16

2⅜" H. x 4⅜" Dia. 1825–1835

After a blown item was removed from a mold, it was reheated and tooled to finalize its form. In the process, the pattern was muted or stretched, making identification difficult today. This is why we read the pattern from the bottom upward. In contrast, because covers were upside down when being blown, their patterns must be read from the finial to the rim. Note that the pattern on the flat of the finial is what one would expect to see on a base. A band of vertical ribs and the band of diamond diapering that would be above the ribs in the mold identifies the pattern as GII-16. When the glass was sheared after removal from the mold, the gaffer left more glass than usual and turned the rim back almost ½". The diameter at which the rim is folded determines the fit of the cover to a particular form of sugar bowl. If you find a blown molded cover with a rim that was cut away and polished rather than folded, be aware that this was not done at the factory. The cover was machined at a later time when married to the wrong bowl. The bowl to this sugar cover has not been found. *The Bennington Museum, Bennington, Vermont*

1297 BLOWN MOLDED DIAMOND DIAPER TAPER TUMBLER

McKearin GII-18

6" H. x 4½" Dia. 1825–1835

Collectors refer to large tumblers as "flips" because they held an alcoholic beverage by that name defined in Webster's Dictionary as "A mixed liquor consisting of beer and spirit sweetened, and also warmed by a hot iron". The heated iron was called a *flip dog*. But the Sandwich sloar book and invoices list all sizes of this form as *tumblers* regardless of capacity or intended use. There are eighteen diamond-shaped indentations on the base of the tumbler in the photo. Reading the pattern from the bottom up, this very large tumbler has a band of vertical ribbing, one horizontal ring, a band of diamond diapering, two horizontal rings and another band of vertical ribbing. The number of rings that separate the bands can vary on any of the blown molded patterns, depending on the whim of the mold maker. This does not change the identification number in the classification system established by the McKearins. It is unusual to find such tumblers with the pattern well defined at the top. When the rim was sheared after the glass was removed from the mold, it was inclined to be rough. Reheating to smooth it often distorted the pattern at the rim. Distortion does not deter from value and can help determine authenticity. This pattern has been extensively reproduced in clear and color. A 1982 catalog of the Imperial Glass Corporation in Bellaire, Ohio, shows a 6" high "Flip Vase" reproduced for the Metropolitan Museum of Art in New York City that can be mistaken for this tumbler. According to the catalog, "This magnificent collection has been so superbly recreated by Imperial that each piece must carry the Metropolitan's hallmark (M.M.A.) in order to distinguish it from the original." Use extreme caution when purchasing because the hallmark can be removed. *Courtesy, Sandwich Glass Museum, Sandwich Historical Society*

1298 BLOWN MOLDED DIAMOND DIAPER TUMBLER

McKearin GII-18

4⅝" H. x 3⅜" Dia. 1825–1835

The pattern known as GII-18 has a band of vertical ribbing at the bottom, a band of diamond diapering in the center and a muted band of vertical ribbing at the top. The common name of the pattern, in this instance *Diamond Diaper*, usually comes from the most prominent motif in the pattern. This tumbler is large and unusually shaped. There are seventeen diamonds on the base. Its lower third is tapered, but the center distinctly bellies out where the single horizontal ring separates the vertical ribs from the diamond diapering. The authors have seen only this one, but do not believe it to be an individual tumbler that became deformed in its making. Except for the addition of an extra horizontal ring above the center band, it matches the GII-18 decanter in *American Glass* by George and Helen McKearin. Several other molds have this distinction, most notably a thistle form decanter in pattern GIII-6. *The Bennington Museum, Bennington, Vermont*

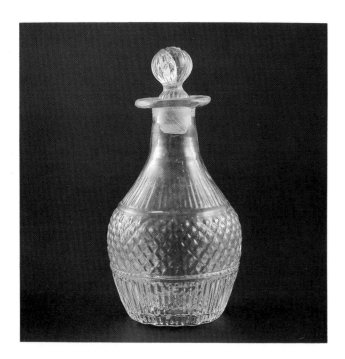

1299 BLOWN MOLDED DIAMOND DIAPER DECANTER WITH HAND-FORMED RIBBED BALL STOPPER
McKearin GII-18
4½" H. x 2¼" Dia. 1825–1835
This decanter is not small enough to be considered a toy. Small decanters were made to hold only one or two drinks. All of these blown molded pieces were blown in full-size molds that retained the pattern on the finished item except where rework was necessary. Even though the same pattern was used on different size decanters, a separate mold had to be made for pieces of different capacity. If a glass blower attempted to increase the capacity of the decanter by expanding it after it was taken from the mold, the pattern would be so muted that the piece would not be saleable. However, the same mold could be used to make a different piece of like capacity such as a cream or a barrel tumbler. This decanter has fifteen diamond-shaped indentations on its base. Its badly damaged stopper decreases its value enormously. *The Bennington Museum, Bennington, Vermont*

1300 BLOWN MOLDED DIAMOND DIAPER CREAM
McKearin GII-18
3⅛" H. 1825–1835
Molded Diamond and *Diamond Molded* were descriptions often used in factory correspondence to describe the patterns known as *Diamond Diaper* to collectors. The flat bottom has a pattern of fifteen diamonds in a circle. The number of diamonds on blown molded pieces does not determine origin; it varies with the diameter of the base and the whim of the mold maker. This cream held an individual serving of heavy cream skimmed from the surface of milk in an era when milk was not homogenized. (Many Sandwich property deeds included the right to keep a family cow on a community pasture on Town Neck. A general store in the village provided a bull to service family cows when necessary for a fee. The use of Henry Vose Spurr's bull as recorded in his store account book is pictured in Chapter 2 of Volume 4.) Cream was commonly used in cereals and on berries, and in coffee when it became a common beverage. Note the size of the opening in the handle. It is large enough to take the finger of an adult, ruling the piece out as an item marketed for children. Toy tableware and toy lamps in blown molded patterns can be seen in Chapter 10 in Volume 3. *The Bennington Museum, Bennington, Vermont*

1301 BLOWN MOLDED DIAMOND DIAPER JUG
McKearin GII-18
6¼" H. x 4⅜" Dia. 1825–1835
It is often claimed that jugs were made from decanter molds, but never that decanters were made from jug molds! So many more decanters have survived that it is difficult to believe that there may have been an equal number of jugs. In almost every pattern, jugs were made in several sizes that do match decanters. Instead of forming the unpatterned glass into a neck and lip, the upper portion was opened to rework it into a rim and spout. The excess glass that was sheared off was dropped into a cauldron of water and saved to be used as cullet. Several styles of handles could be applied opposite the spout: solid, hollow or ridged. The side of the heaviest part of the handle was attached first. Then the tail of the handle was secured and given a curl. Pressure applied to the inside of the handle corrected its form. There are sixteen diamonds on the base.

1302 BLOWN MOLDED DIAMOND DIAPER BOWL ON SUNBURST HIGH FOOT

McKearin GII-18 bowl, McKearin GIII-5 or 6 foot
5¾" H. x 9⅝" Dia. 1825–1835

American glass factories did not have the capability to manufacture objects hollowed both above and beneath unless they molded separate units that were joined together after each was removed from its mold. The joining was done by applying a small gob of hot glass in the form of a wafer to the top of the lower unit while holding the lower unit on a pontil rod, then attaching the lower unit to the bowl. Each unit may have matched in pattern or not; it very probably did not matter to the early 1800's consumer. By understanding the wafer and unit method of construction and learning to identify the patterns separately, a collector can accept as Sandwich any combination of documented Sandwich patterns. The ribs in the upper band on the bowl are normally vertical, but folding the rim outward and stretching the glass to reach its 9⅝" diameter pulled the ribs to the right. The foot has three sunbursts alternating with diamond diaper panels. Its rim is folded under for strength. *Courtesy of The Toledo Museum of Art (Acc. No. 59.61)*

1303 BLOWN MOLDED DIAMOND DIAPER DECANTER WITH HAND-FORMED SUNBURST STOPPER WITH WAFFLE CENTER

McKearin GII-22
6½" H. x 2¾" Dia. 1825–1840

A maximum number of patterns were obtained by combining a minimal variety of banded elements that by themselves were and are uninspiring. However, the right combination of bands well inscribed into a well-maintained mold that was filled on a day when the furnace turned out a good batch of glass could result in a piece such as this small decanter. The lower band of vertical ribs that extend onto the base is very distinct. The diamond diapering is well delineated. The bands of diagonal and vertical ribs on the shoulder still show although muted from reheating to form the lip. The decanter stands straight and the stopper fits well. Early stoppers like this were machined to fit, but were not fitted so well as to require that each stopper be numbered to fit an identically numbered bottle, as was the case in later years. They were routinely interchanged within the household, often being stored in a pantry drawer reserved for stoppers. This is why, almost two hundred years later, we cannot always decide if even a well-fitting stopper is original to the decanter. The waffle effect in the center of this Sunburst stopper is caused by horizontal lines on one side of the stopper reflecting through vertical lines on the other side. See Chapter 6 in Volume 3 for a study of stoppers dug from the Boston and Sandwich Glass Company factory site. *The Bennington Museum, Bennington, Vermont*

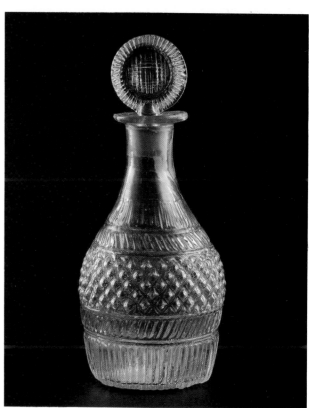

1304 BLOWN MOLDED NAPPIE

McKearin GII
1¼" H. x 6¼" Dia. 1825–1840

This nappie was blown into a dip mold that was a variant of a pattern illustrated on a decanter and designated GII-24 in McKearins' *American Glass*. The nappie has a rayed base of the type originally designated "star bottom". Beginning at the bottom of the pattern, there is a band of vertical ribs, above which is a band of diagonal ribs to the right. Because we are viewing the nappie from above instead of from the side, these horizontal bands appear to be concentric. Next is a narrow band of diamond diapering, a narrow band of inverted squares that more closely resembles a band in GII-46 (Such is the difficulty with a classification system. Combinations exist that were not included.), another band of diamond diapering and finally near the rim a narrow band of diagonal ribs to the left. A band of vertical ribs shown on the shoulder of the decanter was eliminated from the nappie. Nappies, bowls and oval dishes required a gather of glass which resulted in two-thirds waste. A bubble of glass was expanded on the blowpipe and forced into a one-piece, bowl-shaped, patterned mold. After removal, an assistant to the gaffer attached a pontil rod to the outside center of the patterned bubble. The blowpipe was cracked from the upper half and the bubble, now held by the pontil rod, was sheared away ½" above the pattern. This left enough glass to be folded to the outside to strengthen the rim. The glass that was sheared away became cullet that was used in a subsequent batch. *The Bennington Museum, Bennington, Vermont*

1305 BLOWN MOLDED DIAMOND DIAPER

McKearin GII-33

(a) Wine 3¾" H. x 2¼" Dia.

(b) Stopper 3½" H. x 2⅛" Dia. 1825–1830

Some molds had multiple uses. Here is a button stem wine with a bowl that was blown in a mold commonly used for a stopper. The rayed pattern that forms the top of the stopper became the bottom band of vertical ribs on the bowl of the wine. A stem with a shallow knop in its center, called a *button stem* in company records, was applied to the patterned bowl. A base was added and its rim was folded under. The result was a perfectly executed wine. The procedure used to make this button stem wine was used to make a Diamond Diaper candle socket on a button stem as shown in photo 4001. Small tumbler molds were used to make flat-sided bowls for wine glasses. In June 1828, J. H. and H. L. Webb ordered four dozen Fluted and Hooped tumbler bowl wines from the Boston and Sandwich Glass Company. *Courtesy, Sandwich Glass Museum, Sandwich Historical Society*

1306 BLOWN MOLDED DIAMOND DIAPER DECANTERS

McKearin GII

(a) With blown molded ball stopper
   Decanter 8⅜" H. x 4¾" Dia.
   Stopper 3⅜" H. x 2⅛" Dia.
   Combined size 10½" H. x 4¾" Dia.

(b) With pressed mushroom stopper
   Decanter 8¼" H. x 4⅝" Dia.
   Stopper 2⅞" H. x 2½" Dia.
   Combined size 9¾" H. x 4⅝" Dia. 1825–1840

Ignoring the stoppers, compare the decanters and note the variations that would prevent a collector from calling them a pair, although at the time of manufacture they might have been considered. The lowest band on decanter A is fluted as shown in McKearin GII-33 whereas decanter B has wide ribbing like GII-29. The bands of large diamonds separated by ridges such as is shown in GII-32 begin at different heights. The fluted band on the shoulder of decanter A is wider than on decanter B. Yet, variations caused by using different molds may not have mattered at their time of manufacture. Decanters were for the most part made by hand. Too much of a gather blown into a mold resulted in a decanter that was thick and heavy. A smaller gather expanded more fully resulted in a paper-thin, lightweight piece. If two gaffers each made one of a pair, the hand-tooled upper portions varied. The neck might be slimmer and the lip thinner as shown in A. The three snake rings, applied after the decanters were blown, vary in thickness and distance apart. Accept these variations in tableware that was not meant to have great beauty. They were produced and marketed inexpensively. Mushroom and ball stoppers were both listed in early documents and both are correctly used here. Be aware that the Diamond Diaper pattern was reproduced in green, blue and amethyst in the 1920's.

1307 BLOWN MOLDED DIAMOND DIAPER CRUET CASTER WITH HAND-FORMED DIMPLED STOPPER

McKearin GII

(a) Cruet 4⅞" H. x 2" Dia.

(b) Stopper 1⅝" H. x ⅞" W.

(c) Combined size 5⅝" H. x 2" Dia. 1825–1830

The number of banded patterns combined in one mold was limited only by the patience of the mold maker. This caster has five bands, each with a different motif. Reading from the bottom, it has a band of vertical ribbing, a band of diagonal ribbing to the left, a band of diagonal ribbing to the right and a band of diamond diapering. This combination is the same as found on GII-36 and GII-37. However, the fifth band on the shoulder differs. On this unclassified pattern, wide diagonal ribs slant to the right as seen on GII-40, but were pulled and twisted to the left when the slender neck was formed. The rim was flared into two spouts. The flat stopper was made by pinching between dimpled dies. It is original to the cruet.

1308 BLOWN MOLDED SUNBURST-IN-SQUARE DECANTER WITH BLOWN MOLDED DIAGONAL RIBBED BALL STOPPER

McKearin GIII-2 Type 2

(a) Decanter 8⅝" H. x 4⅝" Dia.
(b) Stopper 3⅞" H. x 2¼" Dia.
(c) Combined size 11¼" H. x 4⅝" Dia. 1825–1835

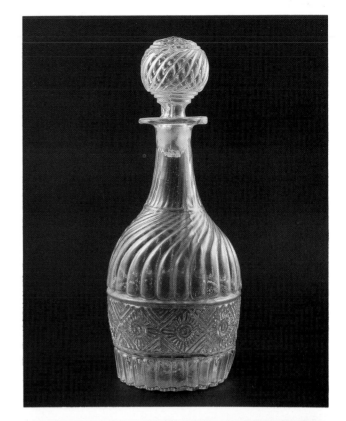

Wide, rounded, vertical ribs comprise the lower band, above which is a band of sunbursts placed on the diagonal bordered by chevrons. An added stripe to the chevron differentiates this pattern from GIII-2 Type 1. Wide ribs continue onto the shoulder and swirl to the right, extending to a horizontal ring. The swirled ribs were molded into the glass; the three vertical mold marks on the sides are easy to find. Narrow vertical ribs on the neck complete the pattern. The matching stopper with wide ribs slanting to the right is original to the decanter. The sunburst-in-square band was made in three styles: completely surrounding the decanter as shown here, interrupted by a molded label indicating the contents, and interrupted by an unmarked label area. The last allowed a metal chain to be hung around the decanter suspending a metal label that spelled out the contents. The ball stopper was made in the same manner as the decanter. It may have overfill on the shank from glass that oozed into the seams of the mold.

1309 BLOWN MOLDED JAM POT ON FOOT

(a) Sunburst pot
   McKearin GIII-4
   3⅜" H. x 4" Dia.
(b) Diamond Diaper cover
   McKearin GII-19
   2" H. x 3¾" Dia.
(c) Combined size 5" H. x 4" Dia. 1825–1835

Although the cover fits the pot, their patterns differ, indicating that they may not be original to each other. However the form of the cover is correct. It has a high dome to take a spoon. Beginning at the finial and ending at the rim, there is a band of vertical ribbing, a band of diamond diapering and a band of ribbing slanting to the left. The pot has an applied foot, above which is a band of vertical ribbing, a band of three sunburst blocks alternating with three diamond diaper blocks and a band of vertical ribbing. The rim was formed into a gallery to accept a cover. This gallery is easily broken. Unscrupulous dealers often machine away the gallery and sell the pot as an open bowl, so examine blown molded bowls carefully. Their rims should not show signs of cutting and polishing. Also examine feet for signs of tampering. *The Bennington Museum, Bennington, Vermont*

1310 BLOWN MOLDED SUNBURST PEPPER CASTER

McKearin GIII-4

4½" H. x 1½" Dia. 1825–1830

This pepper should have a perforated metal cap. It was made to be used in a caster stand with other matching bottles. A wide band of vertical ribbing covers the lower half of the bottle, which was made in a three piece mold. The sunburst motif above, alternating with diamond diapering, is repeated three times around the pepper, once on each section of the mold. Another band of vertical ribbing on the shoulder completes the pattern. Two horizontal rings separate the bands. The fragment on the right of the photo is a matching caster completely melted. Many of these were found in one place at the site of the Boston and Sandwich Glass Company, indicating that an entire tray of them overheated in the annealing leer. Melted pieces adjacent to glass factories aid in determining origin.

1311 BLOWN MOLDED SUNBURST NAPPIE

McKearin GIII-5

1⅝" H. x 10" Dia. 1825–1835

The well-defined patterns illustrate that each piece was blown into a full-size mold rather than having been blown into a smaller mold, removed and further expanded by the blowpipe. This nappie is very large. Each sunburst panel is 4½" long and each diamond diaper panel is 5" long, yet the pattern has clarity. (Smaller nappies were blown into correspondingly smaller molds.) The only parts that are distorted are the sidewalls reheated to fold, or *welt*, the rim. GIII-5 has a lower band of vertical ribbing that matches the ribbing on the rayed bottom. A wide center band alternates diamond diaper and sunburst blocks. Above is a band of diagonal ribbing to the left followed by a band of vertical ribbing. *The number of reproductions made from the 1920's to the present time is staggering.* Beginning and advanced collectors must study Corning Museum of Glass Director Dwight P. Lanmon's articles entitled "Some Blown 'Three-Mold' Suspicions Confirmed" in the 1973 *Journal of Glass Studies* and "Unmasking an American glass fraud" in the January 1983 *The Magazine ANTIQUES*. Extremely well executed reproductions in the 1920's by the Mutzer family include decanters, pitchers, tumblers, celeries, vases, sugar bowls and a blue-rimmed compote. (Authors Barlow and Kaiser are aware of a blue-rimmed jug.) The Clevenger brothers, working in the 1930's to 1950's in Clayton, New Jersey, blew colored jugs and decanters. Imperial Glass Corporation's 1982 catalog pictured a "27 oz. Diamond & Sunburst Pitcher" made for the Metropolitan Museum of Art signed "MMA". A 1990 Sandwich Glass Museum gift catalog showed a cream, decanter and vase with turnover rim marked "SM" or "SGM". *The Bennington Museum, Bennington, Vermont*

1312 BLOWN MOLDED SUNBURST TAPER TUMBLER

McKearin GIII-6

3⅝" H. x 3" Dia. 1825–1830

Enterprising businessmen saw the need for domestic glass bar ware such as tumblers and decanters years before the United States of America became a nation. The demand for drinking vessels so outstripped production that by the time a glass factory was established in Sandwich a ready market was guaranteed. Factory correspondence and entries in the sloar book document numerous orders for plain and pattern, blown and cut articles that could be used in eating places, taverns, hotels and ships. The difference between the pattern in the photo and GIII-5 is the direction of the diagonal ribbing above the sunburst band. The ribs on this tumbler slant to the right. The uppermost band of vertical ribbing was muted when the rim was folded. Rims were always fire polished and/or folded. Examine them when considering a purchase. If a rim was cut and polished, it was done to remove chips. If you buy it, do so knowing that it will be difficult for you to sell. Be aware that three forms of GIII-6 tumblers were reproduced by the Mutzer family in the 1920's in deliberate attempts to deceive the antiques market. Other Mutzer reproductions are creams, including one with a blue rim, sugar bowl covers, salts, celeries, vases, a variety of bowls and a flask. *The Bennington Museum, Bennington, Vermont*

1313 BLOWN MOLDED SUNBURST TUMBLER

McKearin GIII-8

2⅝" H. x 2⅜" Dia. 1825–1835

At times it is difficult to decide whether an item was designed for adult use, child use at the table or child use as a toy. This small tumbler presents such a difficulty. Reading from bottom to top, a band of diagonal ribbing to the right extends onto the bottom. A band of diagonal ribbing to the left is followed by a wide band of three sunburst blocks alternating with blocks of diamond diapering. A band of vertical ribbing above was twisted to the right in the process of reworking to smooth the rim. A straight-sided mold such as was used in the making of this drinking vessel could have been adapted to other forms. If the rim folded and flared out to form a lip, the result would have been a hat salt. A peg lamp was produced by removing the patterned gather from the mold, cracking it from the blowpipe and forming a small diameter rim to accept a whale oil burner. A glass peg applied to the bottom made it ready for use. *The Bennington Museum, Bennington, Vermont*

1314 BLOWN MOLDED SUNBURST DRAM

McKearin GIII-12

2⅝" H. x 1⅛" Dia. 1825–1830

When diminutive pieces such as this are studied, care must be taken to differentiate between toys made for children's use and play and small articles made for adults. This form of adult drinking vessel was used throughout the 1700's and was nearing the end of its popularity when glass manufacture began in Sandwich. The *dram* as a unit of measure could be as little as 1/16 ounce. As a drinking vessel its capacity varied from very little to up to three ounces. Drams were used for beverages with a high alcohol content such as brandy. The production of drams as such was not listed in the early Sandwich sloar book, although New England Glass Company invoices refer to them. It is likely that the Sandwich sloar man listed them as liqueurs. This is a crudely made dram. The shallow ribs above the sunburst are distorted. *The Bennington Museum, Bennington, Vermont*

1315 BLOWN MOLDED SUNBURST PATTY-PAN

McKearin GIII-13

1½" H. x 3⅞" Dia. 1825–1835

The sidewall of a patty-pan is flat or slightly curved but set at an angle to support the edge of a small pie and keep it from crumbling. Patties, now called "tarts", were baked in tin patty-pans and then transferred to glass for serving. Pan-shaped dishes ran the gamut from the 3" diameter toy in photo 3333 to very large blown milk pans that became popular mid-Century. This pattern most closely resembles GIII-13 as categorized in George and Helen McKearin's *American Glass*. The bottom has ribs that radiate from a single ring in the center. Beginning with the lowest band, there are ribs that slant to the right, above which are ribs slanting left. The upper half of the pan is made up of a wide band with three panels of diamond diapering alternating with three panels of a sunburst motif. However, unlike the sunburst center of two concentric rings as shown by McKearin, the sunbursts on this pan have a single ring in their centers. Minor variations such as this occurred when the mold was manufactured. Tooling the rim muted an upper band of ribbing. The outside fold of the rim covers the sunburst pattern to the ringed center. *The Bennington Museum, Bennington, Vermont*

1316 BLOWN MOLDED BULL'S EYE SUNBURST DECANTERS WITH BLOWN MOLDED DIAMOND DIAPER BALL STOPPER

(a) *McKearin GIII-15*

    Decanter 8⅝" H. x 4⅜" Dia.

    Stopper 3¼" H. x 2" Dia.

    Combined size 10⅝" H. x 4⅜" Dia.

(b) *McKearin GIII-16*

    Decanter 7" H. x 3¾" Dia.

    Stopper 3⅛" H. x 1½" Dia.

    Combined size 9" H. x 3¾" Dia. 1825–1835

Both the quart and pint decanters have sunbursts with a target-like pattern of concentric circles in their centers. This combination was named *Bull's Eye Sunburst* by George and Helen McKearin. Three sunburst blocks alternate with three diamond diaper blocks around the body. The seam mark where the mold was opened, although smooth to the touch, is very distinct. The only difference between the decanters in pattern is the band of diagonal ribbing. On decanter A, they slant to the left. They slant to the right on decanter B. Both stoppers are in the common GII-18 pattern—diamond diapering and vertical ribbing. The authors have not seen a Bull's Eye Sunburst ball stopper, although it is possible that they were made. The GIII-16 pattern was one of many patterns blown into molds at bottle factories such as Deming Jarves' New England Glass Bottle Company in East Cambridge, Massachusetts, and Perry, Wheeler and Company in Keene, New Hampshire. When researching the glass sand industry (see Chapter 10 in Volume 2), the authors found a reference that a high grade of glass sand was regularly transported to Keene in 1832. Colorless and artificially colored flint glass could have been made from that sand. However, the Keene works would have had to convert from open pots used in bottle making to closed pots used in flint glass factories. There is no indication that anything other than bottle glass was made in Keene. If a decanter is colorless or artificially colored, it was made in a flint glass factory. If dark amber, olive green, brown or black, it was made at a bottle works.

1317 BLOWN MOLDED SUNBURST TAVERN TUMBLER

McKearin GIII-18

3½" H. x 3" Dia. 1825–1835

Tumblers with sidewalls that are almost vertical were called *tavern tumblers*. An order that accompanied Deming Jarves' letter to William Stutson dated June 8, 1827, included a request from Joseph Leach for "30 doz. ½ pt Tav'n Tumblers". Blanchard and Steele ordered "20 doz. Tale Tav'n Tumblers". *Tale* articles were lighter, less expensive and sold by weight rather than by the piece. Tavern-keepers were licensed to sell liquor to be consumed on the spot. They were required by law to provide beds for guests and fodder for horses and cattle. As the United States expanded and the West was developed, demand for heavier pressed glass increased. The blown molded tavern tumbler went out of favor as did the term. The *bar tumbler* came into being. The tavern tumbler in this photo has a lower band of wide vertical ribs that extend onto the bottom. Three blocks of a sunburst centered with a large unpatterned bull's eye alternate with blocks of diamond diapering. A narrow band of diagonal ribbing to the right followed by a band of faint vertical ribbing completes the pattern. *The Bennington Museum, Bennington, Vermont*

1318 BLOWN MOLDED WAFFLE SUNBURST DISH

McKearin GIII-19

1" H. x 6½" Dia. 1825–1835

Even in his correspondence to factory Superintendent William Stutson, Jarves might have had difficulty describing this dish. He probably would have called it a "bowl, or rather plate". The ribbing on the bottom produces a rayed pattern. Vertical ribbing forms the curved bowl. A horizontal ring delineates the bowl from the band of waffle sunbursts that alternate with diamond diapering to make up the flat, wide rim. Diagonal ribbing to the left can be seen on the outer edge, which is folded. The pattern lacks the additional upper band of vertical ribbing that appears on tall pieces with the waffle sunburst motif. It is apparent that once a pattern was established it was repeated on a myriad of items. Reworking sometimes distorts the pattern and it is difficult to identify. This dish maintained its pattern. Its clarity adds considerable value.

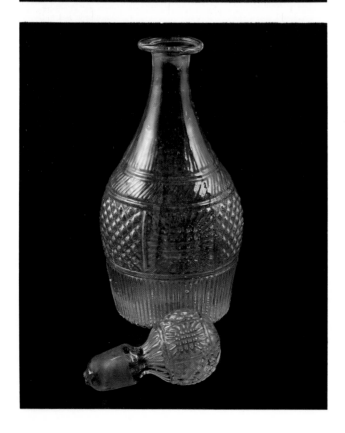

1319 BLOWN MOLDED WAFFLE SUNBURST DECANTER WITH BLOWN MOLDED WAFFLE SUNBURST BALL STOPPER

McKearin GIII-20

(a) Decanter 7" H. x 3¼" Dia.

(b) Stopper 3" H. x 1½" Dia. 1825–1835

Note the marked difference in color between the decanter and stopper. The green tinge was caused by iron oxide in the batch, generally because it was in the glass sand. It in no way is a designation of origin of the finished product. Every glass house could have and did have this occasional problem. If the stopper was not made from the same batch of glass, the contrast in color would be apparent. Even today it would deter from the value of the decanter. The Waffle Sunburst pattern was also made with the band of diagonal ribbing slanting to the left rather than toward the right as shown here. When slanting left, the pattern is GIII-19. Each of these blown molded geometric patterns were also made at other glass houses, some of which were in existence prior to 1825. People in the business of making molds, such as Boston mold makers Enoch Dillaway and E. M. Bartholomew (see pages 144 and 145 in Volume 3), sold their ware to many glass factories. Tumblers in the GIII-20 pattern were reproduced for The Metropolitan Museum of Art in New York City. They are 3½" high and cylindrical—proportionally too narrow for their height when compared to old ones. A set of four sold for $12.50 in 1985.

1320 BLOWN MOLDED TUMBLERS

(a) Diamond Sunburst barrel
   McKearin GIII-21
   3" H. x 2½" Dia.
(b) Diamond Diaper toy taper
   McKearin GII-19
   2½" H. x 1⅞" Dia. 1825–1835

Barrel tumbler A was made in a mold that was also used to make a small decanter. Beginning at the bottom, there is a band of diagonal ribbing to the right, then a band of diagonal ribbing to the left. The wide band at the tumbler's widest diameter has three panels of diamond diapering alternating with three panels of the diamond sunburst. The upper band of diagonal ribbing to the right was muted in the reheating to fold the rim. Most pieces, *but not all*, were blown in molds that had three identical side sections. In this instance, each section had one diamond sunburst panel and one diamond diaper panel. If a piece was blown into a mold, the pattern can be felt on the inside because the hot glass conformed to the contours in the mold. The upper band of toy tumbler B has diagonal ribbing to the left. Above it is a wide area that has no pattern. The gaffer could have made a well-proportioned tumbler bowl wine by adding a stem and foot and shearing away more of the unpatterned glass to fold the rim closer to the diagonal ribs. Both of these pieces have been reproduced.

1321 BLOWN MOLDED DIAMOND SUNBURST DECANTER WITH HAND-FORMED RIBBED BALL STOPPER

McKearin GIII-21

4½" H. x 2¼" Dia. 1825–1840

The lowest band is comprised of diagonal ribs that slant to the right. The ribs extend onto the bottom of the decanter. The second band has diagonal ribbing to the left. The most prominent motif is that of a diamond divided into nine equal parts surrounded by a sunburst. Three diamond sunburst panels alternate with three diamond diaper panels. A wide band of diagonal ribbing to the right completes the pattern. This particular piece was mated to a ribbed ball stopper, but another form of stopper could have been used as well. There are so many patterns, so many base variations and so many stopper forms that it is impossible for us to state that a certain combination was made in Sandwich alone. Even finding a blown molded piece with a mold flaw that matches a like flaw found on fragments dug at the factory site cannot guarantee this. The flaw could have been a defect that occurred in the manufacture of the molds, and identical molds with the same flaw could have been sent to several glass houses. *The Bennington Museum, Bennington, Vermont*

1322 BLOWN MOLDED SUNBURST-IN-SQUARE NAPPIE

McKearin GIII-23

1" H. x 4½" Dia. 1825–1840

The collector and antiques dealer can find a variety of shallow nappies in blown molded patterns. Deep bowls seem to be nonexistent. All of the early pieces have a pontil scar in the center of the bottom. A ring molded as part of the base pattern helps make the rough scar less noticeable. There was no reason to polish, or *punty*, the scar if the dish set steady on the table. Most rims are folded out for ease in washing, but this rim is folded ¼" to the inside, where the remains of food can creep beneath. As the result of reheating to shape the rim, nappies vary in diameter and roundness. One side may be higher than the other. They topple if stacked over four high. The lower band of pattern is vertically ribbed. Above it is the predominant motif of the sunburst-in-square placed end to end. A band of diamond diapering completes the nappie to the rim. Taller pieces of holloware have an additional band of ribbing slanted to the right.

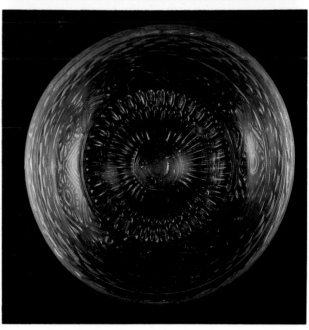

1323 BLOWN MOLDED SUNBURST-IN-SQUARE

McKearin GIII-23

(a) Hat salt 2½" H. x 2½" Dia.

(b) Ink 2" H. x 2¼" Dia. 1825–1835

Hat salt A with its sunburst-in-square motif is one of the most difficult to find. The band of sunbursts around the lower half of the salt can vary in location depending on where the band was inscribed into the mold. There is always a band of vertical ribs below it. Above the band of diamond diapering, there is a band of diagonal ribs that slant to the right. It was almost obliterated when the salt was reheated to fold back the rim and form the brim. Ink B was made in a different mold of the same pattern. Pieces with concave walls are called "waisted" by collectors. The would-be ink was open at the top when it was removed from the mold into which it was blown. The upper edge was rolled in and a circular gob of glass similar to that used to make a small foot was adhered to make a flat top. While still hot, a small hole was made in the center to allow the ink to be filled and a quill pen to penetrate. Because it was impossible to make airtight, its contents evaporated if allowed to stand for a length of time. More practical ink wells fitted with plated caps were available, as documented by an order for "1 Doz. plated Cap Inks" for Thomas Jones, which accompanied a Jarves letter dated July 2, 1827. *Courtesy, Sandwich Glass Museum, Sandwich Historical Society*

1324 BLOWN MOLDED SUNBURST-IN-SQUARE TOY LEMONADE

McKearin GIII-25

2¾" H. x 2¼" Dia. 1825–1835

It is incorrect to refer to this form as a "mug" if it was made during this early period. Up to the 1870's, tumblers with applied handles were marketed as *lemonades*. *Mugs* were tapered—their rim diameter was smaller than that of the bottom. The size of the opening in the handle determines whether this lemonade was marketed for adult or child use. If the hole is large enough to admit a man's forefinger and the lemonade can be lifted to the lips without snapping the handle, adult use was intended. This lemonade could be used by an adult, but with difficulty, so the authors place it in the toy category. The bottom has a pattern of concentric circles. There are only two bands of pattern on the side: the lower third has a band of herringbone, the center a band of sunburst-in-square alternating with diamond diapering. The upper third is unpatterned. Check carefully for damage when buying handled articles. *The Bennington Museum, Bennington, Vermont*

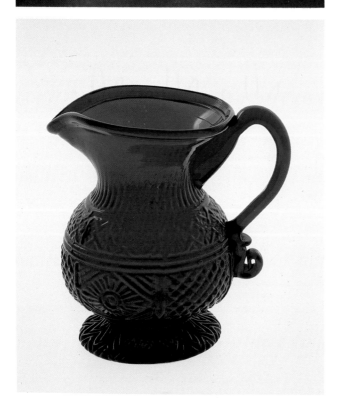

1325 BLOWN MOLDED SUNBURST-IN-SQUARE CREAM ON FOOT

McKearin GIII-26

4" H. x 3" Dia. 1825–1835

This cream was given to The Toledo Museum of Art in 1917 by Edward Drummond Libbey. Libbey had manufactured glass at the New England Glass Works in East Cambridge, Massachusetts, prior to establishing the Libbey Glass Company in Toledo, Ohio. (A brief synopsis of Libbey's relationship to the Sandwich glass industry is included in notes 2 and 6 on page 44 of Volume 3.) Small creams had many uses in a household. They were used on sick trays and for individual servings of cream for cereal and berries. Note the long length of handle attached to the upper part of the cream to provide strength to hold the cream and its contents. Reproductions generally are not fastened so securely. When purchasing creams for your collection, however, check the lower extremity of the handle where it first makes contact with the body. Many are cracked at this weakest point. This is a complicated pattern not frequently found. Beginning at the bottom: a band of herringbone squeezed to form a foot, one horizontal ring, a band comprised of alternating blocks of diamond diapering and sunburst-in-square, two horizontal rings, a band with the sunburst-in-square motif end to end, one horizontal ring and a band of vertical ribbing. *Courtesy of The Toledo Museum of Art (Acc. No. 17.245)*

1326 BLOWN MOLDED SUNBURST-IN-SQUARE CREAM

McKearin GIII-26

4⅝" H. x 2¾" Dia. 1825–1835

To the collector, one of the finest examples of early Sandwich workmanship can be seen in this photo. The cream appears to have been fashioned from a mold also used to produce a half pint decanter. The glass was fairly thick when the rim was folded to the outside; the resulting heavy spout pours well, but the user is left with a drip that must be wiped before the cream can be placed on the table. The handle was applied opposite the spout. No particular attention was paid to the pattern when spouts and handles were formed, so their position in relation to the pattern vary from piece to piece. The tail can cover a sunburst or the diamond diapering. Matching fragments on the right dug from the factory site show the configuration of the handle and the tail applied to diamond diapering. It is possible for creams in this pattern to have clear handles. One in the GIII-24 Sunburst-in-Square is known.

1327 BLOWN MOLDED SUNBURST-IN-RECTANGLE PEPPER CASTER

McKearin GIII-27

4½" H. x 1¾" Dia. 1825–1835

This pepper, designed to be placed in a caster frame, represents most of the elements combined in the sunburst series. There are nine distinct sides, three in each of three mold sections. They go as high as the horizontal rings around the shoulder, above which the pepper becomes circular. A row of herringbone surrounds the lower third, separated from the sunburst rectangles by horizontal rings. The center band is comprised of a sunburst, a sunburst-in-square and diamond diapering. These three elements are repeated three times to cover the nine sides of the pepper. The sunburst-in-square becomes a sunburst-in-diamond when elongated to fill the rectangle. A band of vertical ribbing stops halfway to the rim without the benefit of a horizontal ring. Concentric rings are on the bottom. Look for a matching mustard with a glass cover and a cruet with a glass stopper. The Sandwich Glass Manufactory, followed by the Boston and Sandwich Glass Company in 1826, sold casters separately as well in caster frames purchased from metal manufacturers. One such metalworker was William Carleton. The shipment of pepper tops from Carleton is documented in William T. Mayo's letter to Stutson dated July 11, 1829. "... they were a little smaller than those you now write for. Carleton has 80 Groce.....and Mr. Jarves observed the mould could be altered so as to fit these....."

Fig. 10 BLOWN MOLDED ROMAN ARCH WITH SPRIG OF LEAVES (FLUTE AND SHEAF, FLUTE AND TREE)

McKearin GIV-2 1825–1835

This simple flute pattern was contemporary to the pattern shown on the font of the whale oil lamp in photo 2006. Fragments dug at the site prove Sandwich manufacture, but it could have been used five years earlier at other glass works. An undated New England Glass Company document lists a Tree pattern. The stylized sheaves above the flutes make a fitting motif for holloware meant to hold spirits distilled from grain. (Webster's 1847 Dictionary defines *sheaf* as "A quantity of the stalks of wheat, rye, oats, or barley bound together; a bundle of stalks or straw.") On May 16, 1828, Boston store clerk William T. Mayo forwarded orders to factory superintendent William Stutson. George A. Potter and Company requested "7 doz. Sheaf pattern ½ pint Tumblers, Flute & sheaf" and "1 doz. Sheaf Pattern Wines, to match". Gaffer Edward Haines recorded the making of Flute and Tree tumblers in 1833, providing another tentative name. Tumbler fragments were found in Sandwich. A matching 4" high dram, or knob tumbler, is shown in McKearin's *American Glass* as is a 1⅝" high by 5¾" diameter patty-pan. Descriptions such as "Roman Arch" and "Gothic Arch" were not in known Sandwich documents.

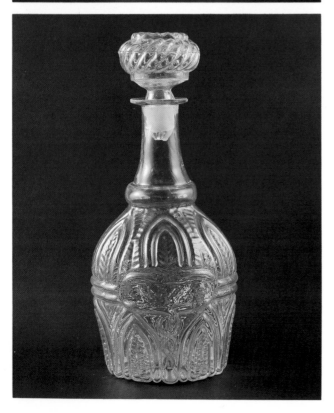

1328 BLOWN MOLDED GOTHIC ARCH WITH DOUBLE SPRAY OF LEAVES (FLUTE AND HUSKED) TAVERN TUMBLER

McKearin GIV-3

3⅛" H. x 3⅛" Dia. 1825–1830

Admittedly, study of Boston and Sandwich Glass Company orders leave many unanswered questions. Whether certain descriptions refer to blown molded patterns or blown and cut designs is unclear. Some popular configurations were copied one from another. Several Flute listings were obvious descriptions of blown molded patterns (i.e., "Flute and Pine Tree" and "Flute and Flute"). Keeping this in mind, the authors suggest that *Flute and Husked* may have been the factory name for the pattern shown here. It is clear from a September 1, 1826, order that "flute pine tree" and "flute husked" are not the same. G. T. and J. Waldron ordered "6 pr. Flint, flute husked qt., Decanters" in addition to Flute and Pine Tree articles. This pattern was identified as Sandwich from tumbler fragments dug from the factory site. We are aware that to date only tumblers have been located in the antiques market. The tumbler mold had twelve pointed flutes and twelve double husks of grain. Eight deep diamonds in the form of an eight-pointed star were on the base. The pattern can be felt inside. *Courtesy, Sandwich Glass Museum, Sandwich Historical Society*

1329 BLOWN MOLDED ARCH (FLUTE AND FLUTE) DECANTER WITH BLOWN MOLDED RIBBED BALL STOPPER

McKearin GIV-6

(a) Decanter 8⅞" H. x 4⅞" Dia.

(b) Stopper 3⅜" H. x 1¾" Dia.

(c) Combined size 11⅛" H. x 4⅞" Dia. 1825–1835

The pattern of this quart decanter may be the one alluded to by Jarves when he forwarded an order on June 8, 1827; along with other articles, Joseph Leach had requested "6 prs. flute & flute Qt. Decanters". The ribbed ball of the stopper appears to be too small in proportion to the decanter. It is the size normally used with pint decanters, so the two units may have been married at a later time. Decanters blown into unusually patterned molds are subject to damage that is often missed. Note the protrusions that, because of the way they were constructed, are the thinnest parts. They do not crack in the usual manner, but bruise in little spider patterns. Bruises greatly reduce value. However, it is not unusual to find irregularities in the area of the reworked lip. Manufacturing characteristics lend individuality that should not devalue antique glass.

1330 BLOWN MOLDED ARCH AND FERN WITH SNAKE MEDALLION (FLUTE AND PINE TREE) DECANTER WITH BLOWN MOLDED DIAGONAL RIBBED STOPPER

McKearin GIV-7

(a) Decanter 8½" H. x 4¾" Dia.

(b) Stopper 3⅜" H. x 2½" Dia.

(c) Combined size 10½" H. x 4¾" Dia. 1825–1835

Fragments of this pattern were dug at the factory site. The earliest Sandwich decanters are easily identified by their light weight and thin walls equal to an eggshell. Through his letters to William Stutson, Deming Jarves stressed the necessity to "make it light". By producing as many articles as possible from each batch, he saw the greatest return on his investment while minimizing shipping costs from out-of-the-way Sandwich. His goal sometimes backfired when wholesalers complained of unnecessary breakage. The slightest bump to this empty decanter or its matching jug can cause it to shatter, so extreme caution is recommended. The neck and lip of the decanter are heavier and will take some abuse. It is unfortunate that this pattern was named the unwieldy Arch and Fern with Snake Medallion before original Boston and Sandwich Glass Company documents were deciphered. The original name *Flute and Pine Tree* was well documented by Barbara Bishop and Martha Hassell in *Your Obdᵗ. Servᵗ., Deming Jarves*, a collection of Jarves correspondence. On September 1, 1826, William T. Mayo, who was Jarves' clerk in the Boston store, sent to Jarves an order from G. T. and J. Waldron that included "Flint, flute pine tree" pint and quart decanters and "flute & pine tree" wines. Note that the pattern on the decanter has the trunk of a pine tree, missing on the similar GIV-2 and GIV-3 flute pattern. The label area is bordered by two entwined snakes facing each other. Rather than describing the decanter's intended contents, a row of X's runs horizontally through the center. When this pattern is found with a specific molded label such as "WINE", "RUM", "CHERRY", or "BRANDY", it is extremely rare and value is greatly enhanced. The "GIN" label has been found upside down. Unless specially ordered, most Sandwich decanters had unmarked labels so as not to limit sales. They were labeled by metal identification tags hung by a chain. The stopper is the one most often combined with the decanter. Both units and a matching jug (pitcher) were reproduced in clear and color by the Pairpoint Glass Company in Sagamore, Massachusetts, for the Sandwich Glass Museum gift shop and are marked "SM" or "SGM". The lines of the reproductions are static. There is no form to the rim of the jug. Be aware that the identifying monogram is easily removed.

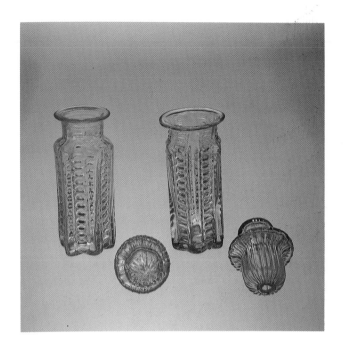

1331 BLOWN MOLDED MUSTARD CASTERS WITH BLOWN MOLDED RIBBED ACORN STOPPERS

McKearin GV-1
(a) Mustard 4" H. x 1¾" Dia.
    Stopper/cover 2¼" H. x 1½" Dia.
    Combined size 5¼" H. x 1¾" Dia.
(b) Mustard 3⅞" H. x 1¾" Dia.
    Stopper/cover 2½" H. x 1¾" Dia.
    Combined size 5" H. x 1¾" Dia. 1825–1830

Most of the patterns classified as GV are deeply molded and flamboyantly overdecorated with curves and figures rather than straightforward, confined patterns held in check. They are generally called *baroque*, although the Baroque Period in art, music and architecture is considered to have been 1550–1750. These attractive mustard casters have columns of horizontal ovals separated by wide, deep ribs. They are part of a six-caster set that was purchased in its original frame. Note the large opening that the acorn plug of the stopper fits into. The plug does not provide a tight fit; the stopper rests lightly on the lip of the mustard. Evaporation or drying out of the contents was not a problem when good household habits were followed. Mustard was purchased "ready-mixed" or dry. Articles in newspapers and periodicals suggested that only the amount of dry mustard needed for one meal or one day be prepared. The blown molded acorn stoppers predate pressed stoppers that have a spoon slot. Study the stoppers. They can sometimes be found in box lots and, when returned to their rightful positions on mustard casters, can increase the value of the mustard by five or six times.

1332 BLOWN MOLDED CASTERS IN SIX-HOLE FRAME

McKearin GV-1
(a) Cruet 4¾" H. to rim (replaced stopper) x 1¾" Dia.
(b) Peppers 4⅞" H. x 1⅞" Dia.
(c) Mustards (see previous photo) 1825–1830

This set of six casters was found complete in the soft pewter frame. It consists of one vinegar with a replaced blown molded tam-o'-shanter stopper, three peppers with brass perforated shaker caps and two mustards with blown molded acorn stoppers. The walls of the casters are thinner than an eggshell, so they take very little abuse. A great many casters in this pattern were dug at the Sandwich factory site, discarded because they cracked. A caster set with three peppers should be acceptable to a collector; the family from whom it came may have used a variety of mild and hot, white, black and red peppers. The average home had several caster frames, enough casters to fill them and a dozen or more spare cruets, peppers and mustards. Extra cruets may have held soy sauce and pepper sauce, a condiment made by steeping small red peppers in vinegar. Extra mustards held horseradish and small servings of jelly for the breakfast table. The metal frame was the carrier by which the casters were taken from the food safe or pantry to the table. Similar rectangular stands may have five large rings for casters.

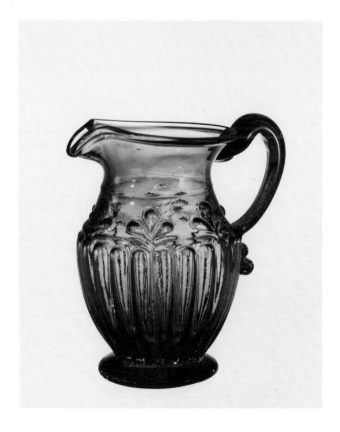

1333 BLOWN MOLDED TREFOIL AND RIBBING JUG OR CREAM

McKearin GV-3
5" H. 1835–1845

Broad, rounded ribs encircle the body, above which are three-lobed devices. The rim of the foot has a soft scallop. There is a rough pontil mark from holding the article when the spout was formed and the sturdy handle attached. Patterned molds were designed for the blowing of several articles that held a specified capacity. If a cream exists, logic dictates that the Boston and Sandwich Glass Company used the same mold to make a small decanter and a wide-necked water bottle. This piece is transparent blue with a red cast. *The Corning Museum of Glass, Corning, New York*

Fig. 11 BLOWN MOLDED PLUME
McKearin GV-4 1835–1840
This pattern is usually found on tumblers, two sizes of which were inexpensively reproduced for The Metropolitan Museum of Art. In 1985, a set of four reproduction bar tumblers 3⅝" high sold for $12.50. A set of six tall tumblers 5¼" high were $24.00. Generally speaking, even if the museum's logo "MMA" was removed, an experienced eye can differentiate between clear glass made in the 1820's and the icy brilliance of modern glass. Note the similarity of the plume motif in this blown molded pattern and the pressed Plume and Acorn pattern. When well-liked by the public, patterns and designs were carried over to other production methods.

1334 BLOWN MOLDED SHELL AND RIBBING DECANTERS WITH BLOWN MOLDED BALL STOPPER
McKearin GV-8
(a) Quart with unpatterned stopper 1" H. x 4½" Dia.
(b) Pint with ridged stopper 9⅛" H. x 3⅜" Dia. 1825–1835
It is interesting to test the holding capacity of early decanters. They were molded slightly over the required capacity. For example, when a quart decanter such as A is filled with a quart of liquid, the level of the liquid is 1" below the molded ring on the shoulder. The extra capacity was "built in" to allow for variances that occurred when the gaffer reheated and hand finished the neck and lip. Blown molded glass is very rare in color, so the pieces with matching stoppers shown in this photo are extremely valuable. The bottom of both decanters are plain. Quart decanter A was reproduced in clear for The Metropolitan Museum of Art. It retailed for $27.50 in 1985. The original name of GV-8 and the similar GV-9 is not known. The variant GV-9 is called *Shell with Diamond*. It has a small diamond between and below the coils of two shells and vertical ribbing on the neck. *The Bennington Museum, Bennington, Vermont*

1335 BLOWN MOLDED SHELL AND RIBBING JUG
McKearin GV-8
4⅝" H. 1825–1835
The same pattern appears as in the previous photo. Collectors and dealers often speculate whether or not a jug could have been made from a decanter mold. In the opinion of the authors, there was no such thing as a decanter mold. Glass companies purchased holloware molds of certain capacity such as gill, half pint, pint and quart. Different forms of like capacity were blown in the same mold, i.e., pint decanters and pint jugs were blown in a pint mold, quart decanters and quart jugs were blown in a quart mold. The final form required by the customer resulted from hand work that was done after the article was taken from the proper capacity mold. If it was a decanter, the neck was drawn up and the rim was flared into a lip to accept a stopper. If a jug, the neck was expanded to make a wide opening with a spout. Note that the horizontal ring above the ribbing is no longer convex, but was flattened during expansion. The ridged handle was attached in a separate operation. It is interesting to experiment with antique jugs and creams by attempting to pour liquid from them. (If you do so, do not hold them by their brittle handles.) The shape of the spout varies from jug to jug, and it is the shape that is critical to its effectiveness. After pouring milk, cream or water, some spouts stop the liquid abruptly and do not drip. Others drip and some even drool back upon the body, soiling table linens. The jug acquired by a collector for its beauty may be a jug that was pushed to the back of the pantry shelf because it was unserviceable. *The Bennington Museum, Bennington, Vermont*

1336 BLOWN MOLDED GUILLOCHE AND RIBBING DECANTER WITH BLOWN MOLDED DIAGONAL RIBBED STOPPER

McKearin GV-12

(a) Decanter 7⅜" H. x 4½" Dia.
(b) Stopper 3¼" H. x 2½" Dia.
(c) Combined size 9⅝" H. x 4½" Dia. 1825–1835

This intermediate size decanter was blown in a six gill or 1½ pint capacity mold. Sometimes the neck was expanded to a larger diameter to make a water bottle, which had no stopper. As shown here with a narrow neck and stopper, it would have been called a *1½ pint decanter*. The continuous interwoven curved lines surrounding the center is a decorative design known as *guilloche*. It is exposed to damage from anything pushed against it, so check for bruises when purchasing and use care in storing. Note the band of tiny dimpled checks faintly molded between the shoulder ring and lowest neck ring. They almost disappear when stretched to form a water bottle. The foot was molded in one piece with the body.

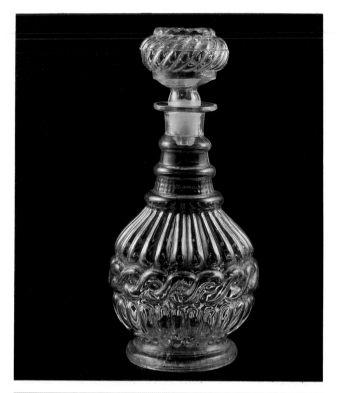

1337 BLOWN MOLDED HEART AND CHAIN DECANTER

McKearin GV-13

8¾" H. x 4½" Dia. 1825–1835

Of all blown molded patterns manufactured in this time period, this is the least impressive. The depth of the pattern in the mold was minimal, a lack that is apparent in the finished product when compared to GV-14 which follows. Note the difference in depth of the five-lobed plume centered in the heart on the decanter in this photo and the three- and five-lobed plumes on GV-14. Other elements such as the chain surrounding the body below the heart are weak. It is likely that the mold itself was less expensive for glass companies to purchase. Certainly, less was charged for the completed decanter. Like most early decanters, the Heart and Chain one is usually found with a replaced stopper. The original stopper was probably ribbed. To determine an appropriate replacement, study the stoppers on other Sandwich decanters in this chapter and the stoppers dug at the Boston and Sandwich Glass Company site as pictured in Chapter 6 of Volume 3.

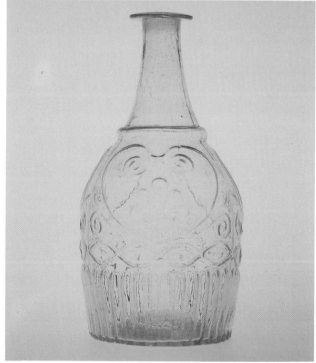

1338 BLOWN MOLDED GUILLOCHE, PLUME AND RIBBING

McKearin GV-14

(a) Decanter with blown molded diagonal ribbed stopper 9¼" H. x 4⅜" Dia.
    Stopper 3¼" H. x 2½" Dia.
    Combined size 11" H. x 4⅜" Dia.
(b) Jug or cream 4½" H. x 2⅞" Dia. 1825–1835

The GV-14 pattern combines elements from GV-12 and GV-13. The guilloche that surrounds the center of the GV-12 decanter now appears on the shoulder. Hearts resting on their sides form a chain around the center. They and the five-lobed plume repeat elements found on GV-13. A trefoil is enclosed in each heart. Tiny dimpled checks visible on GV-12 between the shoulder and neck rings are all but obliterated on this GV-14 quart decanter. The molds in which the quart decanter and the half pint jug or cream were blown each had four identical sections. Although three sections were more common, molds with two sections and four sections were manufactured when called for by the design of the pattern. Regarding blown molded holloware, decanters and pouring pieces go hand in hand because the same capacity mold was used to make both articles. When pouring pieces are small, differentiating between a cream and a jug becomes a judgment call. One would think that a cream would have a matching sugar bowl, but a sugar bowl would be considered an extreme rarity. In the opinion of the authors, it sets up a challenge to collectors. Look for all of these patterns on unusual pieces, constantly keeping in mind the many similar pieces that were manufactured by other houses at a later time. A similar pattern called *Scroll* by "milk glass" collectors was made in opaque white, blue and yellow-green by Challinor and Taylor of Pittsburgh and Tarentum, Pennsylvania. Scroll bowls, tumblers and tankards are common.

1339 BLOWN MOLDED CORNUCOPIA (PEACOCK TAIL)

McKearin GV-17

(a) Jug 7¾" H. x 5" Dia.

(b) Decanter with blown molded diagonal ribbed stopper 9¼" H. x 4¾" Dia.

    Stopper 3⅜" H. x 2⅝" Dia.

    Combined size 11½" H. x 4¾" Dia. 1825–1835

Collectors, dealers and auctioneers usually call this pattern *Cornucopia* or *Horn of Plenty*. A New England Glass Company invoice dated May 2, 1829, referred to Cornucopia decanters. It is similar to a French pattern illustrated in an 1840 Launay Hautin & Compagnie catalog. The Paris firm referred to it as *Tail of Peacock*. It is shown here on two articles, each blown in a different mold. The decanter has two horizontal rings molded around the bottom whereas the jug has none. Sixteen "eyes" of a peacock tail can be counted around the jug and fourteen around the decanter. Both pieces have a scale pattern above each "eye". The scales are repeated in every other curve beneath the "eyes". Both pieces were made in three-section molds, but in both instances only two of the sections were identical. The third section was narrower, accounting for the reason why the number of "eyes" cannot be divided by three. The blown molded Cornucopia pattern is thought of as the forerunner to the pressed Horn of Plenty (Comet) pattern. It is a good example of a popular motif used for a long period. The stopper is a probable replacement. A pressed mushroom stopper with matching "eyes" was marketed with the decanter. The similar GV-18, believed to have been used only on whale oil fonts, can be seen in photo 2044.

PRESSED CUP PLATES

1827–1860

The custom of placing a cup on a small auxiliary plate while coffee or tea cooled in a saucer was established before the Sandwich Glass Manufactory opened in 1825. Having made the statement, the authors admit that little documentation exists depicting when and where the practice became socially acceptable. Nineteenth Century paintings and prints of gentlemen making merry illustrate decanters and stemware, with wine glasses upturned in bowls to rinse them between servings. Guides on etiquette show well-laden tables for formal occasions, every serving dish and utensil in place. The cup plate is noted by its absence in both sources. It is generally agreed that the cup plate had its place, but its place was probably in the homes of rural America. This is evidenced by a letter dated July 29, 1828, that accompanied a July 26 New England Glass Company invoice for boxes and cases of glass consigned to William E. Mayhew and Company of Baltimore, Maryland. The invoices are now preserved at the Maryland Historical Society in Baltimore.[1] Henry Whitney, who succeeded Deming Jarves as agent of the New England works in East Cambridge, Massachusetts, instructed the Mayhews that the cases, which contained blown molded tumblers and lamps, were intended for export. Disposition of the boxes, which contained only 3½" and 4" diameter plates, was left to the Mayhews' discretion. The authors believe that the 3½" diameter plates were cup plates and the 4" diameter plates may have been toys, which were made in several sizes.

English potters made cup plates that matched china tableware sets. Antiques dealers expert in the field of china and porcelain, when questioned by the authors, concurred that the china cup plates are most often found in the transfer patterns and strong colors that were made for export to America. The plates seldom match the lighter-hued patterns preferred in England. Again referring to the New England Glass Company invoices to William E. Mayhew and Company, one dozen firestone[2] cup plates were listed on June 6, 1829.

The earliest cup plates manufactured in the Boston area were free-blown and blown molded, but they may have not been made in quantity because they were not as strong as

pottery. Newspaper advertisements of the New England Glass Company appearing in 1819 and 1820 issues of the *Boston Commercial Gazette* itemized blown molded holloware and dessert plates, but not cup plates. Glassware retailers Davis and Russell advertised a long list of obviously free-blown and blown molded articles in the May 18, 1822, issue of the *Old Colony Memorial and Plymouth County Advertiser*. It even included "Mould Patty Pans", but plates for cups were not mentioned. However, blown molded cup plates were documented by an order that accompanied a letter written by Boston and Sandwich Glass Company Agent Deming Jarves to his factory Superintendent William Stutson on October 17, 1827. The New England Glass Company ordered from the Boston and Sandwich Glass Company "4 doz. 2d size Mo. Split Cup Plates" and "6 doz. 1st size Mo. Split Cup Plates".

The term *split* in flint glass factory language was interchangeable with *groove*. The molded pattern may have been a type of V-groove that when translated onto a circular plate appeared as a muted pattern that today would be called *ribbed*, or *rayed*. Two blown molded pieces that may be cup plates are shown in photos 1289 and 1290. Their pattern is known as *Diamond Diaper*. The authors hesitated to place them in this chapter because their dimensions, 4¼" and 4" in diameter respectively, are larger than the documented sizes of 1820's cup plates.

Other Boston and Sandwich Glass Company papers refer to first and second size cup plates. Orders that accompanied a July 2, 1827, letter to the factory included one from Thomas Jones for three sizes of cup plates that were to be sent to New Orleans, Louisianna. Jones ordered "2 Doz. 1st Size Cup Plates", "6 Doz. 2d Size Cup Plates" and "6 Doz. Toy Size Cup Plates". The toy cup plates were the smallest. Two pressed examples shown in photos 3342 and 3343 are 2¾" and 2⅛" in diameter respectively. First and second size, listed in the Boston and Sandwich Glass Company factory sloar book as "No. 1" and "No. 2", would have been 3" and 3½" in diameter. Those were standard flint glass industry sizes as shown on New England Glass Company invoices of merchandise consigned to

Authors Raymond E. Barlow and Joan E. Kaiser examine the Albert C. Marble cup plate collection. *Photograph by John H. Belding, courtesy of Worcester Historical Museum, Worcester, Massachusetts.*

William Mayhew and Company. On April 18, 1829, Mayhew purchased "3 Doz. 3 in Cup Plates" and "3 Doz. 3½ in Cup Plates". Of course, slight variations in diameter were common due to the hand-folding of free-blown and blown molded plate rims, the primitive techniques of stamping out and/or "slumping" pressed glass and the warping in the annealing oven of both types. (The "slumping" of glass is described in Chapter 6.) Other changes occurred in the molds. Cap rings might have been interchanged that varied in width and thickness. Replacement molds were crafted by a different maker. Patterned dies on the plunger were cleaned or recut.

Not all 3" and 3½" diameter plates were designed as underplates, or coasters, for tea and coffee cups. Though outside diameters may agree with glass factory records, the diameters of the plate bottoms on which the cups rested are often too small. This fact was not emphasized by Lacy glass scholars Ruth Webb Lee and James H. Rose in their impressive study of cup plate patterns published in 1948 in the book *American Glass Cup Plates*. Lee and Rose used as their nucleus photographs of a cup plate collection that had been assembled by Albert C. Marble, an industrialist from Worcester, Massachusetts.[3] Mr. Marble had noted every pattern that had been brought to his

attention, and every variant of that pattern, no matter how minute. Lee and Rose recorded changes in form and the number of rim scallops in an effort to determine the origin of each plate based on the design of the cap ring, or cover plate, and the location from which each plate seemed to emanate. *American Glass Cup Plates* provides the collector with a marvelous study of the evolution of mold design, pressing techniques and pattern dating. However, Lee and Rose failed to consider several aspects that Barlow and Kaiser believe are critical to the study of glass, the most important are the answers to two questions. First, did the finished product fulfill the objectives of the mold designer working to specifications supplied by the glass company? And second, did the finished product satisfy the requirements of the customer? If the answer to both questions is "yes", then the center of the plate must be larger than the bottom of average Nineteenth Century tea and coffee cups. *If a cup does not fit, the plate is not a cup plate.*

The dual function of small plates can be proven by flint glass company account books and catalogs. A study of the 1825–1828 Sandwich factory sloar book showed unbelievably large quantities of toy plates. Yet, comparatively few are found in the antiques market today. It is our contention that many pieces that were intended to be toys have been reclassified by collectors and writers into the cup plate category. The *Cape Cod Glass Company List of Glass Ware*, reprinted in full on pages 108–110 in Volume 3, provided a parallel example of dual use in their listing of 3" diameter nappies under *Toys*. A separate heading *3-in. Nappies* itemized three pressed patterns: Acorn, Comet, and Flute and Split. At an antiques show today, the patterned nappies would be purchased by a collector of pressed tableware. They would be ignored by the glass toy, or "miniature", collector, who could rightfully place them on his toy shelf and increase their value by doing so.

Study a sizable collection of cup plates and look at them from the standpoint of strength to withstand the daily abuse of a cup. (Keep in mind that the custom of pouring a hot beverage from a spoutless, handled or handleless cup into a deep saucer was a rural one that was probably messy. We suspect that a guest entertained in a Boston, Philadelphia or New York City hotel would have been properly reprimanded.) Some cup plates are thick and sturdy. Others are light in weight with intricate patterns and the thinnest of rims, raising the question of their purpose.

The marketing in earnest of glass cup plates began with the invention of the pressing machine, as described in Chapter 6. The years 1827 through 1830 saw keen competition between Massachusetts glass companies as they increased production to meet the demand for the stronger pressed articles. Deming Jarves' correspondence with William Stutson on June 8, 1827, demonstrated their demand.

> Toy and Cup Plates are wanted, but have them made light. Light B. S. Lamps on Toy and 2d size Cup Plates sell well.

The button stem lamps alluded to by Jarves are the cup plate base lamps shown in photos 2031–2035 and 2038. Cup plate molds provided weighted feet for whale oil lamps and occasionally for candlesticks. Pressed Diamond Check (Checkered Diamond) cup plates were referred to by Jarves as early as September 8, 1827.

Letters accompanying the Mayhew invoices show the spirit of rivalry that propelled the pressing of glass to the forefront. In the previously mentioned July 29, 1828, letter to William E. Mayhew and Company, Baltimore consignees of glass from the New England Glass Company, Agent Henry Whitney suggested that the boxes of small pressed plates be disposed of immediately, "as the South Boston Company have copied our patterns and Mr. Jarves will do the same probably." On August 9, 1828, Whitney sent another consignment of plates and recommended "...that you take a little pains to get these plates off to the trade now while Jarves Factory is repairing. Soon he will commence again and be filling your market with them." On August 16, 1828, boxes of plates were again sent with Whitney's instructions to saturate the market by reducing the price to below cost. "...we hope you will be able to dispose of before Mr. Jarves fills your market with them."

These few consignments over a short period of time constituted thousands of 3½" and 4" plates with scalloped rims in patterns called *Planet* and *Star Bottom*. Whitney's letters illustrate two facts that are important to the documentation and attribution of cup plates, both of which were largely ignored by Ruth Webb Lee and James H. Rose in their book *American Glass Cup Plates*. First, most patterns can be attributed to more than one flint glass factory. Irrefutable documentation linking a piece to its place of origin, such as fragments dug at a factory site or its prominence in the family collection of a glassworker, does not eliminate the possibility of other manufacturers. Second, the area in which a cup plate is found in quantity cannot be used as evidence of the place of manufacture. Note the number of Planet and Star Bottom plates that filtered into the market from one Baltimore consignee alone. The New England Glass Company and the Boston and Sandwich Glass Company had agencies in major cities throughout the United States, Canada, South America, Europe and Africa.

It is true that certain areas produced glass with certain characteristics, such as the large beads and bull's eyes on Pittsburgh products. However, a difference on a cup plate rim of one or two scallops or the addition or subtraction of a minor design element is not enough to change attribution. It has never been necessary to count the hundreds of scallops on a large pressed Lacy plate. It is not necessary to count them on a small one. There is no better way to frighten a beginning collector than to burden him with useless information.

The popularity of cup plates reached its height during the Lacy era. They were a convenient size to be sold as commemoratives and souvenirs of significant fund-raising events such as an election campaign or the restoration of a ship to her former glory. Although no documentation has surfaced to substantiate this point, the authors believe that such plates that were molded for special purposes were not carried as glass company inventory. Plates with ships known to have been excursion vessels may have been sold on board to the traveling public. Researching the occasion for which plates were designed enables us to date the pattern on their borders. Most historical cup plates depict events that took place in the 1830's and 1840's. Conventional plates with matching patterns were therefore produced at that time. Their use as cup plates was documented by Kenneth M. Wilson in his book *New England Glass and Glassmaking*. Mr. Wilson quoted Catherine A. Beecher's 1842 publication *A Treatise on Domestic Economy*.

> Tea-cup mats or small plates, are useful to save the tablecloths from dripping tea or coffee...a cup-mat or cup-plate, should be set to each plate.

The production of small plates for specific use with cups seems to have ended by 1860. No cup plate commemorated the presidency or death of Abraham Lincoln, which took place in the 1860's. Nor are there plates about persons or events connected with the Civil War. A study of catalogs from the Pittsburgh, Pennsylvania, firm of McKee and Brothers[4] shows the cup plate's demise. Only one cup plate was illustrated in their catalog that was printed between the spring of 1859 and the spring of 1860. It carried a Diamond pattern and was listed as a "3 in. Dia^d Cup plate". The plate remained in McKee and Brothers catalogs printed over the next decade, but was shown as a "3 in. Diamond Plate". The Cape Cod Glass Company, which operated between 1864 and 1869, listed 3" diameter plates in three patterns under the heading *Plates*.

The advent of the Civil War in 1861 may have played a part in changing the dining habits of America's people. Coffee became so scarce that by June 1862 the newspaper *Barnstable Patriot* printed recipes for "hard times coffee", "one dime coffee" and "victory coffee". Barley was first used as a coffee substitute followed by roasted, grated carrots. The March 10,

1863, issue reported food poisoning caused by rye coffee. Whatever the reason, the cup plate as a useful household article vanished from the scene until it became collectable in the Twentieth Century.

Its ease of manufacture and resultant inexpensive selling price made Sandwich glass cup plates ideal targets for reproduction. According to Lee and Rose in *American Glass Cup Plates*, they first appeared in the 1920's. Many were the product of the Westmoreland Glass Company of Grapeville, Pennsylvania. Lee and Rose reported that an advertisement of cup plate "repros" appeared in a 1947 *Boston Herald* accompanied by a photo of seven cup plates that had been copied from Sandwich antiques. The photo also pictured a larger Washington souvenir plate. The set of eight retailed for $2.50. Authors Barlow and Kaiser believe that all were products of the Westmoreland Glass Company, which in 1950 copyrighted a catalog entitled *Westmoreland Glass Company Handmade Reproductions of choice pieces of Early American Glass*. All eight plates listed by Lee and Rose were included with a ninth under the heading "Authentic Reproductions of Old, Handmade Cup Plates." Excluding the larger George Washington plate, the eight Sandwich reproductions were "Henry Clay", "Benjamin Franklin", "1831" Eagle, "The Wedding Day", Valentine, "Bunker Hill Monument", Heart and Butterfly.

The small plates are still being made to benefit museum gift shops. Some are new patterns and many mimic old ones. Twentieth Century plates lack the brilliance and mold sharpness of Nineteenth Century originals. Rim scallops are static and regular in size.

The book *American Glass Cup Plates* is a monumental, detailed study of small plates that were produced in a number of flint glass factories on the Eastern Seaboard and the Midwest. Our book *The Glass Industry in Sandwich* shows only those made by the Boston and Sandwich Glass Company on Cape Cod. For the convenience of glass scholars who are familiar with Lee and Rose's study, the plates are shown in the order assembled by Lee and Rose, using their numbering system.

THESE SIMPLE HINTS WILL HELP YOU IDENTIFY SANDWICH CUP PLATES

All Sandwich cup plates are flint glass. They ring when pinched between the thumb and finger.

If the center of the plate is too small for a cup, the piece is not a cup plate.

Cup plates with large beads and bull's eyes on the rim were not made by the Boston and Sandwich Glass Company.

Cup plates with a rope ring, or cable pattern, separating the border from the scalloped rim were not made in Sandwich.

If a historical plate is inscribed with a date or depicts an event that occurred after the 1850's, it is not a Sandwich cup plate.

Reproductions were generally made from poor quality, lackluster glass that will not ring. Rim scallops have soft edges, unlike the brittle sharpness of old plate rims.

NOTES TO CHAPTER 8

1. The New England Glass Company invoices, letters and bills of lading for articles shipped to William E. Mayhew and Company are dated November 25, 1826, to September 19, 1829. Several were discussed by Helen McKearin in the September, October and December 1947 issues of *The Magazine Antiques* and by Kenneth M. Wilson in his book *New England Glass and Glassmaking*. Copies for authors Barlow and Kaiser's study were provided by the Maryland Historical Society, Baltimore, Maryland.

2. According to Webster's 1847 *An American Dictionary of the English Language*, *firestone* is defined as "Iron pyrites" and "A kind of freestone which bears a high degree of heat." It is better known to us as *ironstone*.

3. The Albert C. Marble cup plate collection is at the Worcester Historical Museum, Worcester, Massachusetts.

4. Five McKee and Brothers catalogs were published as *M'Kee Victorian Glass* by The Corning Museum of Glass, Corning, New York.

1340 PRESSED CUP PLATES
Diamond Check (Checkered Diamond)
Lee-Rose 57
(a) ½" H. x 3½" Dia.
(b) Fragment
Rayed
(c) *Lee-Rose 13* ½" H. x 3¾" Dia.
(d) *Lee-Rose 10* ½" H. x 3" Dia. 1827–1832

These three plates are among the oldest pressed in Sandwich. Fragments of each were dug from the site by Francis (Bill) Wynn. Correspondence to Deming Jarves dated September 8, 1827, referred to Checkered Diamond cup plates and on October 17, 1827, Jarves informed William Stutson that they sold well. Of early Sandwich cup plates, Diamond Check is the most common. At times it is found with one side thicker than the other, a characteristic caused by the plunger entering the mold at an angle. The large Rayed plate C with five concentric rings in the center may not be for a cup. In the opinion of the authors, some plates now included in cup plate collections were produced as toy plates. Although sloar books and invoices clearly differentiated between cup and toy plates, we cannot do so today. Cup plate D also carries a rayed pattern, but the center has three concentric circles. Rays on the bottom were repeated on the upper surface of the border. When combined with the rays, concentric circles molded beneath the border give the effect of tiny squares.

1341 PRESSED RAYED WITH FAN CUP PLATE
Lee-Rose 15
⅝" H. x 3½" Dia. 1827–1832

Authors Barlow and Kaiser were privileged to photograph the cup plate collection of Worcester, Massachusetts, resident Albert C. Marble. Marble's collection formed the basis of Ruth Webb Lee and James H. Rose's *American Glass Cup Plates*. The paper labels and arrows on the plates were part of their collaborative effort and were not removed for the purpose of this study. This primitive cup plate has a decided pink tinge thought to be the result of too much manganese mixed into the batch. Its thickness and pattern of concentric circles, rays and fans pressed by a two-part mold put it into the earliest years of pressed glass manufacture. We assume that cup plates with no rim configuration were the first to be pressed; however, it is an assumption. No one knows for sure which mold was first perfected during the middle months of 1827. A Lee-Rose 15 cup plate base lamp is shown in photo 2034. *Albert C. Marble Cup Plate Collection, Worcester Historical Museum, Worcester, Massachusetts*

1342 PRESSED STRAWBERRY DIAMOND CUP PLATES
(a) Fan border
 Lee-Rose 20
 ½" H. x 3½" Dia.
(b) Sheaf border
 Lee-Rose 48
 ½" H. x 3¾" Dia. 1828–1832

Here are two applications of the Strawberry Diamond motif. On cup plate A, it is presented as an overall pattern. On cup plate B, it extends from a ring enclosing an eight-pointed star. The ring made this cup plate a likely candidate as a plate base for a lamp font or candle socket because it would confine a scar left from a pontil rod. The rim configuration of cup plate A forms the top of the fifteen fans that alternate with tiny Diamond Checks. The sheaves of wheat alternating with stars on cup plate B are well inside a scallop and point rim. Both plates were designed before the advent of the cap ring, or cover plate, as described in Chapter 6. Boston office clerk William T. Mayo referred to "scallop cup plates" in a letter to William Stutson on May 29, 1828. Note the underfill of rim B caused by an insufficient amount of glass placed in the mold at the time of manufacture, giving the cup plate unique character that adds to its value.

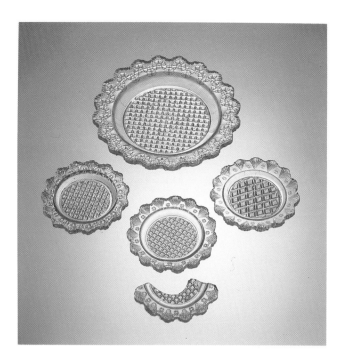

1343 PRESSED PLATES
(a) Diamond Check (Checkered Diamond) plate
 ¾" H. x 5½" Dia.
(b) Diamond Check (Checkered Diamond) and Fan cup plate
 Lee-Rose 54
 ½" H. x 3¼" Dia.
(c) Diamond Check (Checkered Diamond) and Fan cup plate
 Lee-Rose 53
 ½" H. x 3½" Dia.
(d) Strawberry Diamond and Fan cup plate
 Lee-Rose 20
 ½" H. x 3½" Dia.
(e) Fragment 1828–1832
Cup plate patterns were carried over onto plates as large as 9" diameter and ½" thick. All three cup plates B, C and D are smooth on the usable upper surface except for a beaded chain near the rims of fifteen fans. Fragment E was dug from an area of the factory yard where most of the glass dated to the late 1820's.

1344 PRESSED PLATES
(a) Diamond Check (Checkered Diamond) and Fan cup plate
 Lee-Rose 54
 ½" H. x 3¼" Dia.
(b) Rayed Star and Fan plate
 ½" H. x 4⅛" Dia.
(c) Stippled Pinwheel plate
 ¾" H. x 5" Dia. 1828–1832
There is no question that plate A is an underplate for a cup, but we cannot be certain of the uses to which plates B and C were put. In their book *American Glass Cup Plates*, Ruth Webb Lee and James H. Rose arbitrarily chose 4½" as the diameter of a plate too large for cups. Plates approaching 5" diameter were called *toddies* by Lee and Rose, suggesting they were underplates to protect furniture and table linens from toddy, a mixture of liquor and sweetened water. Our research shows 9" diameter plates used under lamps as discussed in Chapter 6. And because Boston and Sandwich Glass Company records show production of toy plates in quantity, determining function is tentative at best. All three patterns shown here were molded beneath the plates except for a beaded chain defining the rims. All three patterns and variants can be found in cup plate sizes.

1345 PRESSED SHEAF CUP PLATE
Lee-Rose 30
¾" H. x 3½" Dia. 1832–1835
It is believed that this pattern was made for many years because amber was not a desirable color when pressing first got underway. The color occurred naturally from iron in raw materials. It was acceptable when made at a bottle works such as Deming Jarves' New England Glass Bottle Company but not from a flint glass works priding itself for the lack of naturally-occurring minerals in favor of a brilliant, colorless product. The central pattern is a star made up of six diamonds enclosed by concentric rings. The eleven devices that complete the bottom are called "lance points with bricking" by Lee and Rose. A variant has twelve. Fifteen sheaves on the border extend into well-rounded scallops. Note the chain of beads on the upper surface of the rim. We have seen the plate with and without the beads. Variation may not have been deliberate, but merely oversights by busy mold makers hand tooling patterns into individual molds. The dark spot is a large pot stone. *Albert C. Marble Cup Plate Collection, Worcester Historical Museum, Worcester, Massachusetts*

1346 PRESSED SHEAF CUP PLATE BASE
Lee-Rose 32
¾" H. x 3¼" Dia. 1830–1832

Numerous variants occur in cup plates with the Sheaf of Wheat pattern. This one is believed to be the only one that has sixteen sheaves and rim scallops. Each sheaf is bisected one-quarter of the way up by a binder. The position of the binder varies in the Sheaf series. The rim is ⅜" thick in places and the plate would have made a good weighted lamp base had it not separated from its stem. The central pattern of eight petal-like lobes enclosing a divided square or diamond was obliterated when the plate was fused to the stem. When purchasing a cup plate, make sure you understand whether you are acquiring a true cup plate, which does not show traces of rework, or a base broken away from a whale oil lamp. The green streaks are *gall*, or *sandever*, usually skimmed from the surface of hot glass in the pot. If the lamp had been completed without breaking, it may have been sold as a second because of this defect. *Albert C. Marble Cup Plate Collection, Worcester Historical Museum, Worcester, Massachusetts*

1347 PRESSED SHEAF CUP PLATE
Lee-Rose 37
⅝" H. x 3¼" Dia. 1830–1835

This is a true cup plate. Its diameter is within documented dimensions. Its patterned underside shows no sign of having been attached to a stem or wafer; the central pattern is distinct. The smooth upper surface has no scar from having been held by a pontil rod. The authors have not encountered a fiery opalescent cup plate attached to a lamp stem. The above telltale signs generally apply to clear examples. However, anything is possible. Note the change in position of the binder when compared to the previous example, and the addition of stipples or fine diamond point that when annealed become muted to resemble stipples. Other variants have stippled borders and all eight leaves in the center are veined. The tiny Strawberry Diamond devices between the leaves are common to Sandwich Lacy pieces. *Albert C. Marble Cup Plate Collection, Worcester Historical Museum, Worcester, Massachusetts*

1348 PRESSED SHEAF CUP PLATE
Lee-Rose 45
⅝" H. x 3½" Dia. 1830–1835

The central pattern of this bright, fiery opalescent cup plate is an eight-lobed ornament enclosing a square of fine diamond point. Eight diamonds surround the ornament. A wide band of stippling extends to a rope table rest. The cup plate was pressed upside down in a three-piece mold consisting of a plunger, receiver and wide cap ring. The sheaf and rope pattern on the underside of the border was on the cap ring. A seam line running along the outside of the nineteen scallops was made by the cap ring joining the receiver. The rim rope pattern was also on the receiver. The cap ring and receiver generally failed to meet properly at this juncture, so irregular and incomplete rope rims often resulted. This particular cup plate is one of the better ones. *Albert C. Marble Cup Plate Collection, Worcester Historical Museum, Worcester, Massachusetts*

1349 PRESSED STRAWBERRY DIAMOND AND FAN CUP PLATE
Lee-Rose 46
⅝" H. x 3½" Dia. 1827–1830
The thickness of the glass and the intensity of its color are the reasons why the pattern pressed into the lower surface cannot be seen when the cup plate sets on the table. The cup plate was placed upside down to be photographed. Although the glass is very dark amethyst, it appears to be black. In the opinion of the authors, this was the intent at the time of manufacture. The plate was pressed in a mold that had no cap ring. The central pattern is an eight-lobed ornament with a square of fine diamond point. It is enclosed by a rope ring. An allover pattern of Strawberry Diamond covers the bottom. There is no table rest. Fine diamond point enclosed in fans extend into each of fifteen large rim scallops. The upper surface of the plate is smooth. *Albert C. Marble Cup Plate Collection, Worcester Historical Museum, Worcester, Massachusetts*

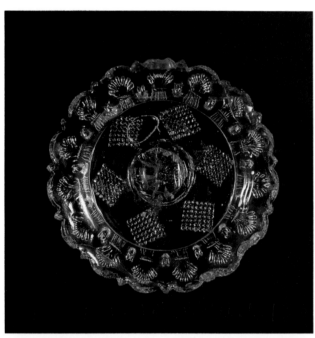

1350 PRESSED STRAWBERRY DIAMOND AND SHEAF CUP PLATE BASE
Lee-Rose 50
¾" H. x 3¾" Dia. 1828–1832
This base is a fragment that was dug at the site of the Boston and Sandwich Glass Company. It is slightly larger in diameter than the cup plate of this time period and may have originally been a child's toy plate. The surface that would have been the upper surface of the plate has a scar from a pontil rod in its center. On the patterned bottom is a broken stem that at one time supported a whale oil lamp font or a candle socket. As a plate, it will not set on the table. The star center protrudes because of necessary rework to attach the stem, an operation that muted the pattern. The ring surrounding the star may have been a deliberate attempt to confine the scar when the plate was used as a base. Six large strawberry diamonds complete the bottom. The border has fifteen sheaves of wheat that alternate with hearts. Large rim scallops above the sheaves alternate with points. On a variant designated Lee-Rose 51, the bottom has a stippled ground.

1351 FREE-BLOWN CONICAL HAND LAMP WITH PRESSED STRAWBERRY DIAMOND AND SHEAF CUP PLATE BASE
Lee-Rose 50
6⅝" H. x 3¾" Dia. 1828–1832
The base of this whale oil lamp matches the above dug fragment. It was pressed in a mold and after removal was held on the end of a pontil rod fastened to its smooth surface. A stubby spool stem was attached to the patterned surface. A bladed meresè or wafer, one of five wafer types routinely employed by Sandwich glassmakers (see page 43 in Volume 2), connected the spool stem to the conical font. A handle was fashioned by applying a length of hot glass to the upper portion of the font and crimping it with pressure at the tail. If the plate had not been intended for a lamp base, there was no need to attach it to a pontil rod. It would have been carried directly to the annealing leer. This lamp is beautifully proportioned to set securely on a table with little danger of falling over. The handle contributes to its scarcity. *Spencer Museum of Art, University of Kansas, Lawrence, Kansas. William Bridges Thayer Memorial*

1352 PRESSED CUP PLATE

Lee-Rose 61

½" H. x 3⅜" Dia. 1828–1832

This is a thick, shallow piece which, according to Lee and Rose, was made before the invention of the cap ring, or cover plate. Whether by intention or accident, it is pale blue with splotches of opal. A great deal of experimentation was going on at this time at the Boston and Sandwich Glass Company factory in Sandwich as well as other flint glass works. Some colored pieces made it to market, but the bulk of Sandwich production was in the clear glass called *flint*. Most cup plates in the antiques market today are clear. An example, such as is shown in this photo, even though uneven in color, is rare and valuable. *Albert C. Marble Cup Plate Collection, Worcester Historical Museum, Worcester, Massachusetts*

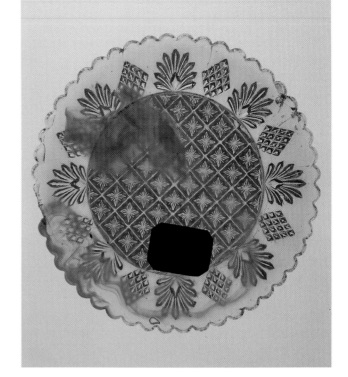

1353 PRESSED STAR CUP PLATE

Lee-Rose 65

⅜" H. x 3⅜" Dia. 1828–1832

Here is another thick, early cup plate. The pattern of five-pointed stars interspersed with divided diamonds is molded beneath the plate. The beaded chain at the rim of seventeen scallops is molded on the upper surface, which is why the two patterns appear to overlap on some scallops. Documents prove the existence of scallop plates as early as May 29, 1828. On that day, clerk of the Boston office William T. Mayo wrote to Sandwich factory Superintendent William Stutson about a Mr. Underwood, who wanted "5, 6 & 7 inch Scallop Plates" for the South American market. Also, "I spoke a few days since of altering bottom to scallop cup plates." There are several bubbles in this plate that do not deter from value unless they are broken through the surface of the glass. Take special care to protect cup plates with bubbles by placing padding between them and not stacking them too high. *Albert C. Marble Cup Plate Collection, Worcester Historical Museum, Worcester, Massachusetts*

1354 PRESSED ACORN CUP PLATE

Lee-Rose 82

⅝" H. x 3⅝" Dia. 1830–1835

The extremely detailed patterns of acorns, leaves and roses that appear on silver blue cup plates and salts were executed by a mold maker who was an artist in his own right. The silver blue sheen brings out the detail. A tiny five-petaled flower is in the center, perhaps designed around a center dot needed to inscribe the concentric rings of minute stipples. Twenty-three well-formed acorns surround the shoulder and twenty-three oak leaves cover the border. Concentric rings cover the underside from center to rim. If pressed in transparent glass, the concentric rings would clash with the acorns and leaves. Having only been found in white and blue to date leads us to believe the mold was designed for opaque pressing only. The mold had a wide cap ring that met the receiver at a place where a fin, or overfill, caused scratches on the table. Look for factory grinding to remove the fin. The cup plate has been found with traces of gilding probably applied by Boston women decorators employed by the Boston and Sandwich Glass Company. A silver blue Lee-Rose 85 cup plate matches one of five variants of a silver blue round pedestal salt as shown in photo 1460. L. W. and D. B. Neal, authors of *Pressed Glass Salt Dishes of the Lacy Period 1825–1850*, believed it to be an underplate for the salt, a conjecture that poses several possibilities. As there was no need for an underplate for a dry condiment such as salt, either Lee-Rose 85 is a cup plate and Neal RP 1 through 4 are salts, or the units combined are neither. *Albert C. Marble Cup Plate Collection, Worcester Historical Museum, Worcester, Massachusetts*

1355 PRESSED BASKET OF FLOWERS CUP PLATE

Lee-Rose 88
⅝" H. x 3¾" Dia. 1829

Albert C. Marble must have been pleased with the documentation that accompanied this wonderful opaque white specimen. A note was with the cup plate. "This plate was one of two that was given to Mrs. S(uiter) Allen after she went to house-keeping. Aug. 29, 1829—Given to me Aug. 29, 1879 (Golden Wedding)." If only the note stated "cup plate"! It was made in a two-piece mold that became obsolete soon after the invention of the cap ring. It has a pinwheel center with concentric rings covering the remainder of the bottom. Eight wide baskets were molded into the border, which has a rope rim. *Albert C. Marble Cup Plate Collection, Worcester Historical Museum, Worcester, Massachusetts*

1356 PRESSED BASKET WITH FRONDS CUP PLATE

Lee-Rose 90
⅝" H. x 3¾" Dia. 1830–1835

Unlike the previous cup plate that was pressed in a mold comprised of a plunger and receiver, this similar plate was pressed in a three piece mold consisting of a plunger, receiver and cap ring, or cover plate. (See Chapter 6 for detailed information about the evolution of pressing molds.) It is known that the cap ring was in use by 1830. A small pinwheel is in the center, surrounded by rings. Eight baskets on the border are completely different in proportion to those of the plate in the previous photo. Each basket has two fronds ascending upward and curling in the direction of the side of the basket. A thin rope surrounds the rim. *Albert C. Marble Cup Plate Collection, Worcester Historical Museum, Worcester, Massachusetts*

1357 PRESSED CUP PLATE

Lee-Rose 174
⅝" H. x 3⅝" Dia. 1830–1840

Note how busy the patterns became as the Lacy period reached its height. Many hours were spent perfecting the mold in which the roped, scalloped plate was pressed. Eight stippled sectors surround a central bull's eye, the space between them tapering toward the center. Above each section is an open fan. The combination of one sector and fan resemble an ice cream cone, a device seen on other Lacy articles such as the Shield tray in photo 1053. The fans alternate with ovals divided into sixths. Rows of tiny squares cover the shoulder between a rope table rest and rim. The plate was made in clear flint as well as white and blue. *Albert C. Marble Cup Plate Collection, Worcester Historical Museum, Worcester, Massachusetts*

1358 TOP VIEW OF ABOVE CUP PLATE

If a new collector was not familiar with the silver blue of the 1800's, he might pass up this plate if it was resting right side up. In clear glass, the pattern of eight sectors and open fans is easy to see, but is completely lost when manufactured in an opaque color. This is an extremely rare plate that is valuable even though damaged. However, when the *Barlow-Kaiser Sandwich Glass Price Guide* is studied, be aware that prices are given for perfect pieces.

1359 PRESSED CUP PLATE
Lee-Rose 177A
⅜" H. x 3⅜" Dia. 1830–1845

It is often stated that the tiny background dots called *stippling* were intended to hide the poor quality of early glass. This is only partly true. New furnaces and conversion to coal for fuel improved quality and yet, throughout the 1830's, intricacy of patterns increased. Stipples were a way of varying texture as well as covering defects. There are six versions of this pattern, one of which has the thick roped scallop rim of photo 1357. The plate shown in this photo has very fine stippling, finer than necessary to merely cover defects. It served the same purpose as frosting. The rim design shows that this central pattern, enclosed by C-scrolls and a border of alternating bull's eyes and five-lobed shells, was produced in the East and Midwest. *Albert C. Marble Cup Plate Collection, Worcester Historical Museum, Worcester, Massachusetts*

1360 PRESSED CUP PLATE
Lee-Rose 228A
⅜" H. x 3½" Dia. 1830–1845

The structured, geometric patterns of earliest pressed articles gave way to freer patterns of flowers and scrolls. Diameter and thickness was controlled by the now-common cap ring. When purchasing cup plates in sets, a buyer was assured of matched pieces as was customary in china and porcelain. Interchangeable cap rings varied rim configuration. On this rim, a large scallop alternates with two small ones. Study the elements of this pattern. The beaded scrolls and tiny five-petaled blossom between them can be found on numerous Lacy pieces ranging in size from small toys to the largest objects shown in Chapter 6. (See Chapter 10 in Volume 3 for a study of Sandwich toys.) *Albert C. Marble Cup Plate Collection, Worcester Historical Museum, Worcester, Massachusetts*

1361 PRESSED CUP PLATE

Lee-Rose 229

½" H. x 3⅜" Dia. 1830–1845

The four-petaled blossom appearing in the center of Lee-Rose 228A was repeated five times on the border of this cup plate, alternating with acanthus leaf sprigs. A lone blossom in the center is on a ground of "watchcase stippling", made by engine turning arcs that result in a very fine diamond point. When annealed, except for the arcs, diamond point is difficult to differentiate from stipples inscribed one at a time. The machined background was and is used in the making of watches. *Albert C. Marble Cup Plate Collection, Worcester Historical Museum, Worcester, Massachusetts*

1362 PRESSED CUP PLATE

Lee-Rose 229A

½" H. x 3⅜" Dia. 1830–1845

This pattern of blossoms and leaves repeats that of the previous plate, but another cap ring changed the configuration of the rim. This rim has fifty-six small scallops all the same size. Note that all of the rim configurations documented as products of the Boston and Sandwich Glass Company are rather simple. Bold configurations and large beads are characteristic of Lacy glass molded in Pittsburgh, Pennsylvania, houses. Cup plates have been traced to the Union Flint Glass Company located in the Kensington section of Philadelphia, Pennsylvania. The Kensington works has not yet been thoroughly researched and attribution is tentative at best. *Albert C. Marble Cup Plate Collection, Worcester Historical Museum, Worcester, Massachusetts*

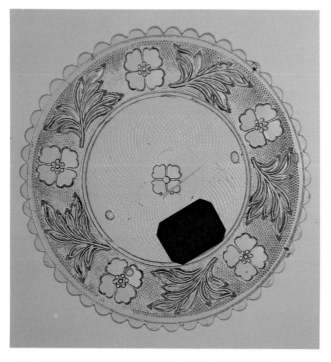

1363 PRESSED CUP PLATE

Lee-Rose 229B

½" H. x 3⅜" Dia. 1830–1845

Again the pattern is repeated, this time with a rim of forty-nine even but slightly larger scallops. These minor differences are important to the dedicated cup plate collector, but perhaps less so to the collector of a wide range of Sandwich products. The number of rim scallops was incidental at the time of production. The authors believe that too much emphasis is placed on it. The straight line interfering with the central blossom is an accepted manufacturing characteristic that was called a "straw mark" before glass production processes were researched. It is a scar seen on most pressed articles made during the 1800's. A gather of glass on the end of a rod was suspended over the mold receiver. A glassworker approximated the amount required and cut it off with shears, allowing it to drop into the receiver. The glass cooled and hardened at the point of the cut and never again reached a high enough temperature to be obliterated. *Albert C. Marble Cup Plate Collection, Worcester Historical Museum, Worcester, Massachusetts*

1364 PRESSED CUP PLATE

Lee-Rose 236

½" H. x 3½" Dia. 1830–1845

Three scrolled hearts were arranged outside a central triangle. The hearts were flanked by C-scrolls extending to a plain table rest. On the border, six large blossoms alternate with six leaves. They are separated by twelve scrolled flowers. The circle surrounding the border is the mold mark created by a seam between the patterned plunger and the scalloped cap ring. Eighty-one even scallops surround the twelve-sided rim. At the time of manufacture, the commercial mold making facility had little regard for the number of scallops per inch. Certainly a glass company when ordering a mold did not specify a particular scallop configuration. Mold sections were mixed and matched when shipped to any factory that required them.

1365 PRESSED CUP PLATE

Lee-Rose 243

⅜" H. x 3½" Dia. 1830–1845

A tiny cross with dot center divides four lobes of a quatrefoil. The lobes were intended to be leaves. These each have a midrib, but a rare variant has leaves with a midrib and diagonal veins. The bottom is covered with an overall pattern of stippled circles enclosing five-pointed stars. The remaining spaces between the circles are filled with larger dots. The border has four devices, each with a dart center and scrolls ending at a five-pointed star. Four groups of three leaves alternate. Stippling extends from a smooth table rest to a scallop and point rim. Several scallops and points are incomplete because glass did not fill the cap ring. This is a desirable defect to a glass scholar studying construction methods. When purchasing articles that appear to have under-fill, examine closely to determine that the rim was not machined to remove chips. We cannot say with certainty that fiery opalescent was deliberately manufactured by 1830. The mold was likely cast in the early part of the decade. *Albert C. Marble Cup Plate Collection, Worcester Historical Museum, Worcester, Massachusetts*

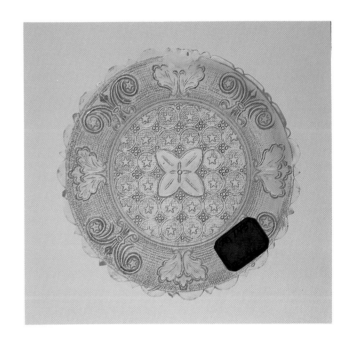

1366 PRESSED SHELL CUP PLATE

Lee-Rose 247

⅝" H. x 3½" Dia. 1835–1850

This twelve-sided plate was made in clear and several shades of green. Its central pattern is a pinwheel enclosing a seven-petaled rosette. The curved stems facing each other, flanked by sprigs of three leaves, are a simplified motif known as Princess Feather Medallion. Two medallions and two ornaments complete the bottom. Stippling used here and there add texture. Twelve shell-like ornaments surround the border. The cup plate is the smallest article pressed in the Shell pattern. A larger plate is shown in photo 1088. *Albert C. Marble Cup Plate Collection, Worcester Historical Museum, Worcester, Massachusetts*

1367 PRESSED CUP PLATE

Lee-Rose 256

⅝" H. x 3⅝" Dia. 1835–1850

The central pattern is made up of four C-scroll ornaments alternating with darts. A small dart extends from the center of each ornament. A chain of beads acts as a table rest. Scrolls repeated on a convex border converge over a stippled device similar to that of a tableware pattern known as New England Pineapple. Background stippling stops short of an evenly-scalloped rim. A variant with a scallop and point rim has stippling extending to the very edge.
Albert C. Marble Cup Plate Collection, Worcester Historical Museum, Worcester, Massachusetts

1368 PRESSED CUP PLATE

Lee-Rose 257

½" H. x 3½" Dia. 1830–1835

A five-pointed star enclosed by an eight-lobed rosette makes up the center of a quatrefoil. Each lobe of the quatrefoil is a veined leaf. A plain ring separates the quatrefoil from an outer pattern of scrolls forming medallions enclosing two five-pointed stars and two shields. The table rest is plain. Scrolled ornaments and small leaves are combined on the border. This cup plate has a rim of fifty-three scallops, but a variant has fifty-four. Note the overfill or fin of glass that protrudes beyond the rim. The pressure of the plunger forced the hot glass into the seam of an ill-fitting mold. This cup plate is unusually crude to have been accepted for sale at the time of manufacture, but the overfill adds considerably to value today.

1369 PRESSED CUP PLATES

Lee-Rose 258

(a) Clear

(b) Translucent white ½" H. x 3⅜" Dia. 1830–1835

A four-petaled blossom forms the center of a beaded quatrefoil. Four U-shaped chains of beads extend to a plain table rest. Four lily-like devices complete the central pattern. Eight scrolled leaves make up the border. The rim has seventy-six even scallops, but a variant has forty-eight. This was accomplished by interchanging cap rings. Note how translucent and opaque colors destroy the effect of the pattern when the plate rests on a table. The more transparent the color, the more pronounced the pattern. This color barrier is the reason so few colored cup plates are found. The difference in price between clear and colored plates is substantial, with color being at least five times greater.

1370 PRESSED PINE TREE CUP PLATE

Lee-Rose 260

½" H. x 3½" Dia. 1830–1832

The arrow was placed on the plate when James H. Rose and Ruth Webb Lee studied Albert C. Marble's collection. It points to the odd double line that separates the geometric elements and fans of this unusual pattern. A variant, also with a stippled scallop and point rim, has wide, single lines separating each element. The vegetation on the border is similar to that on a blown molded pattern originally listed as *Flute and Pine Tree* and now called *Arch and Fern with Snake Medallion*. The randomly-spaced stipples are exceptionally crude. Although the plates were pressed after the invention of the cap ring, the pattern probably was not replaced when the molds wore out. Lee and Rose did not record a colored example. If some are known, they are very rare. *Albert C. Marble Cup Plate Collection, Worcester Historical Museum, Worcester, Massachusetts*

1371 PRESSED SCROLL WITH LILY CUP PLATE

Lee-Rose 262

½" H. x 3⅜" Dia. 1835–1850

Scrolls forming a heart medallion enclose a three-petaled blossom known as the "Sandwich lily". They alternate with four fine diamond point triangles or half-diamonds, which are elements often combined with scrolls and lilies on Sandwich Lacy toy dishes as pictured in Chapter 10 of Volume 3. The background is stippled. There is a dot in the very center, missing in a variant that is otherwise identical. Around the border, six fleur-de-lys alternate with quatrefoil, also on a stippled ground. The rim has sixty-six even scallops. This cup plate is pale blue, an unusual but not unheard-of color in this time period. The color is often passed by at an antiques show or flea market because it is usually thought of as only a Depression Era color from the early 1900's. A pale blue whale oil lamp can be seen in photo 2103. *Albert C. Marble Cup Plate Collection, Worcester Historical Museum, Worcester, Massachusetts*

1372 PRESSED CUP PLATE

Lee-Rose 269A

½" H. x 3½" Dia. 1835–1850

Four large leaves extend from a seven-petaled rosette or blossom in the center. Two rose sprigs and two blossom sprigs are between them. The ground is smooth to a rope table rest. A complicated border pattern is made up of a pair of rose sprigs flanking an ornament composed of four pointed petals alternating with four diamonds. It is repeated four times around the plate. Each rose sprig has two leaves that match the rose leaves of the central pattern. The border stipples stop short of a rim of fifty-three scallops. There are a number of variants. Some have stippling in the center or on the rim scallops. The variations were manufactured by combining plungers, receivers and cap rings in various ways. Each element of pattern on this peacock blue plate was used on other Sandwich objects, so study them in detail. The rose leaves are in a horizontal band on the peg lamp in photo 1222. The pointed petal and diamond ornament of the border was executed in a larger size to cover the center of other cup plates. Scrolls and blossoms repeat those on smaller plates known to be toys as shown in photo 3344. It is very likely that some cup plates were also marketed as toys for children. *Albert C. Marble Cup Plate Collection, Worcester Historical Museum, Worcester, Massachusetts*

1373 PRESSED CUP PLATE

Lee-Rose 271

½" H. x 3½" Dia. 1830–1845

A chain of beads enclosing a central diamond connects four fleur-de-lys that extend to a plain table rest. The background is heavily stippled as is the border. There are four short, wide medallions on the border, two enclosing stipples and two enclosing a pair of six-petaled rosettes. The medallions alternate with four tree-like elements. The rim of this cup plate has seventy even scallops. The variant Lee-Rose 271A has fifty-two even scallops. There is also a difference in the stippling that surrounds the bead-enclosed diamond center. The plate can be found with a green or blue tinge caused by iron oxide that found its way into the batch. Characteristics that were production defects often increase antique value.

1374 PRESSED OAK LEAF CUP PLATE

Lee-Rose 272

½" H. x 3½" Dia. 1830–1840

The most prominent motif on this cup plate is the four deeply indented oak leaves in the center. They are surrounded by beaded ornaments on a stippled ground. The table rest is smooth. On the border, four rosettes are positioned above the oak leaves. The beaded double scroll repeated twice on the border is called *Ram's Horn* by collectors. Well-executed stippling covers the bottom and border. There are several variants that differ in minute detail such as the shape of the oak leaves and the form of the plate itself. This plate designated Lee-Rose 272 has forty-three even scallops. (In the text of *American Glass Cup Plates*, the number of scallops is given as forty-two, but forty-three can be counted in the photo.) Some have a rope rather than smooth table rest. Because of an ointment or pomade box brought to the authors' attention and shown in the following photo, the beaded scroll Ram's Horn pattern can be accurately dated.

1375 PRESSED ACANTHUS LEAF OINTMENT OR POMADE BOX

(a) Box 1½" H. x 4" Dia.

(b) Cover ¼" H. x 4" Dia.

(c) Combined size 1⅝" H. x 4" Dia. 1829–1831

This ointment or pomade box A is the earliest commercial piece we have seen, although it is similar to those shown in Chapter 9 of Volume 3 entitled "Covered Containers for Specialized Use". The beaded scroll on the side of the box, sometimes called *Ram's Horn*, appears on the previously shown Lee-Rose 272 cup plate. Six-pointed rosettes enclosed in the scroll were pressed into larger Sandwich pieces. The five-leaved sprig extending from the Ram's Horn is repeated on the cover B. Concentric circles on the cover are surrounded by a beaded circle that separates a border of the aforementioned five-leaved sprig alternating with scrolled acanthus leaves. This cover pattern is identical to the border pattern of a cup plate designated Lee-Rose 96. The rim is beaded. Although damaged, the cover is an extremely important document as shown in the photo that follows.

1376 COVER OF ABOVE BOX

Molded beneath the Lacy cover is the name and address of the manufacturer who ordered the container to be made. The cover reads "N. SMITH. PRENTISS. WHOLESALE PERFUMER. No. 12. EXCHANGE STREET. NEW YORK." *Longworth's American Almanac, New York Register, and City Directory* listed Nathaniel Prentiss as a perfumer at 28 John. A separate listing revealed that N. Smith Prentiss was also a perfumer. (Without extended study of the family genealogy, the authors hazard a guess that N. Smith Prentiss was also a Nathaniel, possibly a son using his middle name to distinguish himself from his father.) N. Smith Prentiss relocated his business several times, his address coinciding with Nathaniel Smith's only in the 1826–7 directory. From 28 John, he moved to 12 Exchange, the address molded into the Lacy cover, as he was listed in the 1828–9, 1829–30 and 1830–1 directories. By the time the 1831–2 directory was published, N. Smith Prentiss moved to 24 William, where he remained for several years. In the opinion of the authors, problems in pressing deep cylindrical pieces precluded the manufacture of this box much before 1829. It may be possible to find this cover marked with the name of another perfumer. By changing the mold pieces into which the name was inscribed, the glass factory accommodated other manufacturers with the same box.

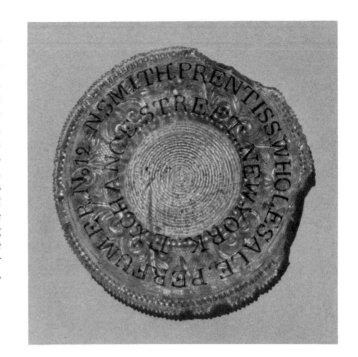

1377 PRESSED OAK LEAF CUP PLATE

Lee-Rose 275

½" H. x 3½" Dia. 1830–1840

This cup plate represents a smaller version of the Oak Leaf nappies in photos 1016–1020. The central pattern is a four-petaled blossom. It is enclosed by a beaded ornament from which extends four poorly-defined, flat oak leaves. The leaves alternate with four trefoil on a stippled ground. The table rest is smooth. The border pattern is called *Scrolled Leaf*. Seven S-shaped leaves have blossoms at each end. The scrolled leaves alternate with devices resembling double-ended, three-lobed sheaves. The border is stippled to a complicated edge that repeats the three lobes of the sheaves just inside a rim of forty-two deep scallops. It is difficult to find some of these early Lacy pieces without damage. The *Barlow-Kaiser Sandwich Glass Price Guide* reflects the value of perfect pieces. *Albert C. Marble Cup Plate Collection, Worcester Historical Museum, Worcester, Massachusetts*

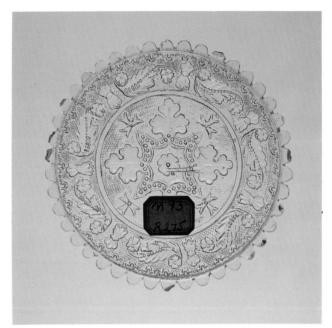

1378 PRESSED CUP PLATE

Lee-Rose 277

½" H. x 3⅜" Dia. 1835–1845

The center is made up of a seven-petaled rosette encircled by twelve dotted beads. The whole is surrounded by a circle from which radiate three diamond darts. The three arcs have a sawtooth or zigzag pattern which is replaced by a chain of beads on a variant. The remaining space on the bottom of the plate is filled with three diamonds that have diamonds within. The background is stippled to a narrow rope table rest. A variant has a wide rope rest. The border pattern is made up of four brackets, each enclosing four diamonds over which is a pair of scrolled leaves. Two concentric circles of stipples surround the border just inside a rim of fifty-eight even scallops. In addition to the variants noted, there can be slight changes in stippling, dimensions and form. The plate in this photo was made in several colors, all extremely rare today. *Albert C. Marble Cup Plate Collection, Worcester Historical Museum, Worcester, Massachusetts*

1379 PRESSED HAIRPIN CUP PLATE
Lee-Rose 285
½" H. x 3¾" Dia. 1830–1840
Hairdressers of today would not recognize the hairpin from which the border pattern derived its name. Hairpins were large enough to hold long hair that was coiled on top of the head. They preceded bobby pins that tamed "bobbed" hair. The hairpin was rounded at the top and cinched above curved sides. In 1948, Ruth Webb Lee and James Rose stated, "This was and still is one of the most popular patterns ever made." It still stands today as the single most desirable Lacy pattern. It was made in a number of articles as described in detail in Chapter 6. The central pattern of squares is typically eastern. Another Hairpin cup plate with a central pattern of a riverboat encircled by an undulating grape vine is believed to be a Midwest product.

1380 PRESSED ROSETTE CUP PLATE
Lee-Rose 291
⅜" H. x 3⅛" Dia. 1835–1850
Labels placed on the cup plate by Albert C. Marble, Ruth Webb Lee and James H. Rose obscure concentric rings that make up the center of a ten-petaled rosette. The little ground remaining is stippled. A plain table rest separates the rosette from a border of thirteen five-pointed stars on a ground of distinct stipples. This plate is soft amethyst; others have been located in off-colors. There are sixty-two scallops. *Albert C. Marble Cup Plate Collection, Worcester Historical Museum, Worcester, Massachusetts*

1381 PRESSED CUP PLATE
Lee-Rose 311
½" H. x 3¾" Dia. 1830–1835
One cannot determine time of production based on the amount of stippling. Although stipples covered poor quality, it had other purposes. Other than stipples, there was little an 1830's mold maker could do to vary the texture of inexpensively made pressed pieces. Here a six-petaled rosette surrounded by bull's eyes is on a stippled ground. In contrast, the border has stippled diamonds on a smooth ground. The rim was formed by an early cap ring configuration of twenty-three large scallops alternating with two small ones. The number of bull's eyes and diamonds demonstrates the lack of design concept afforded cheaply-produced articles. There are eleven bull's eyes and twelve diamonds.

1382 PRESSED INTERLOCKING WEDDING BAND CUP PLATE

Lee-Rose 313

½" H. x 3½" Dia. 1830–1835

According to private records belonging to Boston and Sandwich Glass Company employee descendants, cup plates were pressed in a pattern factory-named *Interlocking Wedding Band*. Although the pattern was not illustrated, the cup plate in this photo most closely matches the title. A waffle pattern completely covers the bottom of the plate. The table rest is wide and plain. The rim configuration of one large scallop alternating with two small ones should be repeated twenty-five times. The flat area where scallops are missing was caused when hot glass did not penetrate into the cap ring. This underfilled rim was a manufacturing fact of life that should not be considered damage. Value is not diminished. An advanced collector will pay more because of it.

1383 PRESSED CUP PLATE

Lee-Rose 319

½" H. x 3¼" Dia. 1835–1850

Numerous blown and pressed fragments dug from the Sandwich site have no pattern. Once broken away from the original article, they are difficult to identify. The authors believe that plain tableware was produced to complement china and porcelain settings. And a plate such as this was also possibly marketed as a toy. A bull's eye is in the center. Two concentric rings form the table rest. Two concentric rings delineate the border inside a rim of sixty-six scallops. Note the line running from the center of the border, caused by shears that cut off the correct amount of glass to be dropped into the mold receiver. The shears, being cool, hardened the glass into a permanent scar. The scar is mistakenly called a "straw mark", thought to have been made when the article was released onto a bed of straw. However, straw cannot mark glass. If glass was soft enough to take an impression from straw, it was hot enough to burn the straw rather than be scarred by it. Similar plates were molded with the names of advertisers known to have been in business in the 1840's. Manufacture of the plate in this photo was not limited to Sandwich.

1384 PRESSED STAR CUP PLATE

Lee-Rose 321B

⅜" H. x 3⅛" Dia. 1830–1840

A five-petaled rosette in a circle forms the center of a large five-pointed star. An S-shaped element is between the star points. The table rest is plain, and other than concentric circles, so is the border. The rim has fifty-two scallops. Other cap rings were used with the star pattern, so expect to see the plate with various rim configurations. *Albert C. Marble Cup Plate Collection, Worcester Historical Museum, Worcester, Massachusetts*

1385 PRESSED CUP PLATE

Lee-Rose 324
½" H. x 3¼" Dia. 1835–1855
The central pattern is comprised of a rosette with twelve petals varying in length that resembles a twinkling star. Four of the petals, or rays, extend almost to the table rest, dividing the bottom of the plate into quarters. An elongated eight-petaled rosette is molded into each quarter. Elongated stars such as this were molded into the bottoms of salts and toy dishes. Flame-like ribs, or rays, extend from the table rest onto the border. The rim has sixty-six scallops. This satisfying pattern and several variants were produced by the Boston and Sandwich Glass Company in quantity. Clear and opal are considered common; amethyst and amber are scarce. The evenness of color indicates production into the 1840's, after opal was perfected. The size of the center dot can vary and may be surrounded by a circle. In the cup plate in this photo, there are eight shorter rays between the longest rays on the border; a variant has seven. This is a fine specimen in very good condition.

1386 PRESSED GOTHIC ARCH CUP PLATE

Lee-Rose 328
½" H. x 3½" Dia. 1840–1850
This pale blue cup plate is shown as Lee-Rose 328 in *American Glass Cup Plates*, but its description in the text is in error. In the center are concentric circles from which extend rays of varying length. The border has fourteen simple Gothic arches. There is a small dot between the arches. The rim has sixty-four scallops. The plate was also manufactured with a dot in the center and with dots nearer the scalloped rim. Lee and Rose's obvious error is evidenced by their caution to "count serrations carefully on these plates." A very pale green plate is also in the Marble collection. *Albert C. Marble Cup Plate Collection, Worcester Historical Museum, Worcester, Massachusetts*

1387 PRESSED BUTTERFLY CUP PLATE

Lee-Rose 331
½" H. x 3¼" Dia. 1835–1850
The butterfly in the center is surrounded by stippling. The table rest is plain. Eight stemmed blossoms make up the border pattern, each stem having a bud and a leaf. Note that each blossom has six petals except the blossom below and to the right of the butterfly. This blossom has seven petals. The Butterfly plate has been extensively reproduced. All blossoms on the reproduction have only six petals. The old cup plate in this photo has sixty-six scallops on the rim. A shear mark can be seen running diagonally through the butterfly.

1388 PRESSED SUNBURST (STAR BOTTOM) CUP PLATE

Lee-Rose 332B

½" H. x 3⅝" Dia. 1835–1850

We cannot document the evolution of mold design by the presence or absence of stippling. While a Boston and Sandwich Glass Company catalog from this time period has not surfaced, there are lessons to be learned from catalogs illustrating glass articles manufactured in France. The same patterns could be ordered with and without a stippled, or "sand", surface. The cup plate in this photo has no stippling, yet was produced during the Lacy period. The rayed star in the center has fourteen points. The seven long ones extend toward seven border rosettes elongated to conform to the space available. The rim has sixty-three very shallow scallops. There are variants with differing rim configurations. Canary fragments of this pattern were unearthed at the Sandwich factory site.

1389 PRESSED STAR BOTTOM CUP PLATE

Lee-Rose 333

¼" H. x 3½" Dia. 1830–1845

Rayed patterns such as that molded into the bottom of this cup plate go by various descriptions. When molded into the sidewall of blown items, they are called *sunbursts*. Commonly referred to as a *rayed star* when molded into pressed pieces such as this, the pattern was described as *star bottom* on early New England Glass Company invoices. This glass factory description carried throughout the Nineteenth Century. An 1874 Boston and Sandwich Glass Company catalog illustrated *star bottom* Late Blown ware. The star pressed into this cup plate has six points with a total of thirty-six rays. Six eight-petaled rosettes on the border alternate with six seven-pointed fan-like elements. Fifty-nine scallops form the rim. The bottom of the plate is 2" in diameter, large enough to accept a china cup. Some cup plates are not truly circular due to stretching, shrinking and warping in the annealing leer. Accept variations in dimensions. No reference book in the world can record every minute detail, some of which have little bearing on attribution and documentation.

1390 PRESSED BIGLER (FLUTE AND GROOVE) CUP PLATE

Lee-Rose 364

⅜" H. x 3⅜" Dia. 1835–1855

This is an early pattern originally called *Flute and Groove* that eventually evolved into the well-known *Bigler*. The sixteen rays molded into the bottom of this plate extend to a plain table rest. Sixteen flutes and V-grooves complete the border. The authors find it interesting that the diameter of the bottom varies so much from plate to plate. We cannot be sure that all of the plates shown here were intended for cups; many may have been marketed as toys. However, cup plate researchers who preceded Barlow and Kaiser based their judgment on rim diameter regardless of whether the bottom was large enough to support a cup. Note the larger rim scallops on the left with one protruding. It appears that the mold designer, when making the cap ring, had difficulty with spacing. Under the eye of a more experienced mold maker, this plate could have had sixty rather than fifty-nine scallops. Note also the ever-present shear mark across the center.

1391 PRESSED BIGLER (FLUTE AND GROOVE) CUP PLATE
Lee-Rose 366
⅜" H. x 3¼" Dia. 1840–1855
Fragments dug at the site of the Boston and Sandwich Glass Company show a number of Bigler (Flute and Groove) variants. The center of this plate is a bull's eye from which radiate fourteen heavy petals, turning the center "star" into a rosette. The flutes on the border are wider than on the previously shown cup plate, so more closely resemble the flutes of Bigler as we know it. There are twelve flutes and alternating grooves. The rim has no scallops; neither does the Bigler nappie shown in photo 1140. When considering any cup plate or toy plate for purchase, examine the rim to determine whether it was pressed in a smooth-rimmed mold or was afterward machined to remove scallop chips. The small diameter bottom again brings up the question of original intended use. Is this piece a cup plate or is it another article that matches Bigler nappies that were made in larger sizes and sometimes fastened to a foot as shown in photo 1441?

1392 PRESSED CONCENTRIC CIRCLE CUP PLATE
Lee-Rose 373
½" H. x 3½" Dia. 1830–1840
An allover pattern of twelve concentric rings covers this plate from the center to the rim of seventy-three very small scallops. The sixth ring from the center is the table rest. Fragments of this pattern dug at Sandwich indicate a larger plate was also made with a center ring approximately ½" in diameter. It, too, had twelve rings, so a complete plate would be larger in diameter by ¼". Were they both cup plates? Though the authors cannot provide an answer, we raise the question hoping a future historian will.

1393 PRESSED FINE RIB (REEDED) CUP PLATE
Lee-Rose 397
⅜" H. x 3" Dia. 1850–1865
Here is another little plate included by Lee and Rose in *American Glass Cup Plates*. The star bottom is only 1¾" in diameter. The glass is clear and brilliant and matches the myriad of tableware pieces identified in a late 1860's New England Glass Company catalog as *Reeded*. All three Fine Rib (Reeded) plates in author Kaiser's collection are far too thin to be subjected to the abuse of a heavy resting cup. Although the catalog illustrated seventy forms, this plate was not included. A 3" diameter Diamond plate was listed as a cup plate by Pittsburgh's McKee and Brothers in their 1859/60 catalog, but the word *cup* was dropped in later catalogs. This Fine Rib pattern was made by most flint glass works in the New England area. The plate has forty-four scallops.

1394 PRESSED CUP PLATE

Lee-Rose 404

½" H. x 3½" Dia. 1850–1860

Fragments of this pattern were retrieved from the Boston and Sandwich Glass Company factory site in this size plate as well as larger dishes. An allover pattern of squares divided diagonally into triangles covers the plate's bottom. The table rest is plain. Concentric rings alleviate an otherwise unpatterned border. Unlike most small plates, the fifty-six rim scallops are convex on their upper surface. A canary example is known.

1395 PRESSED HEART AND SHEAF CUP PLATE

Lee-Rose 425

⅝" H. x 3½" Dia. 1828–1832

For the convenience of cup plate collectors, the authors are presenting these photos in the order established by Ruth Webb Lee and James H. Rose in *American Glass Cup Plates*. This is a departure from Barlow and Kaiser's format of earliest to latest. Here is a thick plate that was pressed before a *cap ring*, or *cover plate*, was designed to standardize rim thickness. The plate was pressed as a flat disk, then "slumped" into final form as described in Chapter 6. Four overlapping hearts make up the central pattern surrounded by a band of an allover pattern of Strawberry Diamond. The plate sets flat on the table with no defined table rest. Nine hearts extending to the rim alternate with nine sheaves. Above each sheaf are three dots which in variants are missing or elongated. Changes such as these and the gauge of stippling in no way reflect point of origin, but merely point up individual handwork afforded each mold. A Boston and Sandwich Glass Company invoice dated March 26, 1830, listed "dotted heart" cup plates. *Albert C. Marble Cup Plate Collection, Worcester Historical Museum, Worcester, Massachusetts*

1396 PRESSED HEART AND DIAMOND CUP PLATE

Lee-Rose 439C

½" H. x 3½" Dia. 1835–1845

Eight stippled elements resembling Peacock Eye (Peacock Feather) are arranged in a pinwheel. Each "eye" encloses a diamond and extends to a rope table rest. Fourteen stippled hearts and overlapping diamonds with stars make up the border. The rim has fifty-seven scallops and a variant has fifty-five. Compared to Pennsylvania production, Sandwich rim configurations were relatively unimaginative. There are no large beads or bull's eyes. Once the cap ring came into being, pattern stopped short of the rim. *Albert C. Marble Cup Plate Collection, Worcester Historical Museum, Worcester, Massachusetts*

1397 PRESSED VALENTINE CUP PLATE

Lee-Rose 440B
½" H. x 3¼" Dia. 1830–1850
Two hearts in the center of this plate are pierced with an arrow and lying on top is the wand of an angel. Folklore has it that the Angel of Love and Affection pointed the wand and Cupid, the God of Love, shot the arrow that brought love and affection to a chosen couple. Five-petaled blossoms complete the center to a beaded circle inside the table rest. The border has four lyres, each enclosed in a Princess Feather Medallion. The stipples are fine and closely spaced. This rim has twenty-four large scallops alternating with two small ones, but the plate can be found with even scallops as well. Its popular Valentine connotation made this piece an ideal plate for a reproduction which has coarse stippling, an uneven beaded circle and generally crude detail.

1398 PRESSED HEART CUP PLATE

Lee-Rose 447
½" H. x 3½" Dia. 1835–1855
This attractive plate has one large heart in the center and fourteen hearts around the border, all on a background of concentric circles. There were several legends circulating about why certain plates have a particular number of hearts, none of which stand up to criticism. In this instance, fourteen were the number of hearts required to satisfactorily fill the allotted surface. The plate in this photo has seventy-four scallops; others have seventy-three. Fragments matching it and its variants were found in clear, canary, green and several shades of blue. *Albert C. Marble Cup Plate Collection, Worcester Historical Museum, Worcester, Massachusetts*

1399 PRESSED HEART CUP PLATES

(a) Clear *Lee-Rose 455*
⅝" H. x 3⅞" Dia.
(b) Opal *Lee-Rose 459C*
½" H. x 3⅜" Dia. 1835–1855
Heart border plates enjoyed wide popularity and were manufactured by the Boston and Sandwich Glass Company during a long period of time. Replacement of worn molds resulted in subtle differences even when manufactured by the same mold company. The central pattern is a rosette made up of four pointed oval petals alternating with four stippled darts. The two plates in this photo are stippled to a rope table rest. The clear plate A has twelve hearts in the border and a rim of forty-eight scallops. Note the large diameter center, much larger than the bottom of a cup. The opal plate B has a border of thirteen hearts and forty-one rim scallops. Another plate has stars between the hearts. Scallops can number from forty-one to eighty-one. Were all of these cup plates? Were some underplates or coasters to protect furniture from stains—a type of glass doily? Were they marketed as dinner plates for children's tableware? Whatever their purpose, accept all of the many variants as Sandwich. However, be aware that thirteen heart cup plates with stippled centers were reproduced several times. In 1980, the Sandwich Glass Museum offered one for $4.50.

1400 PRESSED HEART CUP PLATE

Lee-Rose 459M

½" H. x 3¾" Dia. 1835–1855

This is the bottom view of a cup plate that has twelve hearts on the border and forty-three scallops on the rim. It is believed that this is the only cup plate that was pressed in opaque green. The pattern cannot be seen through the plate. Documents as late as 1855 list "old Heart cup plates", but we cannot tell from them the size and Heart pattern of the "old" one. *Albert C. Marble Cup Plate Collection, Worcester Historical Museum, Worcester, Massachusetts*

1401 PRESSED HEART CUP PLATE

Lee-Rose 467A

½" H. x 3¾" Dia. 1835–1855

There are stipples in the diamond darts of the rosette, but the center is otherwise smooth. The table rest is plain. Thirteen stippled hearts make up the border. The rim has forty-eight scallops, but a variant is known that has 102. Ruth Webb Lee and James H. Rose in *American Glass Cup Plates* presented cup plates in great detail. The slightest change in diameter gave rise to another variant. As a result, collectors specializing in cup plates attach great importance to minute differences. Although cup plates were circular when they came out of their molds, few stayed that way after annealing. Expect to see warping and dimension changes. Understanding manufacturing limitations will help you to enjoy collecting without being burdened by unnecessary detail. *Albert C. Marble Cup Plate Collection, Worcester Historical Museum, Worcester, Massachusetts*

1402 PRESSED HEART CUP PLATE

Lee-Rose 477

½" H. x 3¼" Dia. 1845–1855

Here is another Heart plate known to have been produced at the Boston and Sandwich Glass Company. Four plain hearts and a center circle enclosing a dot are on an unevenly stippled ground. The table rest is plain. The border has twelve stippled hearts on an unpatterned ground. Sixty-six scallops make up the rim. Inattention to detail probably indicates late manufacture, yet we cannot say that with certainty. As in every manufacturing business, there were different markets for varying quality levels. Perhaps the hundreds of cup plates required by a public eating house did not have to meet the high standard of a retail customer, so a cheaply-made mold would do.

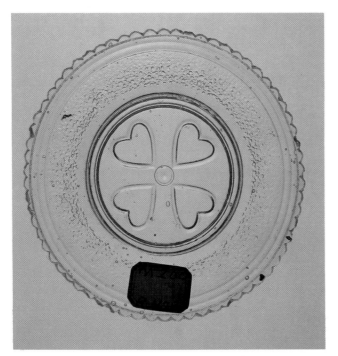

1403 PRESSED HEART CUP PLATE

Lee-Rose 478
½" H. x 3¼" Dia. 1835–1855
Here again are four hearts and a circle around a central indentation. No time was spent stippling the bottom. The table rest is plain. The border is a wide band of ill-placed stipples that resembles the pebbly texture of patterned tableware such as Beaded Medallion (Beaded Mirror). The rim has sixty-six scallops. Lack of detail may indicate a worn mold. Note the wide range of mold workmanship and glass quality throughout the Boston and Sandwich Glass Company's cup plate production. *Albert C. Marble Cup Plate Collection, Worcester Historical Museum, Worcester, Massachusetts*

1404 PRESSED SUNBURST (STAR BOTTOM) CUP PLATE

Lee-Rose 500
½" H. x 3¼" Dia. 1835–1850
Pressed plates with rayed centers are designated *Sunburst* by collectors. The pattern mimics the Sunburst motif on blown molded articles. Glass factory documents indicate the term *star bottom* was used as a catch-all description for rayed patterns pressed and blown molded into the bottoms of flat pieces and holloware. The number of rays vary as do the number of rings in the center. The plate in this photo has three concentric circles in the center and two on the border just inside the rim of forty-eight scallops. *Albert C. Marble Cup Plate Collection, Worcester Historical Museum, Worcester, Massachusetts*

1405 PRESSED SUNBURST (STAR BOTTOM) CUP PLATE

Lee-Rose 511
½" H. x 3" Dia. 1835–1850
Eighteen rays extend from a central dot. Concentric circles form a shallow border pattern. Twenty-two rim scallops alternate with points. The mold did not fill with glass, so the rim is not complete. Though Sunburst plates are devoid of stippling, they were produced concurrently with plates known as Lacy. This plate is deeper than some. We are sure they were also sold as toys. *Albert C. Marble Cup Plate Collection, Worcester Historical Museum, Worcester, Massachusetts*

1406 PRESSED SUNBURST (STAR BOTTOM) CUP PLATE

Lee-Rose 522

½" H. x 3¼" Dia. 1835–1850

Barlow and Kaiser record the number of scallops and points on the rim to aid collectors who rely on Lee and Rose's study that based attribution on minute details of rim configuration. We may therefore have placed too much emphasis on scallop count. You will note minute detail such as this has never been necessary in the attribution of large pressed articles. Many flint glass factories used the same mold making firms who sent their products to every glass works that ordered them. While certain details were characteristic of certain areas, the absence or presence of a stipple or scallop do not, in the opinion of the authors, determine the factory in which a piece was pressed. This unusual Sandwich red-amber cup plate has twenty rays around three concentric rings. It should have sixty-six scallops, but five were underfilled.

1407 PRESSED SUNBURST (STAR BOTTOM) CUP PLATE

Lee-Rose 530

⅜" H. x 3½" Dia. 1835–1850

On this yellow-green cup plate, there are twenty-one rays around a center of three concentric circles and a dot. Again, the border is plain except for concentric circles. The rim has sixty-five scallops. The simple pattern and wide color range allowed the Sunburst plates to be combined with any number of china and porcelain tableware sets. This color was not common to Sandwich, but is not unheard-of. Olive and yellow-green candlesticks were made during the same time period. Small items such as cup plates and salts were often made from puddles of good glass that remained in the bottom of the pot. *Albert C. Marble Cup Plate Collection, Worcester Historical Museum, Worcester, Massachusetts*

1408 PRESSED SUNBURST (STAR BOTTOM) CUP PLATE

Lee-Rose 537

½" H. x 3¼" Dia. 1835–1850

It is believed that the perfection of opal flint glass did not come to Sandwich until the late 1830's. This plate has three rings around a central dot and twenty-four rays. The border has two concentric rings close to the plain table rest and two near the rim of sixty-five scallops. The line that bisects the rays is a scar left by shears when a glassworker cut away the required amount of hot glass, approximating the amount needed. It is often mistakenly called a "straw mark".

1409 PRESSED SUNBURST (STAR BOTTOM) CUP PLATE

½" H. x 3¼" Dia. 1835–1850

This is a seldom seen cup plate that was not recorded by Lee and Rose or included in Rose's notes as compiled by John E. Bilane in *Cup Plate Discoveries Since 1948*. The pattern covers the allotted space nicely. Three rings enclose a central dot. Twenty-six rays extend almost to a ring inside the table rest. Eighteen large and eighteen small scallops make up the rim, inside of which is another ring. This rim of alternating scallops is less common than other configurations. Although the Boston and Sandwich Glass Company produced all of the plates shown here, manufacture by other flint glass houses cannot be excluded.

1410 PRESSED SUNBURST (STAR BOTTOM) CUP PLATE

Lee-Rose 546

⅜" H. x 3" Dia. 1835–1850

The previously shown Sunburst cup plates have rays in their star bottoms equal in length. This one has twelve long rays alternating with twelve short ones. A dot and one ring make up the center. The plain table rest is exceptionally wide. The border is unpatterned to a rim of thirty-six scallops. As you can see, any number of scallops were used on molds purchased by the Boston and Sandwich Glass Company and probably other flint glass factories as well. Unlike many plates made in the Pittsburgh, Pennsylvania, area, the scallops do not surround large beads or bull's eyes. *Albert C. Marble Cup Plate Collection, Worcester Historical Museum, Worcester, Massachusetts*

1411 PRESSED SUNBURST (STAR BOTTOM) CUP PLATE

Lee-Rose 550

½" H. x 3½" Dia. 1830–1845

Here is a Sandwich fiery opalescent plate that does not have a dot in the center. Eighteen long and short rays alternate in the star bottom. The table rest is plain. Concentric rings evenly divide the border. There are fifty-three scallops on the rim. Simple patterns of the Sunburst group affords us opportunities to explore the numerous minor variations that occurred at the hands of mold makers and glass factory machinists. Some were the result of mold repair and were of little consequence at the time of production. *Albert C. Marble Cup Plate Collection, Worcester Historical Museum, Worcester, Massachusetts*

1412 PRESSED "HENRY CLAY" CUP PLATE

Lee-Rose 562A

½" H. x 3⅜" Dia. 1832–1852

The appearance of political figures on cup plates helps pinpoint dates of cup plate production. Henry Clay was a colorful American statesman who was born in Virginia on April 12, 1777, to parents who were slave owners. He was licensed to practice law in 1797 and soon moved to Kentucky, where he became active in political affairs. Elected to the United States House of Representatives in 1811 and chosen speaker, he was a proponent of the annexation of Canada to the United States. He developed a war program against England that resulted in the War of 1812, and advocated a protective tariff system in 1823. The opposition of Senator John Randolph to Clay's views about politics and slavery led to a comical duel between them that was related in the April 15 and 22, 1826, issues of the *Old Colony Memorial and Plymouth County Advertiser*, a newspaper published in Plymouth, Massachusetts. The duel took place on the banks of the Potomac River in Washington without the knowledge of Clay's wife. The only damage was to Randolph's flannel gown, which was cut by Clay's ball. It was believed that the duel would diminish Clay's popularity in northern states. However, he was a Senator throughout the 1830's and a presidential candidate for the 1832 election, which he lost to Andrew Jackson. As a presidential candidate for the Whig nomination in 1840, he lost to William Henry Harrison. He was the choice of his party in 1844, but lost the election to James K. Polk. He was a candidate at the 1848 Whig convention, but lost to Zachary Taylor, who was elected president. Although some believed he was the greatest man of his time and country, he died a Senator on June 29, 1852. Several cup plates commemorate Henry Clay's campaigns. This one is thought to be from 1832. Here he is facing right, his portrait enclosed by a ring outside of which are his name and a wreath. The border is made up of ten five-lobed shells on a stippled ground that extends in points to a rim of forty-nine scallops. *Albert C. Marble Cup Plate Collection, Worcester Historical Museum, Worcester, Massachusetts*

1413 PRESSED "HENRY CLAY" CUP PLATE
Lee-Rose 565B
½" H. x 3⅝" Dia. 1832–1852
The numerous fragments from the site of the Boston and Sandwich Glass Company prove the manufacture of many thousands of Henry Clay cup plates. Some fragments were of a plate with the Clay bust but no name. There were at least eight variations with the name and one with the N in "HENRY" reversed. On this blue plate, the portrait facing left, lettering and star combine to make up the central pattern, enclosed by a rope ring. The scrolled pattern between the rope ring and plain table rest resembles a chain of Princess Feather (Prince's Feather). On the border, four fine diamond shields are flanked by fruit-filled cornucopia. Seven cornucopia have an oval fruit, thought to be a pomegranate, on the side away from the shield. One cornucopia at the lower left has a pomegranate near the shield. The rim has fifty-one scallops. It can easily be found in shades of blue and green as well as clear. Reproductions were made over a long period of time in the United States and France.

1414 PRESSED "MAJ. GEN. W. H. HARRISON" CUP PLATE
Lee-Rose 569
½" H. x 3½" Dia. 1841
William Henry Harrison was born in Virginia on February 9, 1773. He studied medicine before receiving a commission in the United States army, which he resigned in 1798. He was appointed secretary of the Northwest Territory and became the Territory's first delegate to Congress. As governor of the Territory of Indiana, he made thirteen treaties with the Indians. After failing in land negotiations with Tecumseh, he set out in September 1811 with an army of nine hundred to punish the Indians. They were met by Indian messengers near Tippecanoe on November 6. It was agreed to hold a council the next day, but Harrison's camp was attacked before daybreak. The Indians were fought off. Harrison was given a major-general's commission in the War of 1812. He was instrumental in creating a navy on the Great Lakes, and defeating a British general and his Indian allies led by Tecumseh, who was killed. Harrison held various political offices after the war and was nominated for president at the Whig convention in December 1839. He won the election and took office in March 1841, but died on April 4, only thirty-one days after his inauguration. This cup plate, marked "PRESIDENT" and "1841" on the drape and tassel border, must have been distributed during the first part of 1841. It was pressed in a mold that had been recut after producing an earlier campaign plate on which "PRESIDENT" and "1841" are omitted. Harrison is depicted in military uniform, facing left, with his birth date beneath. The twenty-six stars represent the twenty-six states of the United States, the twenty-sixth having been annexed in 1837. The rim has sixty-seven scallops. Fragments of the plate were dug from the factory site. Opalescent examples are very rare. *Albert C. Marble Cup Plate Collection, Worcester Historical Museum, Worcester, Massachusetts*

1415 PRESSED "VICTORIA" CUP PLATE

Lee-Rose 578

⅝" H. x 3⅝" Dia. 1837–1838

This plate and a "HENRY CLAY" plate share the same border pattern of four shields flanked by cornucopia, one of which has a pomegranate near the shield rather than on the side opposite. In the United States, "VICTORIA" plates in clear and color are extremely rare, probably because they were pressed at the Boston and Sandwich Glass Company to be exported to England. Victoria, queen of the United Kingdom of Great Britain, was born in London on May 24, 1819, and baptized Alexandrina Victoria on June 24. The death of her uncle William IV on June 20, 1837, raised her to the throne. She chose to be known as Victoria. Her coronation took place on June 28, 1838. Queen Victoria died on January 22, 1901, after a reign of over sixty-three years. This plate is believed to have been ordered to commemorate Victoria's ascension and/or coronation. Her portrait facing left and the name "VICTORIA" is encircled by a beaded rope ring. The rope ring and chain of Princess Feather (Prince's Feather) completing the bottom pattern are like those of the "HENRY CLAY" plate. Twenty-five large scallops alternating with two small ones make up the rim. *Albert C. Marble Cup Plate Collection, Worcester Historical Museum, Worcester, Massachusetts*

1416 PRESSED LOG CABIN CUP PLATE

Lee-Rose 592

½" H. x 3½" Dia. 1839–1841

At the Whig convention in December 1839, William Henry Harrison was nominated for president of the United States. He shared the limelight with vice-presidential candidate John Tyler of Virginia. "Tippecanoe and Tyler too" became the party cry. One end of Harrison's house consisted of a log cabin covered with clapboards, and his table was supposedly well supplied with hard cider. Symbolically, Harrison's and Tyler's endeavor became known as the "log cabin and hard cider campaign". Numerous cup plates were made for this campaign at the Boston and Sandwich Glass Company and other glass works as well. One made at Sandwich is marked "FORT MEIGS", commemorating Harrison's defense of that fort in 1813. The plate in this photo is extremely rare and much sought after. An American flag flies overhead, with a nightcap on the flagpole to symbolize the last drink before retiring for the night. A drinking vessel atop a cider barrel can be seen to the right of the cabin. Smoke pours from the chimney. The border is smooth and the rim has twenty-one large and small scallops. *Albert C. Marble Cup Plate Collection, Worcester Historical Museum, Worcester, Massachusetts*

1417 PRESSED LOG CABIN CUP PLATE

Lee-Rose 594

⅜" H. x 3¼" Dia. 1839–1841

Here is another Harrison-Tyler campaign plate with the central pattern of a log cabin with flag flying overhead, a cider barrel and drinking vessel, and a tree to complete the background. This plate has faint vertical planing on the cabin door, which cannot be seen in the photo. On other plates, the door is plain. The authors are not certain whether the mold maker neglected to plank the door or if that variant was the result of a worn mold that lost its detail. The border pattern is odd in that four adjacent sprigs have blossoms facing outward, and two adjacent sprigs have blossoms and buds turned downward toward the plain table rest. The pattern appears to be out of balance. The rim has sixty-six scallops. Fragments of the plate were retrieved from the Sandwich factory site. William Henry Harrison died shortly after he was inaugurated, so John Tyler assumed the presidency. Tyler withdrew from politics at the end of one term. Little was heard of him until he was chosen president of the Peace Convention which met in Washington on February 4, 1861, in a futile attempt to stave off the Civil War. He was elected a member of Congress of the Confederate States, but died on January 18, 1862, before he took office. *Albert C. Marble Cup Plate Collection, Worcester Historical Museum, Worcester, Massachusetts*

1418 PRESSED SHIP CUP PLATE
Lee-Rose 610A
½" H. x 3⅝" Dia. 1830–1845

The three-masted frigate in the center has not been identified. Collectors are divided in referring to it as the *Cadmus* and the *Constitution*. Actually, it may be neither. The *Cadmus* was the Sag Harbor, New York, ship on which the Marquis de Lafayette made his triumphal return to New York Harbor in August 1824. The United States Frigate *Constitution* is now the flagship of the Atlantic fleet. Her permanent home is in Boston Harbor, where thousands of people visit her each year. The ship that is a part of the plate pattern matches the ship alternating with an eagle on the salt in photo 1454 and an oval dish that is in The Corning Museum of Glass in Corning, New York, and shown in the book *American and European Pressed Glass* by Jane Shadel Spillman. Although there is no confirming documentation, all three historical pieces are thought to have been produced at the time the U. S. F. *Constitution* was reconditioned in the early 1830's. The vessel on the cup plate is surrounded by beads, outside of which are scrolls and leaves enclosing two shields and two stars. The table rest is plain. On the border, two stylized shields enclose a five-pointed star. Four more stars and scrolled leaves complete the pattern to a rim of twenty-three large scallops alternating with two small ones. As on most cup plates, cap ring configuration can vary. It can have twenty-five large scallops alternating with single small ones, fifty-one small ones or alternating scallops and points.

1419 PRESSED "BENJAMIN FRANKLIN" CUP PLATE
Lee-Rose 619
½" H. x 3½" Dia. 1830–1840

The deeper the authors delve into the social structure of the Nineteenth Century, the more we are convinced that people spent their free time in travel, much as they do today. An article entitled "Notes on Historical Glass Cup-Plates", published in the January 1923 issue of *The Magazine Antiques* by Alice Van Leer Carrick, calls attention to the excursion steamship *Benjamin Franklin* that carried six hundred passengers on chartered and regular runs along the coast from Boston, Massachusetts, to Providence, Rhode Island. According to the *Columbian Centinel* of September 10, 1828, she had two engines, three masts and was 144' in length with a ten foot depth of hold. This cup plate may have been sold as a souvenir on board this ship. (Of course, other vessels by the name *Benjamin Franklin* also existed.) The ship depicted on the cup plate is similar to a vessel illustrated in an advertisement for the steamship's passage from Providence, but it should be mentioned that public notices carried a standard cut from the files of the newspaper. The cup plate shows three masts with a flag "BF" on the mainmast. The letter "F" is on the paddlebox. The name "BENJAMIN FRANKLIN" and a chain of beads are inside the rope table rest. The stays supporting the masts are stippled; those ropes are solid on some variants. Some table rests are plain. The border pattern is a complicated one of stars, anchors, diamonds, scrolls, and an eagle with wings outspread. The American shield is on his breast. This variant with forty-eight rim scallops has been reproduced a number of times. One reproduction carried the paper label of the Westmoreland Glass Company of Grapeville, Pennsylvania.

Advertisement for the steamship *Benjamin Franklin*, put into service in September 1828. The name A. J. Allen also appeared in public notices for the steamboat *Lafayette* (see photos 1463–1464). Allen was listed as a stationer in Boston directories and apparently functioned as an agent for ship companies.
Reproduced by courtesy of The Magazine ANTIQUES

STEAM SHIP BENJAMIN FRANKLIN.

CAPT. R. S. BUNKER, will leave Providence on FRIDAY next, 12 o'clock, M. Passengers by leaving their names at the Marlboro' Hotel, or at A. J. ALLEN'S, No. 72, State-street, will be provided with Coaches.   March 11

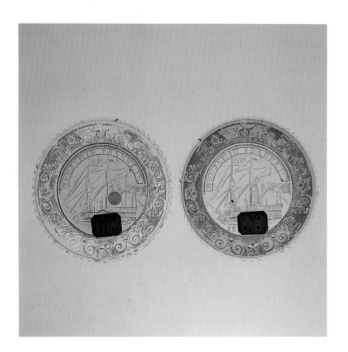

1420 PRESSED "BENJAMIN FRANKLIN" CUP PLATES

Lee-Rose 619A

(a) Silver nitrate center
(b) Silver nitrate border

½" H. x 3½" Dia. 1830–1840

These plates differ from the previously shown one in diameter and rim scallops, which number fifty-nine. Staining glass with silver nitrate was an early decorating technique employed during the Lacy period on large and small pressed articles. The stain was prepared by dissolving silver in nitric acid. When brushed onto glass and fired in a decorating kiln, it turned amber in color. Plate A was stained on the bottom only. Plate B had stain carefully applied on the border, leaving the rim of fifty-nine scallops untouched. A stained, blown lantern engraved by George Franklin Lapham is shown in photo 2416. *Albert C. Marble Cup Plate Collection, Worcester Historical Museum, Worcester, Massachusetts*

1421 PRESSED "BENJAMIN FRANKLIN" CUP PLATE

Lee-Rose 619B

½" H. x 3½" Dia. 1830–1840

This cup plate was pressed in a mold that had a cap ring with fifty-seven scallops. Silver nitrate stain covers the surface except for the table rest and rim. The amber color can vary in intensity depending on the strength of the solution. This example is very bright. Several have been found with stain only on the raised pattern. *Albert C. Marble Cup Plate Collection, Worcester Historical Museum, Worcester, Massachusetts*

1422 PRESSED "CHANCELLOR LIVINGSTON" CUP PLATE

Lee-Rose 628

½" H. x 3½" Dia. 1830–1840

American statesman Robert Livingston was born in New York on November 27, 1746. In 1776, he was sent by the New York State assembly to the Continental Congress, where he was one of five of a committee appointed to draft the Declaration of Independence. He did not sign it, but instead returned to state government. He drew up the state constitution under which he became the first chancellor of New York in 1777. On April 30, 1789, as chancellor he administered the oath of office to George Washington as first president of the United States. Having been granted exclusive privilege of navigating New York waters by steam in 1798, he became a partner and financial backer of Robert Fulton in attempts to perfect steam navigation. After several failures, on August 17, 1807, Fulton's first steamship *Clermont* headed north on the Hudson River bound for Albany, New York. His successful use of the steamboat as a packet ship for freight and passengers led to the building of numerous steam-propelled vessels under his superintendence. One of Fulton's published reports was his 1814 *Advantages of the Proposed Canal from Lake Erie to the Hudson River*. It was the construction of the Erie Canal that spurred Deming Jarves and the Massachusetts Legislature to call for the construction of the Cape Cod Canal through the Town of Sandwich. Fulton died in 1815, about the time the *Chancellor Livingston* was built and named for his former partner, who had died in Clermont, New York, on February 26, 1813. In August 1824 the *Chancellor Livingston* carried the welcoming committee to meet the Marquis de Lafayette, who was aboard the *Cadmus* outside New York Harbor. She later ran between New York and Providence, Rhode Island, and stopped at New Bedford and Nantucket, Massachusetts, in 1830. According to Lee and Rose in their book *American Glass Cup Plates*, she was dismantled in 1834. This plate is one of many variants. The stays, or rigging, can be stippled, solid or a combination of both. Cap ring configuration varies, this one having thirty-eight scallops. Some green plates are swirled with red. *Albert C. Marble Cup Plate Collection, Worcester Historical Museum, Worcester, Massachusetts*

1423 PRESSED "CHANCELLOR LIVINGSTON" CUP PLATE

Lee-Rose 629

½" H. x 3½" Dia. 1830–1840

The *Chancellor Livingston* is identical to the ship depicted in the previous photo except for a boom and rigging at the stern. Her paddle box, three masts, three smokestacks and decks are distinct. She is enclosed by a plain ring and beaded ring inside a rope table rest. The border pattern is made up of two shields, two hearts, scrolls, and large and small stars on a ground of well-defined stipples. This plate without rigging over the stern is more difficult to find in color than the preceding plate. This plate also has thirty-eight scallops. Rims may have as many as sixty-three. It cannot be determined that all such plates were intended to be used on the table for cups. It may be that this was the standard souvenir size during the 1830's and 1840's, as were large pressed platters produced during the latter part of the 1800's by Midwest houses. This plate could have been produced in honor of the vessel's special run to New Bedford and Nantucket and sold aboard the ship or issued in 1834 between the date of Lafayette's death, May 20, and the Boston celebration of his birthday on September 6. According to the *Barnstable Patriot and Commercial Advertiser*, Faneuil Hall was decorated for the occasion with flags of France and the United States, and music was provided by an organ and choir. *Albert C. Marble Cup Plate Collection, Worcester Historical Museum, Worcester, Massachusetts*

Here is the *Chancellor Livingston* as illustrated by line drawing. Note that its angle is the same as it is on the Sandwich plates. Did the pattern designer copy a drawing such as this? If it were possible to trace the origin of patterns on glass, the authors believe it would be found that most were copied from previously published illustrations. The source of this illustration is not known to the Sandwich Glass Museum. Its caption reads, "THE CHANCELLOR LIVINGSTON A PIONEER STEAMBOAT ON THE HUDSON RIVER, BUILT IN 1816, IN SERVICE UNTIL 1828". The latter date is an error.
Courtesy, Sandwich Glass Museum, Sandwich Historical Society

1424 PRESSED "BUNKER HILL" CUP PLATE

Lee-Rose 641

½" H. x 3⅝" Dia. 1840–1845

The Boston and Sandwich Glass Company produced all of the known plates commemorating the anticipated completion of the Bunker Hill Monument in 1841, but there is no way to differentiate the Sandwich plates from those made at other flint glass works in the Boston area. Bunker Hill in the Charlestown section of Boston is connected by a ridge with Breed's Hill. The hills were the scene of a battle on June 17, 1775, during the Revolutionary War. Boston was occupied by the British, so rebel American forces numbering 1500 soldiers planned to seize and fortify the heights of Charlestown. The Americans retreated after exhausting their ammunition in a fierce battle, but their moral victory was great because the British suffered greater losses, proving to the Americans that they were capable of defending their liberties. A granite monument was planned for the Breed's Hill site near where American General Joseph Warren was killed. The cornerstone was laid by the Marquis de Lafayette at a ceremony on June 17, 1825, the fiftieth anniversary of the battle, at which Daniel Webster was the orator. The granite was quarried in Quincy, Massachusetts, and transported downhill by a specially-built, one-horse railway capable of hauling a load of twenty-one tons. (A similar railway was built at the Sandwich glass factory in 1833, as related in Chapter 2.) The monument is in the center of this poorly molded plate. The lettering is difficult to read, but the innermost inscription encircling twelve stars reads, "FROM THE FAIR TO THE BRAVE", referring to the women who raised money to complete the monument. The outer circle reads, "BUNKER HILL BATTLE FOUGHT JUNE 17, 1775". Ten links of chain with small tassels between make up the border. The rim has seventy-six scallops. According to Frederick T. Irwin in his book *The Story of Sandwich Glass*, 2500 Bunker Hill plates were sold at the dedication of the monument. More were needed quickly, so Boston and Sandwich Glass Company workers made one thousand more to be sent to Boston the next morning. If the quality of this plate is poor because the mold was worn or the glass cooled too quickly during the pressing procedure, good examples made under ideal conditions should surface. Yet, the authors have never seen one. Canary fragments were dug at the factory site.

1425 PRESSED "BUNKER HILL" CUP PLATE

Lee-Rose 645A
½" H. x 3⅝" Dia. 1840–1845
This plate can be found with and without the twelve stars in the center. Courses of granite can be seen on the Bunker Hill Monument. The inscription on the bottom is the same as on the previous plate. The drape and tassel pattern outside the plain table rest is similar to that of the 1841 "HARRISON" piece in photo 1414. Beaded circles divide the border into thirds. Between them are molded, "CORNERSTONE LAID BY LAFAYETTE JUNE 17, 1825" and "FINISHED BY THE LADIES 1841". The rim has fifty-three scallops. Despite the 1841 date on the plate, by November, the monument only reached 165 of its 220 foot height. It was completed in 1842 and dedicated on June 17, 1843, with orator Daniel Webster again present. Local glass companies often took part in Bunker Hill celebrations. On June 17, 1875, as reported in the glass industry trade paper *Crockery Journal*, a "creditable display of glass companies" appeared in the procession marking the one-hundredth anniversary of the battle. Foremost was the New England Glass Company of East Cambridge. Horse-drawn barges carried a pot of melted glass and cases of glassware. Glassmakers and cutters wore glass ornaments such as stars and crescents on their clothing. On a reproduction of this plate, there are no tassels between the drapes on the border.

The Monument on Bunker Hill has become an imposing object. It is risen to the height of 165 feet, and may be seen from various points at the distance of many miles. To a spectator in its immediate vicinity, the effect of the simple, unembelished column of granite is a sensation of sublimity. From the top, the view is unexpressibly grand and beautiful; while few persons can stand near its base and look at the top without a feeling of awe and veneration. The work, we believe is now suspended for the season, to be renewed again in the spring, and prosecuted with vigor to its completion. The builder, Mr. Savage, is by contract allowed till October, 1843, to complete it; but from the rapidity, with which he wrought the present season, we have no doubt he will be able to accomplish his labor in the course of the next summer. Twenty or twenty-one courses of stone only are yet to be laid.

Progress on the Bunker Hill Monument's construction was reported in the November 3, 1841, issue of the *Barnstable Patriot and Commercial Advertiser*, a facsimile of which is shown here.

1426 PRESSED EAGLE "1831" CUP PLATE

Lee-Rose 658
½" H. x 3½" Dia. 1831
Fragments of this cup plate were dug in large quantities at the Boston and Sandwich Glass Company site. The eagle's head is facing left and there is the semblance of a shield on his breast. He is perched on a gnarled branch with no olive branch or arrow in his talons. A rope ring separates the eagle from five stars, two olive branches and the date 1831, all on a background of concentric circles. A circle of beads is inside a plain table rest. The border is made up of three scrolled medallions flanked by sprigs of leaves, among which are two leaf-like fleur-de-lys. Small sprigs extend out from the table rest and fill the area below the date. The rim has seventy-eight scallops. This 1831 Eagle plate and its 1832 counterpart may have been made to give to the people who contributed to the restoration of the U. S. F. *Constitution*, also called "Old Ironsides" and "the eagle of the sea". An attempt to dismantle her brought protests from the American populace. She was reconditioned in 1833. It is possible that many of the pieces thought today to be cup plates and open salts were originally manufactured as giveaways and for fund-raising ventures at public events. Many cup plates have Eagle patterns and not all are Sandwich. Some large eagles facing right are from the Midwest. The Sandwich "1831" Eagle plate was reproduced. *Albert C. Marble Cup Plate Collection, Worcester Historical Museum, Worcester, Massachusetts*

1427 PRESSED EAGLE CUP PLATE

Lee-Rose 666

½" H. x 3⅜" Dia. 1830–1845

The central pattern is a small eagle with his head facing right. He holds an olive branch of peace in one claw and the arrows of war in the other. Concentric circles enclosing fine stippling separate the eagle from an outer band of fleur-de-lys alternating with five-petaled rosettes. The border is a combination of elements familiar to other Sandwich cup plates. Three four-petaled blossoms alternate with medallions flanked by leaves. Each medallion encloses a rosette repeated from the bottom of the plate. The rim has forty-nine scallops. One variant has fifty-six scallops. Another has sixty scallops molded in a cap ring that had twelve sides. But the rim is not well delineated and appears more like a poorly-executed circular cap ring with scallops uneven in depth. A large amount of Eagle cup plate fragments were dug from the Sandwich factory site. It must have been a popular pattern. All Lacy cup plates made in Sandwich were manufactured by the Boston and Sandwich Glass Company. When the Cape Cod Glass Works was established in the late 1850's, Lacy glass was out of favor.

1428 PRESSED "THE WEDDING DAY" CUP PLATE

Lee-Rose 697

⅜" H. x 3½" Dia. 1835–1855

Here is an example of what passed for humor in the Nineteenth Century. A lady on the left and gentleman on the right are smiling under the words "THE WEDDING DAY." When the plate is turned 180 degrees, the newlyweds are scowling under the inscription "AND THREE WEEKS LATER." The lady's frilled bonnet becomes her fluted collar. The loosely-designed, flowing floral border pattern and lack of stippling suggests 1840's and 1850's production. The use of these little plates faded out before the Civil War. Very few Sandwich cup plates have a rim configuration of large scallops alternating with a single small scallop. This rim has twenty-one large scallops. This pattern was reproduced. *Albert C. Marble Cup Plate Collection, Worcester Historical Museum, Worcester, Massachusetts*

A typical Cape Cod salt works as pictured in *Pictorial Tales of Cape Cod. Tales of Cape Cod, Inc.*

OPEN AND SHAKER SALTS

1825–1887

Salt was necessary for life from the beginning of time. The fact that it had no substitute is documented in the Holy Bible in Matthew 5:13. It is written that, in his sermon on the mount, Jesus Christ said this to his followers.

Ye are the salt of the earth: but if the salt have lost his savour, wherewith shall it be salted? it is thenceforth good for nothing, but to be cast out, and to be trodden under foot of men.

Salt making is believed to have been the first industry established in America. Colonists of Jamestown, Virginia, erected a works at Cape Charles that sent salt to Massachusetts Puritans in 1633. In Massachusetts, only one person, John Winthrop, had been granted permission by the General Court "to make salt for the Colonie". Beginning March 27, 1656, "none other may make salt within this Jurisdiction for the space of 21 years after this manner, which none hath before known or used".

Early American settlers imported most of their salt, but the British blockade during the Revolutionary War made this almost impossible and certainly unaffordable. In 1777, one hundred years after Winthrop's privilege expired, the Massachusetts General Court gave a bounty of three shillings per bushel to encourage the production of salt by extracting it from boiling sea water. In seashore communities, where salt was also needed for curing fish, commercial saltworks were established at which saltwater was transferred from vat to vat as it was allowed to evaporate by the sun. Only one bushel of salt was derived from 350 gallons of water, so it was essential to find a labor-saving method of conveying water from the sea to the saltworks, usually located on high ground to take advantage of the sun. After hauling by hand and then hand pump, windmills were used with success. Movable covers on vats and troughs protected the water from rain.

According to the November 3, 1827, issue of the *Old Colony Memorial*, the first such works in Massachusetts was on Cape Cod in Dennis, on the north shore adjoining Cape Cod (Barnstable) Bay. The salt industry grew to the point where Dennis alone had 114 saltworks in 1837. Sandwich had eight, which, according to statistics compiled by Town assessors, manufactured only 2670 bushels during the year ending April 1, 1837. Armed with these figures, entrepreneur Deming

Jarves, founder of Sandwich's glass industry who never missed an opportunity to turn a dollar, approached his fellow Board members with an ingenious proposal that would benefit the company as well as himself during hard economic times, following the financial Panic of 1837. At a Board of Directors meeting called for January 11, 1838, Jarves outlined a plan to erect a salt making apparatus on the premises of the Sandwich factory that would evaporate saltwater by utilizing waste heat from a much-needed steam engine.

As related in Chapter 2, the steam engine was required to provide power for an expanding cutting shop. Understandably, the Directors were reluctant to approve its purchase. Jarves suggested that the Boston and Sandwich Glass Company recoup part of the cost by leasing him the waste heat. The sum of $200 was agreed upon, with the understanding that Jarves was to be responsible for the equipment and protective structure. The engine was ordered and set in place. Iron pipes conveyed the heat beneath trays filled with sea water. At the end of the year, the *Yarmouth Register and Barnstable County Advertiser* reported production of ten bushels of salt per day, a figure believed by some to be overestimated. At the time, salt brought $6 to $8 a bushel. There is no further information on the Jarves saltworks. A change in the tariff and expansion of the United States into areas that had natural salt brines and rock salt mines resulted in the decline of coastal evaporating facilities.

Whether from sea or land, the coarsely-milled salt had a tendency to lump and absorb moisture, and so was placed on the table in an open container. Families to whom the lumping was a nuisance made use of soy sauce that was high in salt content. (Soy was placed in a stoppered cruet and/or vinegar caster.) The open container was called a *saltcellar* or simply a *salt*. "Salt Cellars" were listed under *Glass Ware* in an advertisement that appeared in the October 11, 1823, issue of the *Old Colony Memorial and Plymouth County Advertiser*. They were sold by Davis and Russell on Main Street in Plymouth almost two years before glassmaking began in the adjacent Town of Sandwich. Despite the fact that the glass container held only a limited supply of salt, the word *cellar* was in common use as meaning a place of storage. The term used by Sandwich glass works was simply *salt*. During the first full week of production at the Sandwich Glass Manufactory, which began on July 9,

1825, glassmakers turned out 176 blown molded hat salts. The April 1826 factory sloar book documents the variety produced. "Plain salts off foot for cutting", "molded salts" and "molded salts on feet" were the beginning of open salt production that lasted throughout the Boston and Sandwich Glass Company's lifetime. Unless one counts the salt known as *toy hat*, none were made specifically for individual use. Most were quite large—the size that collectors refer to as "master", a term noted by its absence in American glass company catalogs and invoices. (Editor's note: The description *master* in regard to capacity is a carryover from the Fifteenth and Sixteenth Centuries when the largest silver salt was positioned on the table at which the master of the house dined.) Tiny open salts later listed as *individual* came into being when tableware articles were pressed in matching patterns.

Original factory documents that surface from time to time trace the evolution of manufacturing procedures as well as styles, but also attest to research yet to be accomplished. There can be no mistaking the blue salts with feet that were ordered by Russell and Hall of Troy, New York, on September 3, 1826. They and the octagon salt drawn in the sloar book in November 1826 were most assuredly blown molded. But what was the Arratt salt entered in the sloar book in September 1826? Was it blown in a patterned mold named for glassmaker George Arratt, or did the sloar man identify all salts made by Arratt in this manner? In a list of orders that accompanied a June 8, 1827, letter from Agent Deming Jarves to Superintendent William Stutson at the factory was a request from Ezra Stone for round button stem salts "on foot for cutting". The order included a drawing of the intended article. It is possible that this very item is presently in the antiques marketplace unrecognized as Sandwich glass. What was the pressed pattern on the "new Salt Mould" that required a steel plain plunger as dictated by Deming Jarves in correspondence to William Stutson on December 19, 1827? Will we ever know the design of the "cut deep Jackson pattern salts" mentioned in a Jarves letter dated July 25, 1829, that were undoubtedly named for Andrew Jackson? (Jackson was defeated in 1824, but was elected in 1828 to become the seventh President of the United States.)

A little-known early Sandwich manufacturing technique that deserves attention is the production of articles that in their time were called *mottled*. Charles Cotesworth Pinckney Waterman referred to mottled salts when, as friend of the deceased Jarves and former paymaster of the Boston and Sandwich Glass Company, he was asked to prepare a brief history for the Town of Sandwich Centennial box in 1876. Remembering the rivalry between the Sandwich factory and the New England Glass Company in East Cambridge, Massachusetts, Waterman wrote:

> ...we puzzled them with our mottled salts, until we unfortunately sent an imperfect one into the market where the Broken ps of coloured cullet had not been perfectly covered when roll[d] on the marver and being loose they picked it out with a Knife which broke the Charm.

Waterman had described the glass that today is called "spattered" or, erroneously, "end of day". As shown on witch balls in photos 3225–3226, waste glass was crushed and spread on a marver. A bubble of hot glass was rolled over the crushed pieces that penetrated the hot surface and, hopefully, became part of the bubble. The bubble was then shaped into final form by hand tools or was dropped into a pressing mold as shown by the later lamp base in photo 2394. An important dated document recently added to a private collection noted the production of a mottled pepper, which was a bottle with a perforated metal cap. Six dozen mottled peppers were included in an order from Gregory, Bain and Company postmarked Albany (New York) and dated September 3, 1828.

A variety of open salts are available to the salt collector for two reasons. People used an enormous amount of salt, consuming a gallon of water per day to offset it, and the open delivery of salt to the dinner plate continued throughout the Nineteenth Century. The open salts did not match the pepper pot or pepper caster in pattern, nor did the first of the glass shaker salts with perforated metal caps that appeared in the early 1860's. They were indeed first called *shaker salts* rather than salt shakers, hence the title of this chapter. The refined product that was placed in the closed bottle was also marketed in general provisions stores as *shaker salt*. As table manners and eating habits changed with the availability of shaker salt, the pepper bottle came out of the caster set to be paired with a matching salt bottle. Mass production methods dictated that the same shaker bottle placed in glass company inventory could serve both purposes. Whether a bottle was filled with salt or pepper was determined by the style of its metal cap.

The open and shaker salts shown in this chapter represent the various forms and production changes that took place in Sandwich factories. For blown molded patterns, reference is given to the classification system established by George and Helen McKearin in their book *American Glass*. Pressed salts in Lacy patterns are classified according to Logan Wolfe Neal and Dorothy Broome Neal in *Pressed Glass Salt Dishes of the Lacy Period 1825–1850*. Both detailed studies illustrated Sandwich glass as well as glass manufactured elsewhere in the United States and Europe. Without question, neither the McKearins, the Neals nor Barlow and Kaiser were able to show all forms, patterns and designs. We suggest that the reader refer to Chapters 6 and 7 in this volume of *The Glass Industry in Sandwich* for tableware patterns found on salts not shown in this chapter.

THESE SIMPLE HINTS WILL HELP YOU IDENTIFY SANDWICH SALTS

A salt in any documented Sandwich blown molded or pressed tableware pattern can be attributed to Sandwich. Refer to Chapters 6 and 7 for tableware patterns not shown on salts.

Salts with Lacy patterns similar to those on pressed Sandwich salts were also made in France. Generally speaking, French patterns have greater definition and depth.

"Christmas" barrel, Panel and Flute salt bottles were blown into molds. The contour of the inner surface follows the contour of the outer surface of the sidewall. All have a star bottom.

To study designs painted on Sandwich opal shaker salts, refer to decorated lamps, shades and globes in Volume 2, vases in Volume 3, and the reprint of the 1874 Boston and Sandwich Glass Company catalog.

Sandwich glassworkers did not excel in the making of art glass. Blended or shaded colors such as Rubina Verde, Amberina or Peach Blow were not manufactured in Sandwich. The small amounts of Burmese ware *documented* as Sandwich were 1895 experimental attempts by Frederick S. Shirley not found on the open market.

1429 BLOWN MOLDED DIAMOND DIAPER FAN-END SALT

1¾" H. x 3½" L. x 2¼" W. 1825–1830

Fan-end salts were advertised by the New England Glass Company in the October 4, 1819, issue of the *Boston Commercial Gazette*. This type of blown molded square, rectangular and octagonal salts were popular throughout the next decade and were also made by the Sandwich works after it opened in 1825. The Boston and Sandwich Glass Company factory sloar book listed and illustrated molded octagonal salts in November 1826. They were produced by dropping a thick bubble of hot glass into a full-size patterned mold and, after being cracked off above the rim line, were ground smooth in the cutting shop. This salt has a diamond pattern on each side and a large fan on each end that extends from the raised foot to the ribbed rim. Although molded by lung pressure, the pattern cannot always be felt on the inside surface because of the thickness of the sidewall. These early salts are crude by today's standards. They vary in height from one end to the other and rock when on a flat surface. This was caused by uneven heat in the annealing leer. It does not deter from value. Most found at antiques shows have heavy roughage on their rims from hard use. When they left the factory, their rims were perfect. Rim damage greatly affects value because it cannot be corrected by additional machining without changing the height of the rim.

1430 BLOWN MOLDED DIAMOND DIAPER HAT SALT WITH TURNOVER BRIM

McKearin GII-21

2⅛" H. x 2½" Dia. 1825–1835

Although often called "toothpicks", hats were a common salt form in the early years of American glassmaking. During the week of July 9, 1825, the first week of glass production at Deming Jarves' Sandwich Glass Manufactory, 176 molded hats were made. This hat salt is unique because, after folding the rim back upon itself, the gaffer turned it down evenly all the way around. That amount of rework was unusual at a time glassworkers were required to produce a certain amount each week. Reading the pattern from the bottom, there is a band of vertical ribbing, a band of diagonal ribbing to the left, a narrow band of diagonal ribbing to the right and a narrow band of vertical ribbing. The two uppermost bands were muted when the rim was reworked. Unique features such as this brim add to value.

1431 BLOWN MOLDED SUNBURST HAT SALT

McKearin GIII-7

2¼" H. x 2⅝" Dia. 1825–1835

This hat salt has the brim hand tooled in the usual manner. After folding the rim to give it strength, it was tipped down on two opposite sides. The bottom of the salt has a ribbed, or rayed, pattern that can be seen through the lower band of diagonal ribbing to the right. A band of diagonal ribbing to the left is followed by a wide band of diamond diapering panels alternating with the sunburst panels that give the pattern its name. A vertical mold seam can be followed from the left side of the sunburst panel to the bottom, interrupting the pattern of diagonal ribbing.

1432 BLOWN MOLDED DIAMOND SUNBURST SALT

McKearin GIII-21

1¾" H. x 3½" Dia. 1825–1835

Photos cannot do justice to patterns such as this, which is better seen on the decanter in photo 1321. A band of diagonal ribbing to the right and one of diagonal ribbing to the left were distorted when, after removal from the mold, the patterned glass was pinched to form the foot. The band covering the lower half of the bowl is made up of diamond diapering panels alternating with sunburst panels, each sunburst having a divided diamond center. A band of diagonal ribbing to the right on the upper portion of the bowl was pulled to the right in shearing and fire polishing the rim. If the rim was machined, it was done at a later time to remove chips and value is decreased considerably. The *Barlow-Kaiser Sandwich Glass Price Guide* shows how to adjust prices of articles with varying degrees of damage. *Courtesy of The Toledo Museum of Art (Acc. No. 71.17)*

1433 BLOWN MOLDED SUNBURST SALT

McKearin GIII

2¼" H. x 3" Dia. 1825–1835

All blown molded articles that have a galleried rim such as the one on this salt originally had covers. To make the rim, the glass was stretched out to form a wide shelf on which to rest the cover. This eliminated the need to fit a particular cover to a particular salt. Covers were deliberately made to fit loose, so they were still usable if they warped into a slightly oval shape when they were annealed. This sunburst pattern was not classified by George and Helen McKearin in their book *American Glass*. A band of vertical ribbing begins on the foot and extends onto the body followed by a band of diagonal ribbing to the left. The sunbursts alternating with diamond diapering are similar to GIII-13. Collectors sometimes say that pieces such as this were made by hand manipulation after removal from a decanter mold. Documents show that salts were a large part of each week's work, so other molds were not adapted for this use. Future research may disclose that some covered articles included in salt collections today may have been condiment containers for mustard, horseradish or relish. *The Bennington Museum, Bennington, Vermont*

1434 BLOWN MOLDED SUNBURST-IN-SQUARE SALTS

McKearin GIII-25

(a) Galleried rim for cover 2¼" H. x 3" Dia.

(b) Flared rim 1¾" H. x 2¾" Dia. 1825–1835

When these articles were manufactured, a blown bubble of glass was inserted into a patterned mold that had vertical sides. After removal and while still in a molten consistency, the gaffer rotated the patterned article while he drew in the sides by applying pressure with a U-shaped hand tool. The procedure almost obliterated the herringbone pattern in the pinched area above the foot where the surface was rubbed by the hand tool. Regardless of pattern, if you find a similar piece with its pattern distinct in this area, consider that it may be a reproduction. (The problem of Twentieth Century blown molded reproductions is detailed thoroughly in Chapter 7.) Salt A has a galleried rim on which a cover rested. Salt B was hand-tooled into a flanged, or flared, lip and is complete as shown. In reality, salt B should be the greater in value because salt A is only the lower unit of a two-unit article. *Courtesy, Sandwich Glass Museum, Sandwich Historical Society*

1435 BLOWN MOLDED SUNBURST-IN-SQUARE HAT SALT

McKearin GIII-25

2¼" H. x 2½" Dia. 1825–1835

Most flint glass articles were made from batches of clear glass. The first colors to be used at the Sandwich Glass Manufactory and the Boston and Sandwich Glass Company were blue, amethyst and an opaque white called *enamel*. Very few blown molded objects are found in canary and green because production of blown molded ware was curtailed by the time a variety of color came into common use. This hat salt has a pattern of concentric circles on the bottom. The pattern on the sidewall is composed of a band of herringbone, over which is a band of three diamond diapering panels alternating with three panels of a sunburst set at a 45 degree angle. The surface of the glass above the sunbursts is smooth. To make the brim of the hat, the rim was first folded up and over. Then it was tipped downward on opposite sides. Location of pattern elements were not considered when the gaffer fashioned the rim. The sunbursts may not be centered in relation to rim contour.

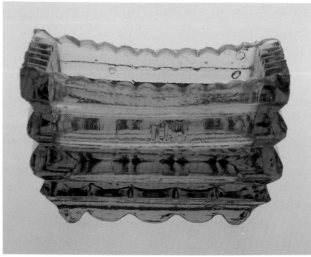

1436 PRESSED SALT

2" H. x 3⅛" L. x 2⅛" W. 1827–1835

This is one of the earliest salts pressed at the Boston and Sandwich Glass Company. Fragments dug at the site indicated large quantities were made there and it is known that the New England Glass Company also produced this pattern. Its form and curved rim follow the forms of blown molded salts and sugar bowls produced in the 1820's. The heavy horizontal ribs resemble free-blown Beehive pieces. Judging from the vertical mold seam marks, the mold opened at all four corners. The study of early salts proves that sophisticated pressing molds came quickly to Sandwich, continuing improvements over the previous decade. Though the mold was designed in the 1820's, color indicates use into the 1830's. Ten dozen "Bee hive" salts were ordered by Thomas Jones to be shipped to New Orleans, Louisiana. The order accompanied a July 2, 1827, letter from Deming Jarves to William Stutson. Whether they were to be pressed or blown was not indicated.

1437 PRESSED SALT

(a) Salt 1⅞" H. x 3⅛" L. x 2⅛" W.
(b) Wooden pattern 1828–1840

Fine detail was possible on wooden patterns, but the simpler the form and pattern, the sooner the mold was made and the sooner production could begin. Since their purpose was to make salt available on the family table, simple containers were all that were necessary. Salt A has a plain rim. Wooden pattern B matches in all respects except the rim, which has a flat block, or Waffle, pattern. Look for salts with both rims. Wooden patterns were not exclusive to Sandwich molds. They were used as models by all mold makers in preparing molds for glass production. *Courtesy, Sandwich Glass Museum, Sandwich Historical Society*

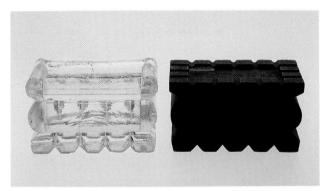

1438 PRESSED SALT

(a) Salt 1¾" H. x 3⅜" L. x 2⅜" W.
(b) Wooden pattern 1828–1840

Heavyweight pieces of tableware were used in public dining rooms on land and ship with little fear of breakage. The niceties of pattern could be overlooked. However, the undulating sides of this salt add to its attractiveness. The plunger that forced the glass into the mold was rounded to give the salt added depth and, therefore, large capacity. A wooden form was made for each mold. After the mold was made, it and the matching wooden pattern was sent to the glass factory. The pattern was stored at the factory until such time as it was needed again in the making of a replacement mold. *Courtesy, Sandwich Glass Museum, Sandwich Historical Society*

1439 PRESSED STRAWBERRY DIAMOND SALT

Neal SD 7
1⅞" H. x 2⅞" L. x 2⅛" W. 1827–1840

If small salts for individual use were made during the 1820's and 1830's, the authors were not aware of them. The allover patterns that completely covered the surface of early pressed salts cannot be found on smaller pieces. Proof that Strawberry Diamond was an early pattern can be found in the order of Thomas Jones that accompanied a July 2, 1827, letter to William Stutson at the Sandwich works. Jones ordered "6 prs Salts no feet, Octagon flang'd, split strawberry diamond and Scallop, Smooth bottom". The allover pattern of diamonds divided into nine fine diamonds is clearly discernible in this photo. It covers all four sides. A sixteen-pointed star is molded into the bottom. Clustered columns make up the corners. A drape motif surrounds the salt on a band below a rim of alternating scallops and points.

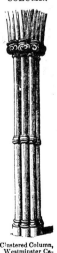

CLUSTERED COLUMN.

Clustered Column, Westminster Cathedral, Eng.

Elements of glass patterns were copied from architecture as illustrated in Webster's 1847 *An American Dictionary of the English Language*. The clustered column, which appears to consist of several columns clustered together, and the scrolled capital above it, make up the corners of the pictured salt. The dictionary illustration was taken from columns on Westminster Cathedral in England.

ARCHITECTURE—Continued.
FESTOON, p. 448.

The festoon in architecture is sometimes composed of an imitation of drapery, similarly disposed, and frequently of an assemblage of musical instruments, implements of war or of the chase, and the like, according to the purpose to which the building it ornaments is appropriated.

The Drape pattern surrounding the salt was known as *festoon* in architecture. In this Webster's dictionary illustration, the festoon was combined with the bucrania, an ornament representing an ox skull. The bucrania was molded into the pressed lamp base shown in photo 2029.

1440 PRESSED STRAWBERRY DIAMOND SALT

Neal SD 9

2⅛" H. x 2⅞" L. x 2⅛" W. 1827–1840

This salt is dark blue with red overtones. Like the salt previously shown, there is a band of vertical ribbing below the Strawberry Diamond pattern on each side and a column at each corner. Button feet end in nipples that can be machined to level the salt, but were not here, although this object is badly warped. A large, extremely deep star on the bottom has twenty points. The band around the top has a chain of horizontal Strawberry Diamonds alternating with simple vertical diamonds. Alternating scallops and points make up the rim. Other variants have bands with ribs, stars or rosettes. Some have rosettes molded into the bottom of the feet, which would be disfigured if the salt was leveled.

1441 PRESSED STRAWBERRY DIAMOND SALT

Neal SD 12

2⅛" H. x 2⅞" L. x 2⅛" W. 1827–1840

Note the mold variants in which Strawberry Diamond salts were pressed. The four sides remain constant, a pattern of squares that, when set at a 45 degree angle, were known as diamonds. Logan Wolfe Neal and Dorothy Broom Neal in their book *Pressed Glass Salt Dishes of the Lacy Period 1825–1850* recorded seventeen variants, not including the wavy-sided salts that follow. The Neals' research and fragments dug at the Boston and Sandwich Glass Company site show most of them to be products of the Sandwich works. Many years of production and replacement of molds account for their abundance. This piece has large, rounded feet that are out of proportion. A sixteen-pointed star is on the bottom. Six-pointed stars surround the salt in the band below the scallop and point rim. *The Bennington Museum, Bennington, Vermont*

1442 PRESSED WAVED AND STRAWBERRY DIAMOND SALTS

(a) *Neal SD 4d* 2⅛" H. x 3⅛" L. x 2⅛" W.

(b) *Neal SD 4a* 2" H. x 2⅞" L. x 2¼" W. 1828–1840

Research by Sandwich Glass Museum Director Barbara Bishop and Historian Martha Hassell, who published their findings in the book *Your Obd*ᵗ*. Serv*ᵗ*., Deming Jarves*, shows that these salts were described at the time of their making as "waved and Diamond". Bishop and Hassell called attention to a letter from Deming Jarves to William Stutson dated June 1, 1829, that included an order from Gregory, Bain and Company of Albany, New York, for twenty dozen "Waved and Diamond Salts". Authors Barlow and Kaiser believe these were the salts in a May 13, 1828, order for six dozen "Wave Salts" for Benjamin Pierce and Son. The Strawberry Diamond salts in this photo have the undulating sidewalls that can be referred to as "waved". Clustered columns make up the corners, from which extend feet that were ¼" high when molded. Often one or more were machined at the factory to level a warped salt. Beneath the bottom of clear salt A is a misshapen eight-pointed star. The pattern beneath blue salt B is a large diamond with one point cut off that encloses an allover pattern of Diamond Check (Checkered Diamond). Variants of these patterns can also be attributed to Sandwich. Both salts have a Banded Leaf pattern beneath their scalloped rims. *Courtesy, Sandwich Glass Museum, Sandwich Historical Society*

1443 PRESSED BEADED STRAWBERRY DIAMOND SALT

Neal OL 15

1¾" H. x 3½" L. x 2⅜" W. 1830–1850

When originally produced by the Boston and Sandwich Glass Company, this salt with raised diamonds separated by beads was available in a number of unusual colors that are rare today. Clear examples are available, but care must be taken to determine that they are old ones. A reproduction was made of lead crystal in Portugal for the Metropolitan Museum of Art in New York. Its quality is such that ringing or tapping it will not differentiate it from the Sandwich salt. The rim of the "repro" has sharp points unlike the salt in the photo that has a rim with a soft contour. The museum's hallmark "MMA" is molded in raised letters that can be removed by unscrupulous antiques dealers. Authors Barlow and Kaiser have unsuccessfully argued for new glass that has lettering indented into the surface that would be difficult to remove without leaving a dished-out punty. *Courtesy, Sandwich Glass Museum, Sandwich Historical Society*

1444 PRESSED STRAWBERRY DIAMOND SALT WITH PAW FEET
Neal OP 2
2⅛" H. x 3¼" L. x 2⅛" W. 1835–1845

Molds became very complicated at the height of the Lacy period. This salt appears to have been made by combining two units, an oval upper unit and a lower unit made up of a rectangular platform with paw feet. However, close inspection reveals four vertical mold seam marks that begin under the center of each paw and extend diagonally across the platform and vertically up the body to the rim. Each paw has five claws. The edge of the platform is serrated. The flat of each diamond is covered with fine diamond point. Large beads follow the rim configuration of eight large scallops. Variants have minor paw changes. *The Bennington Museum, Bennington, Vermont*

1445 PRESSED SHIELD SALT WITH PAW FEET
Neal OP 1a
2" H. x 3⅜" L. x 2½" W. 1835–1845

Note how closely the form of this salt follows the form of the previous paw foot salt. This was a common mold making procedure that allowed the designer to adapt various patterns to the space allotted him once the basic shape was established. It is one more example of the "mix and match" concept that advanced mass production. If you know the forms that were common to Sandwich, and find one with other patterns known to be Sandwich, you may discover combinations that to date have not been recorded. This salt has four scrolled shields that enclose Strawberry Diamonds, two alike on the sides and two that differ on the ends. They alternate with four flower-filled cornucopia on a heavily-stippled ground. The shields closely match the shield on the cream in photo 1042 and certainly date from the same production period. The paws are like those of the nappie on foot shown in photo 1100 and the lamps in photos 2028–2030. If you were aware of the shield, cornucopia and paw, and found them on an oval salt, you could purchase the piece, confident that it was manufactured at Sandwich. A shallow pattern of scrolls and dots on a stippled ground is centered beneath the platform. The upper surface of the platform is smooth. The platform and scalloped rims are serrated.

1446 PRESSED BASKET OF FRUIT SALT
Neal NE 5
2" H. x 3" L. x 2¼" W. 1830–1850

A shallow basket piled high with fruit is on the two long sides of this rectangular piece. Each end has a moss rose sprig with a large five-petaled blossom, two buds and two serrated leaves. Leaves, beads and dots are banded below the scallop and point rim. A large twelve-pointed star fills the bottom. There are many variants that differ in the direction of the basket staves, the beaded basket rim, the way the fruit is piled on the basket, the number of buds on the end sprigs and the banded pattern below the rim. Pattern varies from side to side and end to end on the same salt. Yet all may have come from the same commercial mold making establishment. Those known to have been made at Sandwich have the star bottom, but others are marked "N.E. GLASS COMPANY BOSTON" and "JERSEY GLASS.Cᵒ nʳ.N.YORK". The authors cannot account for the single fragment carrying the letter "G" that was found at the Boston and Sandwich Glass Company factory site. Any explanation is possible including that the factory was inadvertently sent the wrong mold. The unlikely theory was presented that perhaps the Sandwich works manufactured salts for the Jersey works. However, Sandwich manufacture cannot be based on the evidence of one fragment, especially one that was not burnt or otherwise destroyed during the production process. Authors Barlow and Kaiser question whether marked articles were a part of inventory or whether they were given or sold at trade shows and other public events, or if they were salts or taffy containers that were used for salt after they were emptied of their candy.

1447 PRESSED BASKET OF FLOWERS AND ROSETTE SALT
Neal BF 1f
2⅛" H. x 3" L. x 1¾" W. 1830–1840

A single photo cannot do justice to Lacy pieces such as this salt that has end patterns that differ from side patterns. A deep basket on each side is filled with flowers including a five-petaled blossom. A ten-petaled blossom or rosette is on each side of the basket. Scrolls and leaves on the feet and rim combine into sprigs that resemble Princess Feather (Prince's Feather) as depicted on larger articles in Chapter 6. The pattern on both ends combines ram's horn, leaves and five-petaled blossoms. All four sides are stippled. The feet can be machined if necessary. *The Bennington Museum, Bennington, Vermont*

1448 PRESSED BEADED SCROLL AND BASKET OF FLOWERS SALT

Neal BS 2, CD 2

1⅞" H. x 2½" L. x 1½" W. 1835–1845

The molds in which salts were pressed were created by a commercial mold maker who had the mold cast in metal at the foundry of his choice. After the casted mold sections were returned to the mold maker, he inscribed the required pattern into the metal. Each repeat was slightly different than the same motif preceding it. This salt, which is between emerald and apple green in color, demonstrates the individuality of pattern. Both sides have a deep basket with flowers of even height. The rim and bottom of both baskets is delineated by beads. The basket on one side has eight beads at the bottom and eight at the rim. The basket on the opposite side has eight beads at the bottom and nine at the rim. If the baskets were on two different salts, the salts would be considered variants by a dedicated salt collector. In the opinion of the authors, minor pattern changes that were the result of handwork do not a variant make! The ends of this salt have horizontal, alternating rows of beads and rope. A matching pattern in the bottom is one of concentric circles of alternating beads and rope surrounding a small twelve-pointed star. An inner shelf at each end was designed to support a cover in the pattern shown in the following photo. However, the covers are not interchangeable.

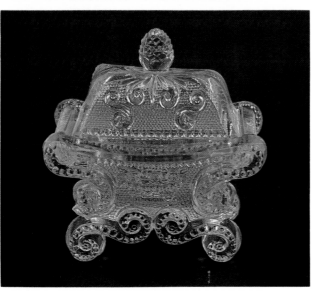

1449 PRESSED BEADED SCROLL AND BASKET OF FLOWERS SALT

Neal BS 3a, CD 2a

(a) Salt 1¾" H. x 3" L. x 1¾" W.

(b) Cover 1½" H. x 2⅜" L. x 1⅜" W.

(c) Combined size 3⅛" H. x 3" L. x 1¾" W. 1835–1845

This Sandwich salt, like the previous piece, has the same pattern of a flower-filled basket and beaded scrolls ending in tiny blossoms. Molded into the bottom is a six-pointed star, flanked by two chevrons, from which radiate serrated rays. The end pattern has a band of eight rounded ribs placed side by side surmounted by a chain of beads. As on the above salt, the protruding uppermost portion is covered with fine ribs, or reeds, and stippling. This successfully hides the inner shelf on which the cover rests. The cover has scrolls on a stippled ground and a pine cone finial. The authors believe that all rectangular salts with inner shelves were shipped from the factory with covers. Covers are so scarce today that their value is much greater than that of the lower unit. As a rule of thumb, the value of the cover is six times that of the salt. If you see a cover alone, purchase it. You will eventually find the lower unit.

1450 PRESSED LYRE (HARP) SALT

Neal LE 3, CD 5

1⅞" H. x 3⅛" L. x 2" W. 1835–1845

A lyre is centered on each side. Two flower-filled cornucopia are beneath the lyre. They are upside down and their flowers form the large scallops near the scroll and rosette feet. Two cornucopia extend from the S-scrolls forming the contour of the corners to the scallops that form the rim. At each end of the salt is a pattern that combines plumes and S-scrolls that repeat the form of the lyre. Molded beneath the bottom are two arcs enclosing rays, outside of which are small diamonds. This salt does not have inner shelves to support a cover, yet it is sometimes found with one as shown in the photo that follows. *Courtesy, Sandwich Glass Museum, Sandwich Historical Society*

1451 PRESSED LYRE (HARP) SALT

Neal LE 2, CD 4

(a) Salt 1⅞" H. x 3⅛" L. x 2" W.

    Cover 1⅝" H. x 2⅜" L. x 1⅜" W.

    Combined size 2⅞" H. x 3⅛" L. x 2" W.

(b) Clear Cover 1⅝" H. x 2¼" L. x 1½" W. 1835–1845

This variant of the Lyre salt has a six-pointed rosette beneath two of the rim scallops. The arcs on the bottom are delineated by a rope pattern, outside of which are beads. Although the salt does not have inner shelves to support a cover, covered salts in clear and blue are occasionally found. The colored salts and covers are well matched and do not appear to have been combined at a later time. Possibly, lower units and optional covers were priced separately and the retail customer purchased the salt with or without its cover, depending on the preference of the family. (It is possible that the covered pieces were used for wet condiments.) As with every colored, covered article, take time to determine that the units are not "married". Slight differences in shade may be the result of thickness of the glass, but a difference in tint indicates a "marriage". If it is determined that the units were later combined, their purchase price should be based on the value of two individual parts. The scroll and stippled pattern is inside the cover and cannot be seen through the blue one. *The Bennington Museum, Bennington, Vermont*

1452 PRESSED EAGLE SALT

Neal EE 1a
2" H. x 3" L. x 2¼" W. 1827–1840
This Eagle salt was made to the specified standard dimensions and configuration geared to mass production. The clustered column corners, scallop and point rim, and band of leaves are those of Strawberry Diamond salts. This "mix and match" method of mold design allowed numerous articles to be added to the Boston and Sandwich Glass Company inventory to give the customer a large selection. The eagle faces left. A shield is at his breast. His talons hold an olive branch of peace and the arrows of war. Thirteen six-pointed rosettes loosely spaced around the eagle may represent the thirteen original states of the United States of America. A variant has smaller rosettes. The placement of the rosettes varies from side to side. A tree is depicted on each end, with four low bushes at the ground line. The number of leaves on the bushes varies from end to end. A sixteen-point star covers the bottom. The salt is devoid of stippling. Six-pointed rosettes beneath each foot may be machined to level the piece. If the salt was leveled at the factory, a minimal amount of glass would have been removed. Beware of salts with stubby feet that may have been altered by an antiques dealer who has chipped feet "repaired" in this manner. This salt was given to The Toledo Museum of Art by Edward Drummond Libbey, who moved the New England Glass Works to Toledo, Ohio (see note 6 on page 44 of Volume 3). Libbey's presentation to the museum may indicate that this pattern was also made at the New England Glass Company. *Courtesy of The Toledo Museum of Art (Acc. No. 17.575)*

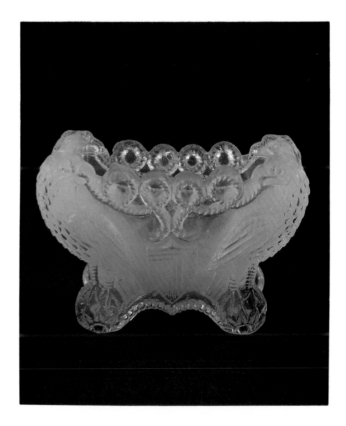

1453 PRESSED EAGLE AND SHIELD SALT

Neal EE 3b
2⅛" H. x 3¼" L. x 2⅛" W. 1830–1845
This American Eagle salt is one of the most attractive patterns pressed at the Boston and Sandwich Glass Company. Two heavily-feathered eagles are back to back, their breasts forming the corner configurations. Each eagle is perched on a ball foot that has a half rosette facing the side. Each eagle's head is turned back over his wing. They hold in their beaks the ends of a rope from which depends an American shield. The coils of the rope form four rim scallops. On each end of the salt, a pointed quatrefoil is surrounded by thirty-two small ones. A twelve-pointed star is molded into the small bottom. A similar salt thought to have been made in Pennsylvania is longer by ½". The rope is replaced by a beaded chain. Leaves on a stippled ground and rounded ribs make up the end pattern of the Pennsylvania salt. *The Bennington Museum, Bennington, Vermont*

1454 PRESSED EAGLE AND SHIP SALT

Neal EE 8a
2" H. x 2⅞" Dia. 1830–1845
The sidewall of this extremely beautiful salt is divided into six panels, each panel having a circular medallion delineated by a rope ring on a ground of fine diamonds. Three medallions enclosing an eagle alternate with three medallions enclosing a three-masted ship. Whether the vessel is the United States Frigate *Constitution* or the *Cadmus* that brought Lafayette to New York in 1824 is not known. It may not be either one. The ship medallion matches that of the cup plate in photo 1418. The eagle with a breast shield, facing left, is repeated as a central pattern on the bottom of the salt. The usual olive branch and arrows are in his talons. The outer portion of the bottom has concentric circles in a pattern of herringbone, or zigzag. The foot with its reeded pattern was molded in one piece with the body. Note that the salt lacks a stem found on later circular articles. The Eagle and Ship salt was made with three rim configurations. With the scalloped rim shown in this photo, the salt matches an oval dish in the collection of The Corning Museum of Glass in Corning, New York, and is pictured in Jane Shadel Spillman's book *American and European Pressed Glass*. Two variants have rims with a flat upper surface, one smooth and one with an intricate chain. *Courtesy, Sandwich Glass Museum, Sandwich Historical Society*

1455 PRESSED CROWN SALT
Neal CN 1b
2⅛" H. x 3⅛" L. x 2" W. 1830–1840
The pattern on the side of this salt is divided horizontally. The lower half is covered by an allover pattern of fine diamond point. An ornament in the middle of the upper half is thought to resemble a crown. It is flanked by scrolls, outside of which are stipples. Scrolls define the contour of the feet and rim. The end pattern combines two fleur-de-lys, one above the other, and brackets on a stippled ground. The bottom of the salt is divided diagonally in four triangles. Two opposite triangles abutting the sides have rays extending from the center. The remaining two are diamond point. Variants have minor differences in the bottom pattern and in the shape of the ribbed band just below the flat part of the rim. *The Bennington Museum, Bennington, Vermont*

1456 PRESSED SALT
1¾" H. x 2¾" Dia. 1835–1850
This hexagonal piece follows the lines of similar ones believed to have been products of European glass houses. However, it was in a private collection of someone who only bought Sandwich glass that could be traced directly back through previous ownership to the Sandwich factory. The collection included this Lacy object with its trefoil ornament in amber, blue and green. Each one held a blown witch ball in a matching color as shown in photo 3233. The authors tend to believe they are salts. We cannot discount the theory that in the Cape Cod area they may have served as witch ball holders. Blown witch ball stands that match witch balls were not a Sandwich product, as far as we can determine. The early Sandwich sloar book documents the manufacture of witch balls, but does not list anything that could be interpreted as being a witch ball stand. Clear examples are known.

1457 PRESSED SHELL SALT
Neal SL 2a
1¾" H. x 3" L. x 2" W. 1835–1850
The most prominent element in this pattern is the large shell in the center of the sides and ends. As was usual during this period, the cartouche pattern determined the configuration of the salt as illustrated by the undulating rim and corners. Small five-pointed fans depend from the rim. The pattern is repeated on the raised foot. The bottom is covered with diamond point. There are a number of variants that show changes in the pattern beneath the bottom and the number of points on the fans. Most interesting from a study standpoint is the gauge of the stipples that cover the remaining surface. Some salts have stippling that is finer than the example in this photo. Others have coarse stippling, perhaps a labor-saving decision by mold makers when the United States was in financial turmoil as the result of the panic of 1837. (The temporary bankruptcy of the Boston and Sandwich Glass Company in 1837 is discussed in Chapter 2.) Few salts pressed in the first half of the Nineteenth Century match other glassware. However, their lines follow the transfer designs of English pottery.

1458 PRESSED SALT
Neal OO 20
1⅜" H. x 2¾" L. x 1⅞" W. 1835–1850
This shallow, rectangular piece with a chamfer at each corner is also shown as a toy in photo 3346. C-scrolls placed end to end form a horizontal chain below a scalloped rim. A three-lobed ornament that resembles a fleur-de-lys depends in the center of the sides and ends. There is a beaded swag below on the sides only. A small lily and diamond are on the narrow panels that separate the side and end panels. Tiny squares are molded beneath the bottom. Vertical ribbing is inside the raised foot. This piece probably was marketed as a salt, but we may never know for sure. In their book *Pressed Glass Salt Dishes of the Lacy Period 1825–1850*, Logan Wolfe Neal and Dorothy Broom Neal listed it only in clear and as very rare. When visiting antiques shops and shows, look through the merchandise of doll and dollhouse dealers for pieces such as this. The piece in this photo is warped from overheating in the annealing leer.

1459 PRESSED STAG'S HORN SALT

Neal SN 1

1¾" H. x 3" L. x 1⅞" W. 1835–1850

The motif in the center of the sides and ends are thought to resemble a stag's head with antlers. Close inspection shows it to be leaf sprigs emanating from a central figure that resembles an urn or a lily. Shallow stipples cover the background, but variants can be found that are not stippled. Examination of French catalogs such as those issued by Launay Hautin & Compagnie reveals that the same patterns were manufactured with and without stippling, called a "sand" finish by the Parisian firm. The rim is a continuous sweep ending in scrolls at the corners. The bottom is rayed. Ribs are molded into the outside surface of the raised foot. *Courtesy, Sandwich Glass Museum, Sandwich Historical Society*

1460 PRESSED FLORAL SALTS

(a) On foot *Neal RP 3*

    2" H. x 3" Dia.

(b) "Off foot" *Neal RD 22*

    1¼" H. x 3" Dia. 1835–1850

All variants of this circular salt are extremely rare. Silver blue salt A has a foot with a rim of twelve even scallops. A variant with this foot has a six-pointed star centered beneath the foot. Another has a foot with nineteen scallops that were poorly spaced on the mold and therefore vary in width. The lower portion of the sidewall has a floral pattern repeated three times around the piece. In the center of each is a rose in bloom. A spray of leaves and blossoms extends from each side of the rose. Fine gauge chains above and below the flowers stand out in bold relief. The upper portion has vertically-placed leaves alternating with elements of two tiny leaves and a blossom repeated from the floral spray. Leaves and five- and six-pointed flowers are pressed into the upper surface of the plain rim. A variant has a rim of small scallops. On occasion, the piece was pressed with a patterned plunger. Within the same article, color appears marbleized from light blue to almost white, giving the pattern great depth. The Boston and Sandwich Glass Company succeeded in translating the cameo-like patterns of Wedgwood pottery onto glass. Blue examples are seldom found in good condition. Clear salt B has a flat bottom. Vertical leaves on the sidewall are seen through the glass. A rope ring is inside the plain rim, but the salt is known with both border patterns. Salt A is shown with an underplate in the book *Pressed Glass Salt Dishes of the Lacy Period 1825–1850*. Authors Barlow and Kaiser cannot be sure the combination is correct. We believe the lower unit is a cup plate identified as Lee-Rose 85.

1461 PRESSED CHARIOT SALT

Neal CT 1

1¾" H. x 2⅞" L. x 2¼" W. 1835–1850

The authors believe that the mold for this silver blue rectangular salt was created at the mold making establishment responsible for the previously shown Floral circular object. Although very rare, undamaged specimens in marbleized blue and opaque white are still available. The salt in this photo has a green streak extending from the head of the charioteer goddess to the right and across the end, caused by gall in the pot of hot glass. Two prancing horses pull the chariot. Flowers spill from a cornucopia at the rear. A beaded shield ornament on each end is flanked by depended leaves and rose blossoms. The figure enclosed by the shield that resembles a dolphin was most likely copied from a picture of a sea horse. In mythology as described in Webster's 1847 dictionary, sea horses were employed by Neptune for drawing his chariot. Pointed ovals and diamonds make up the scallop and point rim. The bottom is a scalloped platform with rings and leaves forming wreaths around a central rosette. A variant has a beaded ram's head ornament with leaves. The feet end in well-rounded rosettes that may be machined to level the salt. Examine the feet closely when considering a purchase. Damaged feet deter from value.

In *myth.*, a fabulous animal depicted with fore parts like those of a horse, and with hinder parts like those of a fish. The Nereids used sea-horses as riding steeds, and Neptune employed them for drawing his chariot.

The tail and scales of a sea horse as illustrated in Webster's 1847 dictionary are clearly defined on the ends of the Chariot salt. Space limitations within the enclosing shield dictated that the pattern maker lower the horse head onto the front hooves. The figure lost its impact as the steed that pulled Neptune's chariot.

1462 PRESSED BEADED SCROLL AND SCROLLED LEAF SALT
Neal MV 1
1¾" H. x 2⅞" L. x 2⅛" W. 1835–1850
This salt is documented as a product of three glass houses, the Boston and Sandwich Glass Company in Sandwich, the Mount Vernon Glass Company in Vernon, New York, and the Mount Pleasant Glass Works in Mount Pleasant, New York. An ornament made up of two beaded C-scrolls back to back is centered on each side. Three lobes extend upward from between them. A chain of beads near the corners forms the vein of a scrolled leaf. The leaves are repeated on the ends and between them is a round beaded ornament with seven lobes extending upward. The scallop and point rim is formed by pointed ovals and diamonds. Beneath the scalloped bottom, a beaded buckle encloses a beaded scroll ornament. Variants have fourteen- and sixteen-point stars. *The Bennington Museum, Bennington, Vermont*

1463 PRESSED "LAFAYET." STEAMBOAT
Neal BT 5
1⅝" H. x 3⅝" L. x 2" W. 1830–1845
This glass replica of a steam-powered paddle wheel boat is the only piece of Sandwich glass known to date that was signed by the Boston and Sandwich Glass Company. If the authors could place themselves in an early Nineteenth Century glass wareroom, we would be surprised if the lady of the house purchased for the dinner table a fleet of vessels marked "LAFAYET." on the paddle box and "B.&.S. GLASS C⁰" on the stern. We doubt that marked steamboats ever saw the inside of a salesroom. Most found today seem to emanate from eastern United States rather than having been distributed throughout the country by glass company agencies. We believe that they were advertising items that were given out either empty or filled with hard candy or taffy. No documentation reveals specific public events where they were distributed, but the number still in existence testifies to large production runs. In addition to the usual trade shows, fairs and parades, there were two Lafayette-related events that could have motivated such a pressed salt. The first was a procession and ceremony that was estimated to have drawn as many as 200,000 people to the heart of Boston. According to the September 10 and 17, 1834, issues of the *Barnstable Patriot and Commercial Advertiser*, September 6 had been set aside to honor the Marquis de Lafayette, who had died the previous May 20. Flags of shipping in the harbor were lowered and the Customs House was closed for the occasion that had taken much preliminary planning. The procession of dignitaries from near and far made its way to Faneuil Hall, which was occupied as a large food market on the lower floor and a gathering hall above that had standing room for thousands of people. The hall was draped in black for "George Washington's friend". A glass boat resembling those that were in New York Harbor when Lafayette returned for a visit in 1824 would have been a fitting memento for those attending. A second possibility is that the glass boat was given to travelers aboard a ship named *Lafayette*. Research disclosed a number of vessels by that name including schooners that plied eastern waters in the 1830's and 1840's and an American brigantine that in the late 1840's was sold to the king of the Hawaiian Islands through the efforts of James Jackson Jarves, son of Deming Jarves. (The history of the Jarves family is related in Chapter 3.) The most logical model for the Sandwich boat was the steamboat *Lafayette* that in 1828 and 1829 plied between Boston and Plymouth and in 1831 from Boston to Hingham. As shown by the vessel's schedule, her number of excursion and scheduled trips during long seasons could account for part of the heavy production of the glass paddle wheel steamboat. She later made trips along the Maine coast and broke up at Eastport, Maine, in 1835.

1464 PRESSED "LAFAYET." STEAMBOATS

(a) *Neal BT 6*
(b) *Neal BT 4d*
1⅝" H. x 3⅝" L. x 2" W. 1830–1845

Several molds were used to make the Sandwich glass steamboat, all having the abbreviated "LAFAYET." molded on both paddle boxes. The star in the center of the paddle box can vary in size. The rim can be serrated as on steamboat A or smooth as on steamboat B. Both in this photo are marked "SANDWICH" on the inside surface of the bottom, but several variants are not. The inside lettering is effective on opaque and dark glass, but is lost on colorless glass because of the pattern beneath. The underside can vary. Several bottoms have a central ornament, sometimes enclosing a star, surrounded by beaded concentric ovals. The outermost oval forms the table rest. Some have a scrolled ornament that may or may not be bisected by "SANDWICH". All but one variant found thus far have molded into the square stern "B.&.S. GLASS C°". The unmarked one has two four-paned windows flanked by two stars. Neither surface of the bottom is lettered. This unmarked variant may have had limited sales because of the many marked steamboats that were given away. It is seldom seen today. When purchasing any boat, make sure the rim was not machined to eliminate chips. This greatly reduces value.

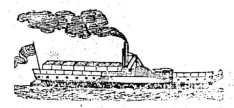

FOR BOSTON & PLYMOUTH.
THE STEAM-BOAT

LAFAYETTE,
CAPT. T. C. HOLMES,

HAVING been thoroughly repaired, will leave the Steam-boat Wharf, Plymouth, and the end of Long Wharf, Boston, on the following days, (weather permitting,) viz :

LEAVE PLYMOUTH,
MONDAY, 27th April, at 8, A. M.
THURSDAY, 30th, 10, A. M.

LEAVE BOSTON,
WEDNESDAY, 29th April, 11, A. M.
SATURDAY, 2d May, 1, P. M.

☞ Passage $1. Freight taken at the usual rates. Light articles of Freight left at N. SMITH'S, No. 71, Long Wharf, will be taken on board free of expense. For further information apply to A. J. ALLEN, No. 72, State-st.
April 18, 1829. 52

Scheduled runs of the steamboat *Lafayette* between Boston and Plymouth were routinely published in the Plymouth newspaper *Old Colony Memorial*. The vessel made two round trips a week in the spring as indicated by the advertisement dated April 18, 1829. July and August ads show an increase to three times a week with extra excursions on special holidays.

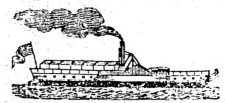

FOR PLYMOUTH & BOSTON.
THE STEAM-BOAT

LAFAYETTE,
CAPT. T. C. HOLMES,

HAVING been thoroughly repaired, will leave the Steam-boat Wharf, Plymouth, and the end of Long Wharf, Boston, on the following days. (weather permitting,) viz :

ARRANGEMENT FOR JULY.

LEAVE PLYMOUTH,
Monday, July 6, at 5, A. M.
Wednesday, 8, " 7, "
Friday, 10, " 8, "
Monday, 13, " 8, "
Wednesday, 15, " 10, "
Friday, 17, " 10, "
Monday, 20, " 6, "
Wednesday, 22, " 7, "
Friday, 24, " 8, "
Monday, 27, " 9, "
Wednesday, 29, " 10, "
Friday, 31, " 10, "

LEAVE BOSTON,
Tuesday, July 7, at 9, A. M.
Thursday, 9, " 9, "
Saturday, 11, " 10, "
Tuesday, 14, " 11, "
Thursday, 16, " 1, P. M.
Saturday, 18, " 8, A. M.
Tuesday, 21, " 9, "
Thursday, 23, " 9, "
Saturday, 25, " 10, "
Tuesday, 28, " 10, "
Thursday, 30, " 1, P. M.

☞ Passage $1—to Scituate 50 cts. Freight taken at the usual rates. Light articles of Freight left at N. SMITH'S, No. 71, Long Wharf, will be taken on board free of expense.
July 4.

[The LAFAYETTE will make an excursion into the Bay for a few hours THIS DAY—leave the wharf, at 12 M. July 4th.]

1465 PRESSED BOAT
Neal BT 9
1¾" H. x 3⅞" L. x 2⅛" W. 1835–1850
This and the previously shown steamboat are the only glass boats known to have been pressed in Sandwich. Fragments in clear and fiery opalescent were dug in filled land in the vicinity of the Boston and Sandwich Glass Company factory. Its stern, keel and stem follows the lines of the "LAFAYET." steamboat, and the beads on the stem resemble those on the Beaded Scroll and Basket of Flowers salt. The sides are a sampler of patterns arranged in horizontal rows. Reading from the bottom are horizontal ribs, diamond point slanting left, diamond point slanting right, diagonal ribbing to the right, raised squares divided diagonally into four triangles, a sweeping horizontal rib from stem to stern and, at the rim, diagonal ribbing or rope. A sixteen-point star covers the stern. The boat was pressed in a two-section mold, its seam bisecting the unpatterned bottom. Glass boats are included in salt collections today, but at the time of manufacture they may have been the forerunner of the covered candy container. In the 1860's, the Cape Cod Glass Company printed a *List of Glass Ware* that included "No. 47 Steamboat" salt. Its placement with salts described as "No. 48 '76 Hat", "No. 53 Shell" and "No. 60 Derby" indicate a figural piece. However, it could have been a salt with a weighted base that was used when dining on board a ship. A weighted base prevented a salt from tipping over in heavy seas.

1466 PRESSED GOTHIC ARCH SALT
Neal GA 2
1⅝" H. x 2¾" L. x 2" W. 1835–1845
This pattern of pointed arches was common at Sandwich and at the New England Glass Company, as were several variants. Each of three Gothic arches on the side of the salt are divided into two arches enclosing fine diamond point. A quatrefoil is centered beneath the uppermost point. The ends have a single, differing Gothic arch with lattice flanked by eight-pointed rosettes. Stippling fills the remaining surface. This salt has a rim of nineteen scallops from corner to corner; variants have sixteen and seventeen. The raised bottom is rayed. The Boston and Sandwich Glass Company also made a Gothic Arch and Heart salt that matches the rectangular dish in photo 1051. A similar salt made in the Pittsburgh, Pennsylvania, area has beads on the edge of the raised bottom and nine large rim scallops on the side. *Courtesy of The Toledo Museum of Art (Acc. No. 17.577)*

1467 PRESSED PEACOCK EYE (PEACOCK FEATHER) SALT
Neal PR 1b
1½" H. x 3" Dia. 1830–1845
This is one of few early pressed patterns that match other tableware items as shown in Chapter 6. The name *Peacock Eye* refers to the "eye" in the feathers of a peacock's tail. Similar patterns manufactured in France were called *queue de paon*, which means "tail of peacock". Each feather on the circular sidewall begins above the raised foot and curves to the left. The eye, or bull's eye, is below a serrated rim scallop that alternates with a point. Each feather carries the same pattern of diamond point. Variants are in the pattern of circles pressed beneath the bottom. The salt in this photo has four concentric circles on the bottom, the innermost a rope ring, a plain ring, and two more rope rings. The table rest is smooth. *The Bennington Museum, Bennington, Vermont*

1468 PRESSED PEACOCK EYE (PEACOCK FEATHER) SALT

Neal PP 2

2⅛" H. x 3⅛" Dia. 1830–1845

This footed circular salt has feathers that curve to the right, but variants curve to the left. As shown in the previous photo, the eyes are below the twelve serrated rim scallops. However, the rim is flared above the eyes. The bottom has six concentric rings, three inside that are plain and three outside that are rope, or cable. Variants have bottoms on which all rings are plain. Others have a rosette made up of twenty-seven rays and two or three beaded circles. Table rests are plain. Similar salts made in the Pittsburgh, Pennsylvania, area replace the convex bull's eyes with eight-pointed rosettes. Their rims are a combination of large and small smooth scallops, while the Sandwich products have serrated scallops alternating with points. *The Bennington Museum, Bennington, Vermont*

1469 PRESSED PEACOCK EYE (PEACOCK FEATHER) SALTS

(a) *Neal PO 6*

   Large concave eyes 1½" H. x 3⅞" L. x 2⅞" W.

(b) *Neal PO 2a*

   Small convex eyes 1⅜" H. x 3½" L. x 2½" W. 1830–1845

The number of variants pressed into small pieces such as salts and mustards as well as large dishes attests to popularity over a long period. Fragments dug from the Boston and Sandwich Glass Company site by Sandwich historian Francis (Bill) Wynn were of articles that differed in center pattern, rim configuration and the allover pattern of fine diamond point and stipples that cover the feathers. The fragments when sorted by Wynn were listed as *Horn of Plenty.* Oval Peacock Eye salts alone vary greatly. The eyes, or bull's eyes, on salt A are concave. Those on salt B are smaller and convex. Some salts have flat eyes. But all eyes are enclosed by a rope ring and extend into an evenly scalloped rim. Beneath the bottom of salt A is a large eight-pointed star with an eight-petaled rosette center. The bottom of salt B is rayed. Variants combine beads and small leaves. Table rests can be smooth as shown in the photo, beaded or serrated. Many salts were made in colors that vary greatly. Color does not determine place of manufacture. All flint glass houses were capable of producing any color required by their customers. *The Bennington Museum, Bennington, Vermont*

1470 PRESSED PEACOCK EYE (PEACOCK FEATHER) SALT

(a) Salt *Neal PO 2*

   1¼" H. x 3½" L. x 2½" W.

(b) Wooden pattern 1830–1845

A study of the wooden pattern necessary for the making of Peacock Eye (Peacock Feather) molds reveals the reason for the many variants. The mold was cast to the basic form of the wooden pattern (i.e., the rise of the foot, the curve of the sidewall and the number of large scallops on the rim). Intricate detail was chipped into the mold by individuals who had different styles and capabilities. The gauge of the fine diamond point, the thickness of the rope rings around each eye and the contour of each eye was left to each mold maker's discretion with no direction from the glass factory superintendent, who, frankly, didn't care. Because there are so few wooden patterns compared to the number of available matching glass articles, they are highly prized by collectors and have become valuable in themselves. *Courtesy, Sandwich Glass Museum, Sandwich Historical Society*

1471 PRESSED SALT

Neal OO 1a

1½" H. x 3" L. x 2¼" W. 1830–1850

Most prominent on this oval salt is the large ring that extends from the bottom to the rim scallop. It encloses diamond point. Two vertical rows of diamond point on each end are confined by a magnet, or horseshoe. The four major elements alternate with columns made up of two raised diamonds that have fine diamond point on their flat surface and a fan that forms a rim scallop. Note the fins of this glass on the rim. This is overfill that was caused when the pressure of the plunger forced hot glass into the seams of the mold. Glass such as this that extends beyond the confines of the rim should not be thought of as roughness. If anything, it adds value in the eyes of an experienced collector. The rectangular bottom has a chamfer at each corner and a sixteen-pointed star that extends to the table rest.

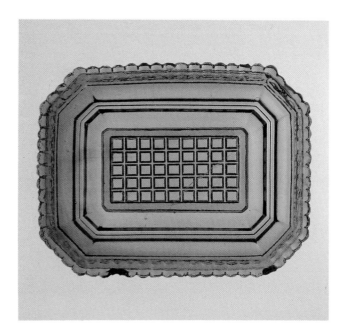

1472 PRESSED INVERTED WAFFLE SALT

1" H. x 3¼" L. x 2½" W. 1840–1850

This shallow salt was the smallest of matching rectangular dishes as shown in photo 1130. Several sizes were made in amber as well as clear. Amber was an unusual color to use on tableware because it was considered to be a bottle color and was not well accepted in the tableware market. The Inverted Waffle pattern on the bottom is enclosed by a plain table rest, both of which would not be seen when the piece was filled with salt. The small rim scallops mimic those of cup plates. Note that a scallop is missing on the upper right chamfer because the mold was underfilled. This manufacturing flaw does not reduce value. However, value is reduced because of the two chips at the bottom.

1473 PRESSED INVERTED WAFFLE SALT

1" H. x 3¼" L. x 2½" W. 1840–1850

This pattern is the same as previously shown, but adapted to oval form. The rim scallops differ in that they are curved on the outer and upper surfaces, making removal from the mold much more difficult. The darkness of the amethyst would hide the pattern if it was pressed into a large, thick, piece such as a sugar bowl or footed nappie. It is free from the usual chips inside the rim and on the scallops.

1474 PRESSED OVAL SALT

(a) Salt 3⅛" H. x 3⅛" Dia.
(b) Wooden pattern 1840–1860

The pattern of ovals repeated six times around the hexagonal salt was used in Europe as well as the United States. The wooden pattern for making the mold was usually made from cherry, but mahogany, birch and nutwoods were also used. Most wooden patterns have blackened with age from the residue of oil that was wiped on before they were surrounded by plaster. For holloware, the mold company also produced a core exact in shape of the inside of the vessel. This became the shape of the plunger that was attached to the piston of the pressing machine as illustrated in Chapter 6. On the wooden pattern in this photo, the horizontal ovals were made of metal and were attached to the wood by tiny brads, and the plaster-of-Paris was cast to this pattern. By repositioning the ovals, a mold with vertical ovals could be made. An unpatterned mold for a hexagonal salt was cast by removing the ovals. *Courtesy, Sandwich Glass Museum, Sandwich Historical Society*

1475 PRESSED LOOP (LEAF) SALT

(a) Salt 2⅝" H. x 3" Dia.

(b) Wooden pattern 1850–1875

This hexagonal salt A has a pattern of a rounded arch on each of six sides. It was made with and without a foot in East and Midwest glass houses. It was shown without a foot in a catalog of Pittsburgh's Bakewell, Pears and Company, where it was identified as *Leaf*. Another salt made at Sandwich is identical except that there are no arches. The molds for both salts were made by using wooden pattern B as a model. Like the previous wooden pattern, this one also has removable metal medallions. As the 1850's approached, glass companies and mold companies collaborated more closely to mass produce glass articles inexpensively. Patterns with only one or two elements eliminated laborious, costly handwork on molds. Hotter furnaces fueled by coal instead of wood resulted in fluid glass easily forced downward by the plunger to form stemmed articles. *Courtesy, Sandwich Glass Museum, Sandwich Historical Society*

1476 PRESSED LOOP (LEAF) SALTS

2¾" H. x 3" Dia. 1850–1870

This versatile pattern lent itself to any article that was circular. It can be seen throughout these volumes on tableware, lamps, vases and colognes. Although known as *Loop*, it is identified as *Leaf* in catalogs of flint glass manufacturers McKee and Brothers in Pittsburgh, Pennsylvania. Because it was produced by any number of glass houses, attribution of a specific piece to the Boston and Sandwich Glass Company is impossible unless it can be traced to the factory through the family of a Sandwich glassmaker or is accompanied by paperwork. On the foot of these beautiful salts, the loops, or leaves, stop short of a plain rim. On the bowl, they extend onto the rim to form six large scallops. Larger articles have more loops, which on nappies may be drastically stretched to increase diameter. The value of colored pieces is many times that of clear. See *Barlow-Kaiser Sandwich Glass Price Guide* for value in a variety of colors. These Loop salts were also made "off foot." *Courtesy, Sandwich Glass Museum, Sandwich Historical Society*

1477 PRESSED NEW ENGLAND PINEAPPLE (PINEAPPLE, LOOP AND JEWEL) SALT

2¾" H. x 3⅛" Dia. 1850–1870

The study of available documents convinces the authors that pressed tableware patterns produced in quantity were assigned names in addition to stock numbers. Two most informative documents are a New England Glass Company catalog and a Cape Cod Glass Company list that date from the late 1860's. (The Cape Cod Glass Company *List of Glass Ware* is reprinted in full on pages 108–110 in Volume 3.) Records that would have shown factory names for Boston and Sandwich Glass Company products have not surfaced to date, many having been lost in a fire that destroyed Boston in 1872. This pattern of a loop depending into a diamond-filled medallion was identified as *Loop and Jewel* by Sandwich glass writer Frederick T. Irwin. Author Ruth Webb Lee and historian Francis (Bill) Wynn referred to *New England Pineapple*, although there is no such thing. This footed salt was pressed as a single unit. Larger pieces may have been produced by pressing two units separately and attaching them with a wafer. *Courtesy, Sandwich Glass Museum, Sandwich Historical Society*

1478 PRESSED FINE RIB (REEDED)

(a) Salt 2⅞" H. x 2⅞" Dia.

(b) Dish with turnover rim 2⅜" H. x 3⅝" Dia. 1850–1875

The original name of this pattern was *Reeded*. Salt A was made in quantity by the Boston and Sandwich Glass Company, the New England Glass Company in East Cambridge and the Union Flint Glass Company in Somerville, Massachusetts. Some pieces were illustrated in Pennsylvania glass house catalogs. The rim has twelve scallops. Note that the same mold was used to produce dish B. When removed from the mold, the feet of both pieces were cup-shaped. They were flared out while the glass was still hot. At this point, salt A was complete and was placed in the annealing leer. To complete dish B, the bowl was stretched out to widen it and the scalloped rim was turned downward. Surprisingly little of the pattern was muted in the hand tooling. Salt A is shown in a New England Glass Company catalog. Dish B is not, so its intended use is not known. It may have been used for nuts or small candy, yet could have still held salt.

1479 FINE RIB (REEDED) SALTS

(a) Pressed open 2⅞" H. x 2⅞" Dia. 1850–1875

(b) Blown molded shaker 2⅝" H. x 2½" Dia. 1870–1880

Because this pattern was widely manufactured over a long period, numerous articles for dispensing salt were marketed. Pressed salt A with its scalloped rim and a pressed individual salt with a star bottom are the most common. Reeded individual salts were listed by the Cape Cod Glass Company. The Kaiser collection includes a flat-bottomed rectangular salt with rounded corners and scalloped rim. Oval ones are known. Production continued into the era when the refinement of salt was such that it could be evenly scattered by shaker salt B. This piece was blown into a mold that had threads on the neck. The narrow ribs extend upward to a horizontal ring that prevented the perforated metal cap from being screwed too tightly. Molded threads did not come into being until the 1860's and the first of those threaded salts were not globe shaped; hence, the late date cited above.

1480 PRESSED PRISM SALT

1¾" H. x 4¼" Dia. 1855–1875

Most pressed glass articles were made by more than one flint glass factory, but the documentation that would prove it has been lost. Therefore, when a catalog is found, articles therein are wrongly attributed to that factory alone. This heavy circular salt is such a piece. It was produced by the Boston and Sandwich Glass Company, but also appears in a mid-1870's catalog published by King, Son and Company, a Pittsburgh manufacturer. The pattern of vertical V-grooves is identified as *Prism*. This large circular salt was illustrated as well as an identical individual one. Shaker salts were intermingled with large and small open salts, indicating that both types were in common use. The market for heavy containers was wide. They were used on ships and trains as well as in restaurants and houses.

1481 PRESSED RIBBED IVY SALT

(a) Salt 2¾" H. x 3" Dia.
(b) Cover 2" H. x 2⅜" Dia.
(c) Combined size 4⅝" H. x 3" Dia. 1855–1875

Large salts for family use are called "master salts", but the authors cannot find the term in catalogs or invoices. Smaller salts are differentiated by the adjective *individual*. Were it not for a salt and cover illustrated in a *Crockery Journal* dated August 12, 1875, the authors would be inclined to believe this Ribbed Ivy piece was for horseradish. However, its proportion is that of a salt large enough to hold more than one meal's supply. The cover prevented hardening. The footed bowl was pressed in a three-section mold, as were many pressed patterns. Two of the six ivy leaves surrounding the bowl were on each of the three sections. The Ribbed Ivy pattern is on the outside surface of the bowl and cover, but the rays on the foot are beneath. This foot was not reworked after the piece was taken from the mold. The finial of the matching cover resembles a tulip. It is repeated on the stopper of a Ribbed Ivy decanter in photo 1218. The cover rests on only a slight shoulder inside the beaded rim. This lack of an inner ridge suggests that the salt may have been marketed with a cover, or open, as it is often found. Because the cover pattern is outside, it is exposed to damage when the cover is in place. Examine covers carefully when considering a purchase. If the cover is damaged, you are only buying the lower unit of a two-unit article.

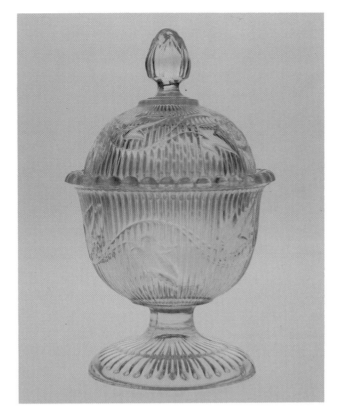

1482 PRESSED GREEK KEY (GREEK BORDER) SALT

2⅞" H. x 2⅝" Dia. 1860–1880

Circular salts with feet and hexagonal stems made during the last half of the Nineteenth Century matched other tableware pieces, all made by the same procedure. Whether a sugar, cream, goblet or salt, they were pressed into a mold and the only rework after removal was to flatten the foot. Around the lower portion of the bowl is a pattern of vertical rounded ribs. Above is a band of Greek Key, also called *Greek Border* at the Boston and Sandwich Glass Company. When sold as it came from the mold, the key pattern was smooth and clear. When the piece was sent to the cutting shop to roughen the raised surface of the pattern, it appeared to be frosted as shown here. Open salts used daily over a long period often have rim chips. Chipped articles that have been machined to remove damage have little value. This pattern was also a product of the Portland Glass Company in Portland, Maine, and the Union Glass Company in Somerville, Massachusetts. *Courtesy, Sandwich Glass Museum, Sandwich Historical Society*

1483 PRESSED CABLE SALT

3⅜" H. x 3" Dia. 1850–1865

In sailing days, *cable* was the name used for twisted rope. Its use as a pattern on glass and ironstone preceded the laying of the first Atlantic Telegraph Cable, which was completed on July 29, 1858, so the authors do not believe it commemorated that event. Heavy segments of Cable extend vertically on the bowl to a rim of alternating medium and large scallops. It completely surrounds the foot, which was molded in one piece with the bowl. This salt did not have a cover, so unused salt had to be dumped back into a storage bin. Individual salts were also made. They are encircled by a Cable ring. *Courtesy, Sandwich Glass Museum, Sandwich Historical Society*

1484 PRESSED MORNING GLORY INDIVIDUAL SALT
¾" H. x 2⅛" Dia. 1865–1880
Morning Glory is a very scarce pattern believed to have been made only by the Boston and Sandwich Glass Company. Only individual salts have been found to date. The leaves and blossoms encircling the tiny article are detailed. Because of its size, the salt was difficult to photograph. We suggest you study the pattern on the large footed bowl in photo 1238. The capacity of the salt is one teaspoon. It is rare in clear and has not been seen in color. Usually bringing top dollar, this one was found at a flea market in a box of assorted salts marked "$2.00 each".

1485 PRESSED SALTS
(a) Canary 2½" H. x 3¾" Dia.
(b) Blue 2¾" H. x 3½" Dia. 1850–1875
These circular Sandwich salts are often confused with similar salts called *Imperial* that were products of Bakewell, Pears and Company and McKee and Brothers of Pittsburgh, Pennsylvania. The McKee salt appeared in their catalogs dated 1859 to 1871, thus helping us to determine the production period of the Sandwich pieces. As shown in the accompanying illustration, the Sandwich salt is concave when viewed from above. The six-lobed bottom resembles a six-petaled rosette when viewed from beneath. The salts were leveled, or *flatted*, by machining the lobes. The thick salts are quite sturdy. Clear examples are easily found and canary now and then. Consider all other colors to be extremely rare.

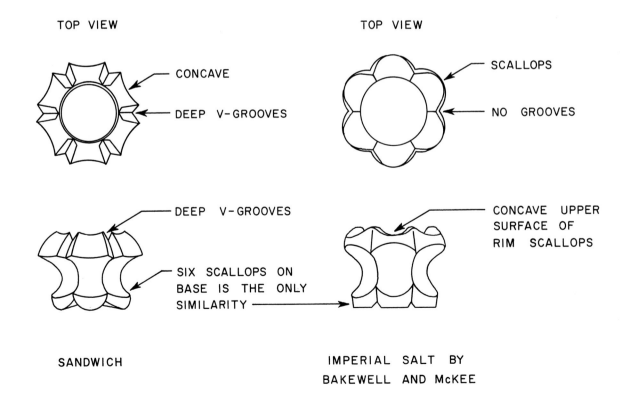

Fig. 12   When viewed from above, the Sandwich salt is concave and has six deep V-grooves. The Imperial salt made in Pittsburgh has six scallops and no grooves.

1486 PRESSED OCTAGON INDIVIDUAL SALTS

⅞" H. x 2" L. x 1½" W. 1850–1887

This sewn, paper-covered box was one of two found in 1952 in the home of John Sise of Portsmouth, New Hampshire. Sise had carried an array of Sandwich glass in his Portsmouth store. Author Barlow discovered the boxes in the Sise attic when descendants disposed of the house. Printing on the side of the cover identified the rectangular salts as "1 DOZ. NO. 180 INDIVID-UAL". The individual salts must have been routinely boxed and sold by the dozen. Another set is known in a similar box marked Jones, McDuffee and Stratton, a Boston glass and china distributor that purchased all of the molds and stock from the Boston and Sandwich Glass Company when it closed. Boxed sets are rare, although the salts themselves are common. The three salts in the foreground were dug at the Sandwich factory. Small checks, or squares, are on the bottom. The chamfer at each corner extends to a triangular foot. Pittsburgh glass company catalogs describe this salt as *Octagon* even though the eight sides are not equal. The salts were in continuous production elsewhere until the 1920's. The second Sise box can be seen in photo 2086.

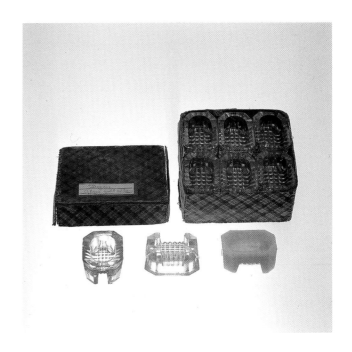

1487 PRESSED DOUBLE SALT

(a) Salt 3¼" H. x 4½" L. x 2¼" W.

(b) Wooden pattern 1865–1887

Double, or twin, salts were late arrivals, but their form persisted into the 1900's. They were pressed in many patterns in the United States and France. This amethyst salt matches quantities of fragments dug at the Boston and Sandwich Glass Company. The wooden pattern is an exact match except that there is no handle. Because the salt was made with several handle variants, a separate handle pattern accompanied the salt pattern to the commercial mold factory. The wooden units were combined, providing a model from which a mold was fabricated. The mold was complex because a special plunger was required to displace the hot glass in two openings while forcing it into the handle cavity. *Courtesy, Sandwich Glass Museum, Sandwich Historical Society*

1488 PRESSED DOUBLE SALT

(a) Salt 3¼" H. x 4½" L. x 2¼" W.

(b) Fragment 1865–1887

Although several glass handles were combined with this double salt, the one shown here and in the above photo is the most common. The blue fragment and large amount of clear ones were dug in an area in which glass known to have been produced between 1865 and 1875 was discarded. In order to dig intelligently, thorough knowledge of factory operation is necessary. For this reason, the authors researched factory expansion, the order in which furnaces and auxiliary buildings were erected, and the dates when land was purchased and filled. For this information, see the keys to each map that accompanies the history of each Sandwich glass company.

1489 PRESSED DOUBLE SALT
4" H. x 4" L. 1865–1887

A different mold was needed when the double salt was to be combined with a metal handle. A pin on the plunger created a center opening through which the handle was bolted. Metal parts, called *furnishings*, were sometimes purchased by the glass company. At other times, articles such as this glass salt without a handle were sent to an assembly house or distributor to be completed before they were offered to the retail customer. A variety of double salts with metal handles were pictured in a Cristalleries de Baccarat catalog thought to date from the early 1900's. Throughout the life of the Boston and Sandwich Glass Company, molds and patterns were purchased or copied from European sources. Other than the convenience of being able to pass the salt around the table by means of a handle, there was little purpose to having salt in twin containers unless the double salt was used as individual salts placed between every two people at the table.

1490 PRESSED DIAMOND (CINCINNATI) INDIVIDUAL SALT
(a) Wooden pattern
(b) Salt 1" H. x 1½" Dia. 1865–1887

Small salts were listed as individual salts in glass catalogs. They held very little salt and were placed beside each person's plate. Exactly when production of this circular salt began is uncertain. It first appeared in a McKee and Brothers catalog in the mid-1860's, where it was called *Cincinnati*. *Cincinnati* was a Honeycomb pattern made in a wide range of tableware pieces. Some Pittsburgh houses called the salt *Diamond*. King, Son and Company refused to take a stand and called it both. The pressed products of American glass houses lost their individuality during the latter half of the Nineteenth Century. While certain patterns were patented and produced at particular factories, a larger percentage of each factory's output was from commercial molds that were available to all houses at low cost. This Diamond salt required no rework after removal from the mold. The wooden pattern matches the glass salt. Look for wooden patterns when you are shopping for antique glass. They sometimes surface inexpensively at large flea markets.

1491 CUT LAPIDARY SALTS
(a) 3" H. x 2" Dia.
(b) 2¼" H. x 2" Dia. 1865–1887

Flat-bottomed and footed cut lapidary salts are pictured on page 42 of the Boston and Sandwich Glass Company catalog believed to have been printed in 1874. They were pressed in a mold and after annealing were sent to the cutting shop. Thirty rays were cut to make the star bottom. All traces of mold seam marks were eliminated when the entire outer surface—the diamonds on the bowl, the panels on the stem and foot, the rims of the foot and bowl—were cut and finely polished. The handwork accounts for the differing heights, although both salts would have been marketed as the same size. These pieces are in the family collection of Henry Francis Spurr. Spurr was head salesman in the Boston office and became factory superintendent in 1882 (see Chapters 1 and 2 in Volume 4). Some of the finest cutting was done during later years.

1492 CUT VESICA SALT

3½" H. x 3" Dia. 1865–1887

The reason that the pressing of glass was so important to mass production is shown by this salt. It and the above Spurr family salts were pressed in one minute. All three were the same shape when removed from the mold, but the salt in this photo assumed an entirely different character after the blank was cut. Vertical grooves cut around the lower portion of the bowl resulted in pointed ovals called *vesicas*. The raised surface between vesicas was serrated. Wide vesicas surround the upper portion. The rim was dished out into pointed serrations. This cut salt also descended through a family of glass company employees, the Laphams. George Franklin Lapham was a skilled cutter whose work can be seen throughout these volumes. His son, George Franklin Lapham, Jr., was a salesman at the Boston store who oontinued at that location after it was taken over by Jones, McDuffee and Stratton.

1493 SILVERED SALT WITH ENGRAVED IVY WREATH

1⅞" H. x 3⅛" Dia. 1860–1887

According to the newspaper *Sandwich Observer* in an article on October 12, 1850, the silvering of glass was a "branch unknown to us", having been patented in England. It was described as glass that "flashes back the light, and is seen best at night, or when surrounding objects are in comparative gloom". The method of plating the inside of a blown, doubled-walled vessel with silver nitrate was first used in America by the New England Glass Company. According to authority Lura Woodside Watkins, they displayed it at the New York Exposition in 1853. Soon it was in use at a number of glass houses. Production at the Boston and Sandwich Glass Company was limited in the 1850's and phased out as the Civil War interfered with factory activity. Production resumed after the war and continued under the management of Sewall Henry Fessenden and Henry Francis Spurr. The open wreath of ivy leaves and tendrils enclosing the name "Abby" was engraved by Joseph Henry Lapham, brother of cutter George Franklin Lapham, for his daughter Abigail. She was born to Joseph and his first wife Mary on March 2, 1842. Joseph died at his Sandwich home on April 23, 1890. *Courtesy, Sandwich Glass Museum, Sandwich Historical Society*

1494 SILVERED SALT WITH ENGRAVED LEAF AND BERRY WREATH

2¼" H. x 2¾" Dia. 1860–1887

This silvered salt was engraved for Melinda Nye Chipman of Sandwich. Her monogram "MNC" is centered in a wreath of two leaf and berry branches crossed at the bottom. Engraved leaves and berries are on the opposite side. The salt was manufactured by blowing an elongated bubble that was caved in to form a double wall. A solution that included nitrate of silver, ammonia and alcohol was poured into the piece through a hole beneath. Heating the salt to about 104 degrees Fahrenheit deposited the solution on the inner surface of the walls. The surplus solution was poured out and alcohol was poured in to clean the residue, followed by a varnish, sometimes shellac. Then the hole was sealed and varnished or waxed to keep the silver nitrate from oxidizing. Examine the seal when purchasing a piece of silvered glassware. When left open to the atmosphere, the silver quickly deteriorates. *Courtesy, Sandwich Glass Museum, Sandwich Historical Society*

1495 BLOWN MOLDED BARREL INDIVIDUAL SALT AND PEPPER BOTTLES IN CASTER FRAME

(a) Blue-green salt bottle

(b) Blue pepper bottle 2⅝" H. x 1" Dia.

(c) Caster frame 4⅜" H. x 4⅛" L. x 2⅛" W. 1877–1887

The blown molded barrel-shaped shaker salt endeared itself to collectors because its perforated metal cap is marked "DANA K. ALDEN, BOSTON. PAT. DEC. 25, 1877". It is known as a "Christmas salt" because of the date, which was a Tuesday. The United States Patent Office received patent applications daily. Regardless of when the paperwork was completed, all patents were dated Tuesday, whether a holiday or not. The patent No. 198,554 for this cap and its rotary agitator was issued to Hiram J. White of Boston. White assigned the patent to Dana K. Alden of Boston, who marketed matching salt, pepper and bitter bottles by the millions. The highly successful agitator prevented salt from caking in the bottle and under the cap. A metal shank was attached to a knob above the cap. Two sets of curved prongs on the shank could be rotated by means of the knob to loosen salt in the bottle. When the knob was pulled up and rotated, the upper set of curved prongs scraped salt that caked inside the cap. These bottles are in an inexpensive stamped metal framed marked "ALDEN SALT CASTER CO. BOSTON, MASS. PATENT APPLIED FOR". Although cheaply made, the frames are very rare and much sought after today. *Courtesy, Sandwich Glass Museum, Sandwich Historical Society*

1496 BLOWN MOLDED BARREL INDIVIDUAL SALT AND PEPPER BOTTLES IN CASTER FRAME

(a) Salt bottle

(b) Pepper bottle 2" H. x 1½" Dia.

(c) Caster frame 4¼" H. x 4⅛" L. x 2" W. 1878–1887

This caster frame has four nipple feet that raise it from the table. It is signed "ALDEN, GRIFFITH & CO. BOSTON, MASS." in a circle. Three-hole frames were made that held bottles for salt, pepper and bitter. This is why every barrel bottle does not have a marked cap. Only the salt bottle cap with large holes is stamped "DANA K. ALDEN, BOSTON. PAT. DEC. 25, 1877". The finial of pepper bottle cap B matches the knob of salt bottle cap A, but is stationary. Two styles of cap were made: these light gauge ones on which the threads can be seen on the outside and heavy gauge britannia ones with a knurled edge and smooth sides as shown on the following bitter bottle. They are not interchangeable. The bottles shown here have higher threaded necks. When screwed down tightly, the metal cap should rest on the horizontal ring molded as part of the bottle. Beginning collectors are inclined to pay more for the bottle with marked cap and rotary salt breaker because they believe that the pepper cap is a replacement. Value is in the matched pair.

Fig. 1.   Fig. 2.

 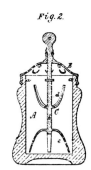

Fig. 3.

UNITED STATES PATENT OFFICE.

HIRAM J. WHITE, OF BOSTON, MASSACHUSETTS, ASSIGNOR TO DANA K. ALDEN, OF SAME PLACE.

IMPROVEMENT IN TABLE SALT BOTTLES.

Specification forming part of Letters Patent No. 198,554, dated December 25, 1877; application filed December 11, 1877.

To all whom it may concern:

Be it known that I, HIRAM J. WHITE, of Boston, of the county of Suffolk and State of Massachusetts, have invented a new and useful Improvement in Table Salt Bottles; and do hereby declare the same to be described in the following specification and represented in the accompanying drawings, of which—

Figure 1 is a side view, and Fig. 2 a vertical section, of a salt-bottle provided with my invention. Fig. 3 is a perspective view of the agitator, to be hereinafter described.

It is well known that table-salt is liable to deliquesce and become hard or cake when in an open bottle or other vessel.

My invention is for the purpose of stirring or breaking up the salt, in order to prevent it from caking in the body as well as in the perforated cover of the bottle. Such invention is also to break up the salt when caked, either in the body or the cover of such bottle.

To this end I use in the bottle a rotary agitator, having a shank extending through the cover, and provided with a knob, such agitator being movable lengthwise, besides being capable of being revolved in the cover by the thumb and forefinger of the hand of a person applied to the knob. This agitator has two sets of curved prongs, one of which projects downward toward the bottom of the bottle, and the other upward toward the cover, all being substantially as represented in the drawings, in which—

A denotes the salt holder or bottle, provided with a perforated cap, B, screwed upon its neck *a*. The agitator C is composed of a cylindrical wire or shank, *b*, a knob, *c*, and two series of curved prongs, *d e*, all arranged in and with the cover, in manner as shown.

By drawing the agitator upward and revolving it, salt that may gather in the cover or stop its holes of discharge may be broken up. So, by depressing the agitator and revolving it within the bottle, salt that may cake in the bottom of such bottle may be broken up. By alternately moving the agitator up and down in the bottle, and at the same time revolving such agitator, the body of the salt may be stirred.

I claim—

The agitator, substantially as described, movable in manner and by means as set forth, in combination and arranged with the bottle and its perforated cap or cover, as specified.

HIRAM J. WHITE.

Witnesses:
R. H. EDDY,
JOHN R. SNOW.

Witnesses   Inventor
S. N. Piper   Hiram J. White.
L. H. Miller   by his attorney.
                          R. H. Eddy.

Hiram J. White's patent No. 198,554 dated December 25, 1877, and assigned to Dana K. Alden. Mechanical devices for breaking up caked salt had been patented since the early 1860's, but more Christmas "table-salt bottles" are found than any other. The pressed bottle illustrated in the patent cannot be attributed to the Boston and Sandwich Glass Company. Note that White's patent attorney was R. H. Eddy, who also served Deming Jarves in that capacity.

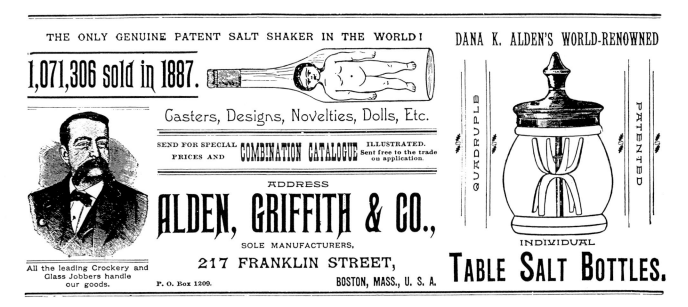

The glass industry trade paper *Crockery and Glass Journal* dated April 19, 1888, had this to say about the article we call the "Christmas salt". "There is nothing meaner nor more exasperating than an individual salt bottle that will not salt. Dana K. Alden's patent shaker, shown by illustration in another part of this issue, contains an ingenious device that overcomes the difficulty and spares the pain of profanity at the same time. Over a million of them were sold in 1887 and there are millions more to follow." It is interesting to note that Alden, Griffith and Company advertisements began after the Boston and Sandwich Glass Company closed. Over the next several years, the number of salt bottles sold the previous year was given. It is obvious that during and after the Sandwich factory closed, the bottle molds were filled at other flint glass works, so it is impossible to distinguish a Sandwich "Christmas salt" from one made at another flint glass house that used the same molds.

1497 BLOWN MOLDED BARREL INDIVIDUAL BITTER BOTTLE
2¾" H. x 1½" Dia. 1878–1887

Only three styles of "Christmas salts" are documented as having been produced by the Boston and Sandwich Glass Company. All three have a star bottom. This barrel bottle has a horizontal ring at the bottom that acts as a table rest and another above the convex wall. The threads on the neck were molded when the bottle was blown; two vertical mold marks begin at the bottom and extend upward through the threads to the machined rim. Bottles retrieved from the Boston and Sandwich Glass Company factory site discarded before the rims were machined proved Sandwich manufacture. The bottle in this photo was fitted with a bitter cap. The liquid was dispensed through a hole in the finial. The cap is lined with leather to prevent the bitter from seeping out around the threads. At the time of manufacture, a set of three bottles in their frame retailed for about 75 cents.

1498 BLOWN MOLDED DECORATED OPAL BARREL INDIVIDUAL PEPPER BOTTLES
(a) Winter scene
(b) Pansy
2½" H. x 1½" Dia. 1878–1887

Prior to the manufacture of glass shakers for salt, salt had been placed on the table in an open container and the pepper shaker was part of a caster set. Therefore, the first of the shakers for salt made in the 1860's did not have matching shakers for pepper. However, by the time opal glass was in style and Dana K. Alden publicized his revolutionary salt breaker, the same container performed both functions merely by changing the cap. These white opal barrel bottles have pepper caps. Pepper bottle A was decorated with a winter scene, a popular Sandwich motif that was executed quickly. Note that Sandwich decorators did not use much white paint. The snow was made by wiping away areas of the floated background. Winter scenes were painted by Edmund Kimball Chipman, Mary Gregory, Annie Mathilda Nye and assuredly other decorators. Pansies such as that on pepper bottle B were considered difficult to execute. Sisters Annie and Sarah Emeline (Lina) Chamberlain were noted for this type of work.

Authors Barlow and Kaiser feel privileged to have in their document collection eight diaries written by Boston and Sandwich Glass Company decorators Mary Alice and Emma Wentworth Gregory, and Emma's autograph book. (The life of Mary Gregory based on the diaries is related in Chapter 14 of Volume 4.) Friends and co-workers personalized the pages with paintings and drawings. This winter scene was drawn by decorator Edmund Kimball Chipman on October 23, 1876. Note the similarity of the house in the background to the house on the above barrel bottle.

1499 BLOWN MOLDED SHAKER SALTS

(a) Panel 3⅞" H. x 1⅝" Dia.

(b) Flute 4¾" H. x 1⅝" Dia. 1878–1887

As previously stated, only three types of shaker salts fitted with Alden's cap have been documented as Sandwich products. All three have a star bottom and a horizontal ring that acts as a table rest. Salt A has ten panels, above which are two horizontal rings. Two mold marks extending through the threads on the neck show that the piece was blown into a mold with two side sections. The cap is marked "DANA K. ALDEN'S WORLD REKNOWNED ROTARY SALT AGITATOR BOSTON MASS. PAT'D DEC. 25-1877." A matching pepper cap is not so marked. According to the April 26, 1888, issue of the *Crockery and Glass Journal*, the Alden salts were gradually being introduced in Australia, France, Germany, Spain and the British Isles. Added proof that not all Alden salts were made in Sandwich lies in the trade paper's statement about a "Queen decorated" salt. Queen's Burmese Ware was the product of Thomas Webb and Sons of Stourbridge, England, working under license purchased from Frederick S. Shirley of the Mount Washington Glass Company in New Bedford, Massachusetts. Salt B has a pattern of flutes, above which are two horizontal rings that differ in diamater. Its salt breaker is missing.

1500 BLOWN MOLDED DECORATED OPAL SHAKERS

(a) Pepper with autumn leaves 3¾" H. without cap, 1⅝" Dia.

(b) Individual shaker with bluebells 2¼" H. without cap, 1¼" Dia. 1870–1887

These opal shakers are from the family of Annie Mathilda Nye, a decorator who began working at the Boston and Sandwich Glass Company in July 1880. The yellow, orange and brown leaves were a common Sandwich motif. The stems were always twisted on the fragments dug at the factory site and on family heirlooms such as the Nye pieces. A large "P" was painted in green on the side opposite the leaves on shaker A. Individual shaker B has a design of little bluebells. All cylindrical shakers documented as Sandwich pieces have metal caps that screw into threaded collars permanently cemented to the rims. However, the molds in which the shakers were blown were commercial ones probably purchased from a New York mold firm that supplied glass works all along the Eastern Seaboard.

1501 BLOWN MOLDED OPAL SHAKER SALTS DECORATED WITH GREAT BLUE HERON

3¾" H. without cap, 1⅝" Dia. 1880–1887

These shaker salts were decorated by Annie Mathilda Nye. At first glance, they appear to be a pair because the great blue herons are facing each other. However, a green "S" was painted on the opposite side of both salts. Miss Nye painted herons on other opal blanks as shown particularly on a vase in photo 3073. She was hired at the age of twenty when the decorating department was expanded under the supervision of Edward J. Swann. Her talent was such that she was still employed by the Boston and Sandwich Glass Company to complete decorating orders after the strike and/or lockout closed the works on January 1, 1888.

1502 BLOWN MOLDED OPAL COMBINATION SET DECORATED WITH WINTER SCENE

(a) Toothpick 2¼" H. x 2½" Dia.
(b) Muffineer 6" H. x 2½" Dia.
(c) Salt 4" H. x 1½" Dia.
(d) Pepper 4" H. x 1½" Dia. 1870–1887

Containers that differed in form but united by common manufacturing and decorating techniques were assembled into *combination sets* as described in a catalog believed to date from 1880. Boston distributors Morey, Churchill and Morey showed three such sets in caster frames. "Pepper and salt pots" even as large as these were referred to as "individual", accounting for the numerous domestic and foreign pieces that appear at every glass show and flea market. The four-piece set in this photo is a documented Sandwich set that could have been decorated by any of several artists that were adept at bleak winter scenes. Labor costs was kept to a minimum by limiting the number of colors, applying one color without blending to a group of containers at a time, and leaving large areas of unpainted snow. Decorator Mary Gregory's distaste for her continual painting of winter scenes (her "especial line") is related in Chapter 14 of Volume 4.

1503 BLOWN MOLDED OPAL SHAKERS DECORATED WITH WINTER SCENE

(a, b) Fragments
(c) Salt 4" H. x 1½" Dia.
(d) Pepper 4" H. x 1½" Dia. 1870–1887

As shown by the opal blanks that were discarded before they were decorated, there is no continuous thread molded into the neck. Metal collars were cemented to the necks. The collars were threaded to accept the perforated caps. Both caps have relatively small holes, but those of cap C are slightly smaller. The cylindrical mold with a horizontal ring below the neck was a common commercial one. Although the authors date them to the closing of the Boston and Sandwich Glass Company, similar pieces may have been produced by one of the small glass companies that attempted to keep the glass industry viable in Sandwich. However, we cannot document winter scenes as having been painted after 1888. Shakers C and D are part of the above combination set. The shadow of the chimney was found on decorated fragments. While not conclusive, it is one clue to help identify Sandwich winter scenes.

1504 BLOWN MOLDED SPANGLE SHAKER SALT

3⅞" H. x 1⅝" Dia. 1880–1887

Termed "spangled" by glass companies, this salt was manufactured by first coating flakes of mica with nitrate of silver and then rolling a partly inflated bubble of hot glass over the particles. The bubble was reheated to incorporate the metallic particles into the surface and was then inserted into the mold that formed the salt. Blue glass with silver flakes was the product of two Sandwich glass works, the Boston and Sandwich Glass Company and the Vasa Murrhina Art Glass Company. Most of the limited production from both sites cracked in the annealing leers because of specific gravity differences between the glass, the mica and the nitrate of silver. When held to a bright light, such internal cracking can be seen in this salt. Perfect pieces found in the antiques market were manufactured by Hobbs, Brockunier and Company of Wheeling, West Virginia. These were the result of experiments by William Leighton, Jr., who was issued a patent for the process on January 29, 1884. Hobbs, Brockunier and Company advertised the dark blue as *lazuline*. John Charles Devoy's similar patent, which he assigned to the Vasa Murrhina Art Glass Company, was granted on July 1, 1884. Before coming to Sandwich, Devoy had been affiliated with the Farrall Venetian Art Glass Manufacturing Company in Brooklyn, New York, where this type of glass was made in 1882. His patent is reprinted in Chapter 8 of Volume 4.

GLOSSARY

ACID CUTBACK Cameo glass, made by treating the surface of cased glass with acid. An acid-resistant design was transferred onto the surface. Acid was applied, which "cut back", or ate through, the unprotected portions of the casing to reveal the glass beneath.

ADVENTURINE See *goldstone*.

AGENCY The office of an agent, or factor.

AGENT One entrusted with the power to negotiate the business of another, usually in a different location.

ANNEAL The gradual reheating and slow cooling of an article in a leer—an oven built for the purpose. This procedure removes any stress that may have built up in the glass during its manufacture.

APPLIED The fastening of a separate piece of glass, such as a base, handle, prunt, or stem, to an article already formed.

APPRENTICE One who was bound by indenture for a specified period to an experienced glassworker or mold maker for the purpose of instruction in the art and skill of creating glassware.

ASHERY A place where potash was made for mixing in a batch of glass.

BARYTES Sulphate of baryta, generally called heavy-spar.

BATCH Mixture of sand, cullet, and various raw materials that are placed in the pot to be heated into metal, or molten glass.

BLANK A finished piece of glass requiring additional work, such as decorating or engraving.

BLOWN GLASS Glass made by the use of a blowpipe and air pressure sufficient to give it form.

BLOWN MOLDED GLASS Glass made by blowing hot glass into a plain or patterned mold, and forcing it with air pressure to conform to the shape of the mold.

BOX A container of any shape and any size (e.g., it could be square, rectangular, circular or oval).

BUTTON STEM A connector between the base and the body of any article, with a button-shaped extrusion in its center.

CANE In *paperweight making*, a bundle of various colored glass rods that are arranged into a design, fused by reheating, pulled until it is long and thin, cooled and then cut into segments.

CASING A different colored layer of glass, either on the inside or outside of the main body of a blown piece, which adhered to the piece at the time it was blown.

CASTOR PLACE The location in the furnace room where large goods were blown, such as apothecary show globes, lamp shades and decanters. The size of such items necessitated that the glassworkers used as a glory hole an empty furnace pot with a widened mouth.

CAVE Ash pit under the furnace.

CAVE METAL Hot glass that flowed into the cave from a broken pot.

CHAIR A term used interchangeably with *shop*. Quoting Deming Jarves in a July 2, 1827, letter to William Stutson, "Do you think it advisable to form another chair for making small articles?"

CLAW FOOT An applied reeded foot resembling a scallop shell.

CLUSTER On *cut glass*, a grouping of similar designs in close proximity.

COMPOTE An assortment of fruit stewed in syrup. In the late 1800's, a long-stemmed, shallow dish, also known as a *comport*, in which to serve compote or fresh fruit, nuts and candies. Both terms superseded *nappie on foot*.

CRAQUELLE Glass that has been deliberately fractured after it has been formed, and reheated to seal the fractures, leaving the scars as a permanent design.

CROSSCUT DIAMOND On *cut glass*, a diamond that is divided into quarters.

CULLET Glass made in the factory and saved from a pot to be used in making future batches. Waste glass trimmed from rims and spouts was dropped into a cullet box. Also, glass items already annealed, either produced in the factory or purchased, and broken to be included in future batches.

CUTTING The grinding away of a portion of the surface of a blank, using wheels and wet sand to produce a design.

DARTER The boy who throws, or darts, dried sticks of wood into the furnace or annealing leer. The sticks were split into 1″ diameter width from 3½′ lengths of pine and oak cordwood.

DECORATING The ornamenting of a blank by painting or

staining it with a non-glass substance.

DESIGN The ornamentation of glass after it has been annealed, by cutting, engraving, etching or decorating.

DIAMOND SQUARES A pattern of perfect squares with equal sides and 90 degree corners set at a 45 degree angle.

DIP MOLD A shallow mold into which a blown gather of glass was dipped to form items such as nappies and dishes.

DONUT On *Trevaise*, the wafer-size glob of glass applied to the base. In most cases, the center of the wafer is dished out, leaving the shape of a donut.

ELECTRIC INCANDESCENT LAMP Original term for the item now called a *light bulb*. The first electric lamps were globe-shaped.

ENAMEL Colored glass made with lead. Most often, the term referred to opaque white glass. However, Deming Jarves noted in an 1867 memo, "Enamelled Glass deep color", meaning that the items listed should be made in color from glass containing lead.

ENGRAVING The process of cutting shallow designs and letters into a blank using a lathe with copper wheels and an abrasive.

ETCHING An inexpensive method of producing a design by using hydrofluoric acid to eat into the surface of a blank.

EXTINGUISHER A cone which, when placed on a burning lamp or candlestick, extinguishes the flame.

FACTOR An agent.

FILIGREE ROD A rod that has spiral or straight threads running through it. Also called *latticinio*.

FINIAL The decorative, terminal part of a newel post, writing pen, etc. The part of a cover used as a handle.

FIRE POLISHING Reheating a finished piece to remove marks left by tools or molds, leaving the article with a smooth surface.

FITTER The lower rim of a globe, shade or chimney that fits onto a metal ring or burner.

FLASHED A method developed during the 1880's of coating pressed and blown molded glass with a layer of colored glass after it was removed from the mold. The *flashed* layer was made from a formula that melted at a much lower temperature than the originally molded piece, so the original piece did not warp. On *cut glass*, a fan-like design located between the points of a fan, hobstar, or star.

FLINT A variety of quartz composed of silica with traces of iron. It is very hard, and strikes fire with steel.

FLINT GLASS Originally made from pulverized flints, it later became glass made from a batch containing lead. The term *flint* continued to be used, however. In the 1800's, it became the factory term for clear glass.

FLOATED In *decorated opal glass*, the method used to apply a solid color background.

FLUTE The hand-crimping of a rim. On *pressed* or *cut glass*, a panel rounded at the top.

FLY The shattering of an article due to uneven cooling in the annealing leer, particularly a problem with cased or flashed glass with layers that expand and contract at different temperatures.

FOLDED RIM A rim on either the body or base of a piece, the edge of which is doubled back onto itself, resulting in greater strength.

FRAGMENTS Broken pieces of finished glass, discarded at the time of production.

FREE-BLOWN GLASS Glass made by blowing hot glass and shaping it into its final form by the use of hand tools.

GAFFER In a group of glassworkers, called a *shop*, the most skilled artisan; the master glass blower.

GASOMETER The place where gas was generated for lighting.

GATHER The mass of hot metal that has been gathered on the end of a blowpipe.

GATHERER The assistant to the master glass blower, who gathers the hot metal on the end of the blowpipe.

GAUFFER To crimp or flute.

GILDING The application of gold for decorative purposes.

GLASS GALL Impurities skimmed from the surface of melted glass. Also called *sandever, sandiver*.

GLORY HOLE A small furnace into which a partly-finished article was inserted for reheating or fire polishing.

GOLDSTONE Glass combined with copper filings.

GREEN GLASS Glass in its natural color, generally used for bottles.

HOBSTAR On *cut glass*, a many-pointed geometrically cut star.

INDENTURE A contract binding an apprentice to his master.

KNOP A round knob, either hollow or solid, in the center of a stem.

LAMP CAPPER The worker who fits a lamp cap, or burner and its accompanying cork or metal collar, to a particular lamp font.

LAMPWORK The making and assembly of leaves, petals, stems, fruit and other small parts from rods of glass that have been softened by heating them over a gas burner. Originally, oil lamps produced the open flame.

LAPIDARY STOPPER A cut, faceted stopper.

LATTICINIO A rod of glass or a paperweight background composed of threads arranged in lattice, spiral or swirl configurations. The threads are usually white. Also, an article of glass made by arranging differently colored rods in a circular configuration and fusing them to a blown gather. The gather is then manipulated into the desired form, such as a creamer or lamp font.

LEER A tunnel-shaped oven through which glass articles are drawn after formation for the purpose of annealing. Also spelled *lear, lehr*.

LIGHTING DEVICE Any wooden, metal or glass primitive or sophisticated contrivance that emits light.

LIME Oxide of calcium; the white, caustic substance obtained from limestone and shells by heat. The heat expells carbonic acid, leaving behind the lime. Documentation shows the Cape Cod Glass Company and other glass factories obtained their lime from oyster shells.

LIME-SODA GLASS Glass made from non-lead formulas that include lime and bicarbonate of soda.

MAKE-DO A damaged item that has been repaired to "make it do" what was originally intended.

MANTLE A chemically treated tube of fabric that produces an incandescent glow when suspended over the flame of a gas burner.

MARBRIE In *blown glass*, a loop design made by looping and trailing threads of glass through another color, such as in paperweights and witch balls.

MARVER Iron plate on which hot glass is first shaped by rolling, in preparation for blowing into its final form.

MERESE A wafer-shaped piece of hot glass, used to connect individual units to make a complete piece, such as the base and socket of a candlestick or the bowl and standard of a footed nappie.

METAL Glass either in a molten condition in the pot, or in a cold, hardened state.

MOLD A form into which glass is blown or pressed to give it shape and pattern. Also spelled *mould*.

MOLD MARKS On glass that has been blown or pressed into a mold, the marks or seam lines left by the edges of the units of the mold.

MOVE A period of time during which a shop makes glass continuously. A glass blower is expected to make ten *moves* each week.

NAPPIE A shallow bowl of any size, whether round bottomed or flat bottomed, which can be on a standard. Also spelled *nappy*.

NEEDLE ETCHING Done by coating a blank with an acid-resisting substance, then inscribing a design into the resist with a sharp needle. The blank is then dipped into hydrofluoric acid, which etches the glass where the design was inscribed.

NIB The writing point of a pen.

OVERFILL On pieces that have been blown or pressed into a mold, the excess hot glass that seeps into the seams of the mold, sometimes creating fins.

PANEL A section with raised margins and square corners.

PATTERN (ON GLASS) The specific ornamentation into which *hot* glass is formed.

PATTERN (WOODEN) Wooden model carved in detail that is sent to the foundry, used as a guide to shape a mold.

PEG On a *lamp*, the unit that holds the oil and is attached to the base with a metal connector.

PICKWICK A pointed instrument used for raising, or "picking", the wick of a whale oil lamp.

PILLAR-MOLDED GLASS Glass made by first blowing a hot gather of glass into a mold with vertical ridges (pillars). A second cooler gather is blown into the first. The hot outer layer conforms to the shape of the mold, while the cooler inner layer remains smooth.

PINWHEEL On *cut glass*, a design resembling a hobstar in motion, its points angled in a clockwise or counter-clockwise position.

PLINTH A square block forming the base for a standard. Also, a base and standard molded in one piece, used as the lower unit of a lamp.

PONTIL MARK Rough spot caused by breaking away the pontil rod or spider pontil.

PONTIL ROD A rod of iron used by glassworkers to take glass from a pot or hold an article while it is being formed. Also called *punt*.

POT A one-piece container in which glass is melted, usually made of clay and able to withstand extreme heat.

POT STONE A gray-white stone deposited in the molten glass at the time of production, according to a Professor Barff, who analyzed pot stones and reported his findings in April 1876. Alumina, an oxide of aluminum present in the clay from which the pot was made, separated from the inner wall of the pot and combined with elements in the glass and solidified.

PRESSED GLASS Glass made by placing hot glass into a mold and forcing it with a plunger to conform to the shape of the mold.

PRISM A pattern or design of deep parallel V-grooves that reflect the light.

PROCELLO An iron spring tool resembling tongs used to expand and contract glass into its final form. Also called *pucella*.

PRUNT A blob of glass applied to the surface of a vessel, for the purpose of decorating or hiding a defect.

PUNT See *pontil rod*.

PUNTIER A glass cutter who dishes out concave circles, sometimes as part of a design and usually to remove the rough mark left by the pontil rod.

PUNTING The process of dishing out a circle with a cutting wheel, usually to remove the mark left by the pontil rod.

PUNTY A concave circle made by dishing out the glass with a cutting wheel.

QUILTING In *art glass*, an all-over diamond design, permanently molded into the piece as it was being blown.

RIBBON ROD A rod that has twisted flat ribbons of glass running through it.

RIGAREE A heavy thread of glass applied to the surface of a piece, giving a decorative rippled or fluted effect.

ROD A straight shaft of glass that will be reheated to form other things. Thin rods are fused together to make canes, and are also softened to supply glass for lampwork. Thick rods are formed into arms for epergne units. Reeded rods are used to form handles and claw feet on Late Blown Ware, as well as nibs for glass writing pens.

SAFE According to Webster's 1847 *An American Dictionary of the English Language*, "a chest or closet for securing provisions from noxious animals". Erroneously called a "pie safe", it was the forerunner of the ice box.

SERVITOR The first assistant to the gaffer in a group of glassworkers called a *shop*.

SHEDDING The flaking of the surface of finished glass, sometimes caused by minute particles of fire clay in the sand. Too much alkali in the glass and moisture in the air drawing out the soda are also contributing factors.

SHELL FOOT See *claw foot*.

SHOP A group of workmen producing glass at the furnace, consisting of a master glass blower and his help.

SICK GLASS Discoloration of the surface of an article.

SILVER NITRATE A stain prepared by dissolving silver in nitric acid. It turns amber in color when brushed onto annealed glass and fired in a decorating kiln.

SLOAR BOOK The book in which an accounting was kept of the output of glass produced by each shop at the furnace.

SLOAR MAN The employee who entered the output of each shop in the sloar book.

SNUFF The part of a wick that has been charred by the flame.

SNUFFER A scissors-like instrument for trimming and catching the charred part of a wick.

SOCKET EXTENSION On a *candlestick*, the section between the socket and the wafer, molded in one piece with the socket.

SPIDER PONTIL An iron unit placed on the end of the pontil rod, consisting of several finger-like rods. The fingers gave support to items that could not be held by a single rod in the center.

STAINED GLASS A finished piece of clear glass that is colored wholly or in part by the application of a chemical dye—most commonly ruby. The article is refired, making the dye a permanent finish.

STICKER-UP BOY The boy who carries hot glass on a V-shaped stick in a group of glassworkers called a *shop*.

STOPPERER The glass cutter who sizes, roughs and polishes the plug of a stopper to fit the neck of a particular object. Also called *stopper fitter*.

STRAWBERRY DIAMOND On *pressed* and *cut glass*, a diamond which is crosshatched. Also the name of a pressed pattern and a cut glass design that utilize crosscut diamonds.

TAKER-IN BOY The boy who carries the hot finished product to the leer in a group of glassworkers called a *shop*. During slow periods, he assists in the removal of glass from the cold end of the leer.

TALE Articles sold by count rather than by weight. In the words of Deming Jarves, "Tale was derived from the mode of selling, the best glass being sold only by weight, while light articles were sold tale."

UNDERFILL An insufficient amount of glass blown or pressed into a mold, resulting in an incomplete product. This is a characteristic, not a defect.

VESICA On *cut glass*, a pointed oval.

WAFER A flattened piece of hot glass, sometimes called a merese, used to join separately made units into a complete piece, such as the base and socket of a candlestick or the bowl and standard of a footed nappie.

WELTED RIM See *folded rim*.

WHIMSEY Unusual, one-of-a-kind item made of glass by a worker in his spare time.

WHITE GLASS Transparent, colorless flint glass.

BIBLIOGRAPHY

UNPUBLISHED SOURCES

Account book of various activities of the Boston and Sandwich Glass Company, such as the company store, sea-going vessels, wages, and wood for construction and fuel. April 17, 1826, to July 1830. Ms. collection in the Tannahill Research Library, Henry Ford Museum, Edison Institute, Dearborn, Michigan.

Barbour, Harriot Buxton. *Sandwich The Town That Glass Built*. Ms. and related correspondence in the Boston University Library, Boston, Massachusetts.

Burbank, George E. *History of the Sandwich Glass Works*. Ms. in the Barlow collection.

Corporate records. Office of the Secretary of State, The Commonwealth of Massachusetts, Boston, Massachusetts.

Correspondence pertaining to the management of the Boston and Sandwich Glass Company and the Cape Cod Glass Company, such as glass formulas, letters, special notices and transfers. Ms. collection in the Tannahill Research Library, Henry Ford Museum, Edison Institute, Dearborn, Michigan.

Correspondence pertaining to the management of the Boston and Sandwich Glass Company, the Boston and Sandwich Glass Company II and the Cape Cod Glass Company, such as glass formulas, letters, statements, etc. Ms. collection in the Rakow Library, The Corning Museum of Glass, Corning, New York.

Correspondence pertaining to the management of the New England Glass Company, such as invoices and bills of lading to William E. Mayhew and Company. Ms. collection in the Maryland Historical Society, Baltimore, Maryland.

Correspondence to and from glass authorities and writers on the subject of glass, pertaining to the excavation of the Boston and Sandwich Glass Company site and the discussion of fragments. Ms. consisting of the Francis (Bill) Wynn papers, now in the Barlow collection.

Dillaway family documents, such as genealogy. Ms. in the private collections of Dillaway family descendants.

Documentation in the form of fragments dug from factory and cutting shop sites. Private collections and the extensive Barlow collection, which includes the former Francis (Bill) Wynn collection.

Documentation of Sandwich glass items and Sandwich glassworkers, such as hand-written notebooks, letters, billheads, contracts, pictures, and oral history of Sandwich families recorded on tape by descendants. Ms. in the Barlow collection, Kaiser collection and private collections.

Documents pertaining to the genealogy of the family of Deming Jarves, including church records. Ms. in the care of City Registrar, City of Boston Vital Records, Boston, Massachusetts. Ms. in the Massachusetts State Archives, Boston, Massachusetts. Ms. in Sandwich Vital Records, Sandwich, Massachusetts. Ms. in the Genealogy Room, Sturgis Library, Barnstable, Massachusetts. Ms. at Mount Auburn Cemetery, Cambridge, Massachusetts.

Documents pertaining to the genealogy of the family of William Stutson, including church records. Ms. in the care of City Registrar, City of Boston Vital Records, Boston, Massachusetts. Ms. in the Massachusetts State Archives, Boston, Massachusetts. Ms. in Sandwich Vital Records, Sandwich, Massachusetts. Ms. in the Genealogy Room, Flower Memorial Library, Watertown, New York.

Documents pertaining to the Sandwich glass industry, such as letters, invoices, statements, photographs, family papers and original factory catalogs. Ms. collection in the care of the Sandwich Glass Museum, Sandwich Historical Society, Sandwich, Massachusetts.

Documents pertaining to the Sandwich glass industry and other related industries, such as statistics from Sandwich Vital Records, information from property tax records, maps, photographs, family papers and genealogy. Ms. in the care of the Town of Sandwich Massachusetts Archives and Historical Center, Sandwich, Massachusetts.

Documents pertaining to the Cheshire, Massachusetts, glass sand industry, such as statistics from vital records, information from property tax records, maps and genealogy. Ms. in the care of the Town of Cheshire, Massachusetts, and the Town of Lanesborough, Massachusetts.

Documents relating to the Cheshire, Massachusetts, glass sand industry, such as original manuscripts and newspaper articles. Ms. in the care of the Cheshire Public Library, Cheshire, Massachusetts, and the Berkshire Athenaeum, Pittsfield,

Massachusetts.

Documents relating to the North Sandwich industrial area, such as photographs, account books and handwritten scrapbooks. Ms. in the private collection of Mrs. Edward "Ned" Nickerson and the Bourne Historical Society, Bourne, Massachusetts.

Documents relating to the Sandwich Co-operative Glass Company, such as account books, correspondence and glass formulas. Ms. in the private collection of Murray family descendants.

Glass formula book. "Sandwich Aug. 7, 1868, James D. Lloyd." Ms. collection in the Tannahill Research Library, Henry Ford Museum, Edison Institute, Dearborn, Michigan.

Hubbard, Howard G. *A Complete Check List of Household Lights Patented in the United States 1792–1862.* South Hadley, Massachusetts: 1935.

Irwin, Frederick T. *The Story of Sandwich Glass.* Ms. and related documents in the Barlow collection.

Kern family documents, such as pictures and genealogy. Ms. in the private collections of Kern family descendants.

Lapham family documents, such as pictures and genealogy. Ms. in the private collections of Lapham family descendants.

Lloyd family documents, such as genealogy. Ms. in the private collections of Lloyd family descendants.

Lutz family documents, such as pictures, handwritten biographies and genealogy. Ms. in the private collections of Lutz family descendants.

Mary Gregory documents, such as diaries, letters and pictures. Ms. in the Barlow collection, Kaiser collection, other private collections, and included in the private papers of her family.

Minutes of annual meetings, Board of Directors meetings, special meetings and stockholders meetings of the Boston and Sandwich Glass Company. Ms. collection in the Tannahill Research Library, Henry Ford Museum, Edison Institute, Dearborn, Michigan.

Minutes of meetings of the American Flint Glass Workers Union, Local No. 16. Ms. in the Sandwich Glass Museum, Sandwich Historical Society, Sandwich, Massachusetts.

Nye family documents relating to the North Sandwich industrial area and the Electrical Glass Corporation. Ms. in the Barlow-Kaiser collection.

Oral history recorded on tape. Tales of Cape Cod, Inc. collection in the Cape Cod Community College Library, Hyannis, Massachusetts.

Patents relating to the invention of new techniques in glassmaking, improved equipment for glassmaking, new designs and styles of glass, and the invention of other items relating to the glass industry. United States Department of Commerce, Patent and Trademark Office, Washington, District of Columbia.

Population Schedule of the Census of the United States. Ms. from National Archives Microfilm Publications, National Archives and Records Service, Washington, District of Columbia.

Property deeds and other proofs of ownership, such as surveys, mortgage deeds, and last will and testaments. Ms. in the Barnstable County Registry of Deeds and Barnstable County Registry of Probate, Barnstable, Massachusetts.

Property deeds and other proofs of ownership relating to the Cheshire, Massachusetts, glass sand industry, such as maps. Ms. in the Berkshire County Registry of Deeds, North District, North Adams, Massachusetts.

Property deeds and other proofs of ownership, such as contracts, mortgage deeds and last will and testaments relating to the Jarves family. Ms. in the Barnstable County Registry of Deeds and Barnstable County Registry of Probate, Barnstable, Massachusetts. Ms. in the Suffolk County Registry of Deeds and Suffolk County Registry of Probate, Boston, Massachusetts. Ms. in the Middlesex County Registry of Deeds, Cambridge, Massachusetts. Ms. in the Essex County Registry of Deeds, South District, Salem, Massachusetts. Ms. in the Plymouth County Registry of Deeds, Plymouth, Massachusetts. Ms. in the Berkshire County Registry of Deeds, North District, North Adams, Massachusetts.

Property deeds and other proofs of ownership, such as mortgage deeds and last will and testaments relating to the Stutson family. Ms. in the Barnstable County Registry of Deeds and Barnstable County Registry of Probate, Barnstable, Massachusetts. Ms. in the Suffolk County Registry of Deeds and Suffolk County Registry of Probate, Boston, Massachusetts. Ms. in the care of City Clerk, Jefferson County Clerk's Office, Watertown, New York. Ms. in the care of Hounsfield Town Clerk, Sackets Harbor, New York. Ms. in the care of Sackets Harbor Village Clerk, Sackets Harbor, New York.

Sloar books, a weekly accounting of glass produced at the Sandwich Glass Manufactory and the Boston and Sandwich Glass Company, and the workers who produced it. July 9, 1825, to March 29, 1828. Ms. collection in the Tannahill Research Library, Henry Ford Museum, Edison Institute, Dearborn, Michigan. May 31, 1887, to December 26, 1887. Ms. in the care of the Town of Sandwich Massachusetts Archives and Historical Center, Sandwich, Massachusetts.

Spurr family documents, such as pictures, handwritten autobiographies, glass formulas and genealogy. Ms. in the private collections of Spurr family descendants.

Vessel documentation records. Ms. in the National Archives and Records Service, Washington, District of Columbia.

Vodon family documents, such as pictures and genealogy. Ms. in the private collection of Vodon family descendants.

Waterman, Charles Cotesworth Pinckney. Notes on the Boston and Sandwich Glass Company, dated November 1876, and deposited in the Sandwich Centennial Box. Ms. in the care of the Town of Sandwich Massachusetts Archives and Historical Center, Sandwich, Massachusetts.

Wright, David F. *The Stetson Family in the Boston and Sandwich Glass Company.* Ms. in the care of the Town of Sandwich Massachusetts Archives and Historical Center, Sandwich, Massachusetts, 1974.

PRINTED SOURCES

Amic, Yolande. *L'Opaline Francaise au XIXᵉ Siecle.* Paris, France: Library Gründ, 1952.

Anthony, T. Robert. *19th Century Fairy Lamps.* Manchester, Vermont: Forward's Color Productions, Inc., 1969.

Avila, George C. *The Pairpoint Glass Story.* New Bedford, Massachusetts: Reynolds-DeWalt Printing, Inc., 1968.

Barber, John Warner. *Historical Collections, being a general collection of interesting facts, traditions, biographical sketches, Anecdotes, &c., relating to the History and Antiquities of Every Town in Massachusetts.* Worcester, Massachusetts: Dorr, Howland & Co., 1839.

Barbour, Harriot Buxton. *Sandwich The Town That Glass Built.*

Boston, Massachusetts: Houghton Mifflin Company, 1948.

Barret, Richard Carter. *A Collectors Handbook of American Art Glass*. Manchester, Vermont: Forward's Color Productions, Inc., 1971.

————. *A Collectors Handbook of Blown and Pressed American Glass*. Manchester, Vermont: Forward's Color Productions, Inc., 1971.

————. *Popular American Ruby-Stained Pattern Glass*. Manchester, Vermont: Forward's Color Productions, Inc., 1968.

Belden, Louise Conway. *The Festive Tradition; Table Decoration and Desserts in America, 1650–1900*. New York, New York, and London, England: W. W. Norton & Company, 1983.

Belknap, E. McCamly. *Milk Glass*. New York, New York: Crown Publishers, Inc., 1949.

Bilane, John E. *Cup Plate Discoveries Since 1948; The Cup Plate Notes of James H. Rose*. Union, New Jersey: John E. Bilane, 1971.

Bishop, Barbara. "Deming Jarves and His Glass Factories," *The Glass Club Bulletin*, Spring 1983, pp. 3–5.

Bishop, Barbara and Martha Hassell. *Your Obd^t. Servt., Deming Jarves*. Sandwich, Massachusetts: The Sandwich Historical Society, 1984.

Bredehoft, Neila M. and George A. Fogg, and Francis C. Maloney. *Early Duncan Glassware; Geo. Duncan & Sons, Pittsburgh 1874–1892*. Boston, Massachusetts, and Saint Louisville, Ohio: Published privately, 1987.

Brown, Clark W. *Salt Dishes*. Leon, Iowa: Mid-America Book Company, reprinted in 1968.

————. *A Supplement to Salt Dishes*. Leon, Iowa: Prairie Winds Press, reprinted in 1970.

Brown, William B. *Over the Pathways of the Past*. Cheshire, Massachusetts: Cheshire Public Library, 1938.

Burbank, George E. *A Bit of Sandwich History*. Sandwich, Massachusetts: 1939.

Burgess, Bangs. *History of Sandwich Glass*. Yarmouth, Massachusetts: The Register Press, 1925.

Burns, Charles. *Glass Cup Plates*. Philadelphia, Pennsylvania: Burns Antique Shop, 1921.

Butterfield, Oliver. "Bewitching Witchballs," *Yankee*, July 1978, pp. 97, 172–175.

Cataldo, Louis and Dorothy Worrell. *Pictorial Tales of Cape Cod*. (Vol. I) Hyannis, Massachusetts: Tales of Cape Cod, Inc., 1956.

————. *Pictorial Tales of Cape Cod*. (Vol. II) Hyannis, Massachusetts: Tales of Cape Cod, Inc., 1961.

Childs, David B. "If It's Threaded...," *Yankee*, June 1960, pp. 86–89.

Chipman, Frank W. *The Romance of Old Sandwich Glass*. Sandwich, Massachusetts: Sandwich Publishing Company, Inc., 1932.

Cloak, Evelyn Campbell. *Glass Paperweights of the Bergstrom Art Center*. New York, New York: Crown Publishers, Inc., 1969.

Conat, Robert. *A Streak of Luck; The Life and Legend of Thomas Alva Edison*. New York, New York: Seaview Books, 1979.

Covill, William E., Jr. *Ink Bottles and Inkwells*. Taunton, Massachusetts: William S. Sullwold Publishing, 1971.

Cronin, J. R. *Fakes & Forged Trade Marks on Old & New Glass*. Marshalltown, Iowa: Antique Publications Service, 1976.

Cullity, Rosana and John Nye Cullity. *A Sandwich Album*. East Sandwich, Massachusetts: The Nye Family of America Association, Inc., 1987.

Culver, Willard R. "From Sand to Seer and Servant of Man,"

The National Geographic Magazine, January 1943, pp. 17–24, 41–48.

Deyo, Simeon L. *History of Barnstable County, Massachusetts*. New York, New York: H. W. Blake & Co., 1890.

DiBartolomeo, Robert E. *American Glass from the Pages of Antiques; Pressed and Cut*. (Vol. II) Princeton, New Jersey: The Pyne Press, 1974.

Dickinson, Rudolphus. *A Geographical and Statistical View of Massachusetts Proper*. 1813.

Dickinson, Samuel N. *The Boston Almanac for the Year 1847*. Boston, Massachusetts: B. B. Mussey and Thomas Groom, 1846.

Dooley, William Germain. *Old Sandwich Glass*. Pasadena, California: Esto Publishing Company, n.d.

————. "Recollections of Sandwich Glass by a Veteran Who Worked on It," *Hobbies*, June 1951, p. 96.

Drepperd, Carl W. *The ABC's of Old Glass*. Garden City, New York: Doubleday & Company, Inc., 1949.

Dyer, Walter A. "The Pressed Glass of Old Sandwich". *Antiques*, February 1922, pp. 57–60.

Eckardt, Allison M. "Living with Antiques; A Collection of American Neoclassical Furnishings on the East Coast". *The Magazine ANTIQUES*, April 1987, pp. 858–863.

Edison Lamp Works. *Pictorial History of the Edison Lamp*. Harrison, New Jersey: Edison Lamp Works, c. 1920.

Farson, Robert H. *The Cape Cod Canal*. Middletown, Connecticut: Wesleyan University Press, 1977.

Fauster, Carl U. *Libbey Glass Since 1818*. Toledo, Ohio: Len Beach Press, 1979.

Fawsett, Marise. *Cape Cod Annals*. Bowie, Maryland: Heritage Books, Inc., 1990.

Ferson, Regis F. and Mary F. Ferson. *Yesterday's Milk Glass Today*. Pittsburgh, Pennsylvania: Published privately, 1981.

Freeman, Frederick. *History of Cape Cod: Annals of the Thirteen Towns of Barnstable County*. Boston, Massachusetts: George C. Rand & Avery, 1862.

Freeman, Dr. Larry. *New Light on Old Lamps*. Watkins Glen, New York: American Life Foundation, reprinted in 1984.

Fritz, Florence. *Bamboo and Sailing Ships; The Story of Thomas Alva Edison and Fort Myers, Florida*. 1949.

Gaines, Edith. "Woman's Day Dictionary of American Glass," *Woman's Day*, August 1961, pp. 19–34.

————. "Woman's Day Dictionary of Sandwich Glass," *Woman's Day*, August 1963, pp. 21–32.

————. "Woman's Day Dictionary of Victorian Glass," *Woman's Day*, August 1964, pp. 23–34.

Gores, Stan. *1876 Centennial Collectibles and Price Guide*. Fond du Lac, Wisconsin: The Haber Printing Co., 1974.

Grover, Ray and Lee Grover. *Art Glass Nouveau*. Rutland, Vermont: Charles E. Tuttle Company, Inc., 1967.

————. *Carved & Decorated European Art Glass*. Rutland, Vermont: Charles E. Tuttle Company, Inc., 1970.

Grow, Lawrence. *The Warner Collector's Guide to Pressed Glass*. New York, New York: Warner Books, Inc., 1982.

Hammond, Dorothy. *Confusing Collectibles*. Des Moines, Iowa: Wallace-Homestead Book Company, 1969.

————. *More Confusing Collectibles*. Wichita, Kansas: C. B. P. Publishing Company, 1972.

Harris, Amanda B. "Down in Sandwich Town," *Wide Awake* 1, 1887, pp. 19–27.

Harris, John. *The Great Boston Fire, 1872*. Boston, Massachusetts: Boston Globe, 1972.

Hartung, Marion T. and Ione E. Hinshaw. *Patterns and Pinafores*. Des Moines, Iowa: Wallace-Homestead Book Company, 1971.

Hayes-Cavanaugh, Doris. "Early Glassmaking in East Cambridge, Mass.," *Old Time New England*, January 1929, pp. 113–122.

Haynes, E. Barrington. *Glass Through the Ages*. Baltimore, Maryland: Penguin Books, 1969.

Hayward, Arthur H. *Colonial and Early American Lighting*. New York, New York: Dover Publications, Inc., reprinted in 1962.

Hayward, John. *Gazetteer of Massachusetts*. Boston, Massachusetts: John Hayward, 1847.

Heacock, William. *Encyclopedia of Victorian Colored Pattern Glass; Book 1 Toothpick Holders from A to Z*. Jonesville, Michigan: Antique Publications, 1974.

————. *Encyclopedia of Victorian Colored Pattern Glass; Book 2 Opalescent Glass from A to Z*. Jonesville, Michigan: Antique Publications, 1975.

————. *Encyclopedia of Victorian Colored Pattern Glass; Book 3 Syrups, Sugar Shakers & Cruets from A to Z*. Jonesville, Michigan: Antique Publications, 1976.

————. *Encyclopedia of Victorian Colored Pattern Glass; Book 4 Custard Glass from A to Z*. Marietta, Ohio: Antique Publications, 1976.

————. *Encyclopedia of Victorian Colored Pattern Glass; Book 5 U. S. Glass from A to Z*. Marietta, Ohio: Antique Publications, 1978.

————. *Encyclopedia of Victorian Colored Pattern Glass; Book 6 Oil Cruets from A to Z*. Marietta, Ohio: Antique Publications, 1981.

————. *1000 Toothpick Holders; A Collector's Guide*. Marietta, Ohio: Antique Publications, 1977.

Heacock, William and Patricia Johnson. *5000 Open Salts; A Collector's Guide*. Marietta, Ohio: Richardson Printing Corporation, 1982.

Hebard, Helen Brigham. *Early Lighting in New England*. Rutland, Vermont: Charles E. Tuttle Company, 1964.

Heckler, Norman. *American Bottles in the Charles B. Gardner Collection*. Bolton, Massachusetts: Robert W. Skinner, Inc., 1975.

Hildebrand, J. R. "Glass Goes To Town," *The National Geographic Magazine*, January 1943, pp. 1–16, 25–40.

Hollister, Paul, Jr. *The Encyclopedia of Glass Paperweights*. New York, New York: Clarkson N. Potter, Inc., 1969.

Hough, Walter. *Collection of Heating and Lighting Utensils in the United States National Museum*. Washington, District of Columbia: United States Government Printing Office, 1928.

Hunter, Frederick William. *Stiegel Glass*. New York, New York: Dover Publications, Inc., 1950.

Ingold, Gérard. *The Art of the Paperweight; Saint Louis*. Santa Cruz, California: Paperweight Press, 1981.

Innes, Lowell. *Pittsburgh Glass 1797–1891*. Boston, Massachusetts: Houghton Mifflin Company, 1976.

Irwin, Frederick T. *The Story of Sandwich Glass*. Manchester, New Hampshire: Granite State Press, 1926.

Jarves, Deming. "The Manufactures of Glass" (numbers 1–8), *Journal of Mining and Manufactures*, September 1852–April 1853.

————. *Reminiscences of Glass-making*. Great Neck, New York: Beatrice C. Weinstock, reprinted in 1968.

Jarves, James Jackson. *In Memoriam James Jackson Jarves*. (Jr.) Published privately, 1890.

————. *Why and What Am I?*. Boston, Massachusetts: Phillips, Sampson and Company, 1857.

Jenks, Bill and Jerry Luna. *Early American Pattern Glass 1850–1910*. Radnor, Pennsylvania: Wallace-Homestead Book Company, 1990.

Jones, Olive R. and E. Ann Smith. *Glass of the British Military 1755–1820*. Hull, Quebec, Canada: Parks Canada, 1985.

Jones, Olive and Catherine Sullivan. *The Parks Canada Glass Glossary*. Hull, Quebec, Canada: Parks Canada, 1985.

Jones, Thomas P. *Journal of the Franklin Institute*. (Vol. 3, rebound as Vol. 7) Philadelphia, Pennsylvania: Franklin Institute, 1829.

Kamm, Minnie W. and Serry Wood. *The Kamm-Wood Encyclopedia of Pattern Glass*. (II vols.) Watkins Glen, New York: Century House, 1961.

Keene, Betsey D. *History of Bourne 1622–1937*. Yarmouthport, Massachusetts: Charles W. Swift, 1937.

Knittle, Rhea Mansfield. *Early American Glass*. New York, New York: The Century Co., 1927.

Lane, Lyman and Sally Lane, and Joan Pappas. *A Rare Collection of Keene & Stoddard Glass*. Manchester, Vermont: Forward's Color Productions, Inc., 1970.

Lanmon, Dwight P. "Russian Paperweights and Letter Seals?" *The Magazine ANTIQUES*, October 1984, pp. 900–903.

————. "Unmasking an American Glass Fraud," *The Magazine ANTIQUES*, January 1983, pp. 226–236.

Lanmon, Dwight P., Robert H. Brill and George J. Reilly. "Some Blown 'Three-Mold' Suspicions Confirmed," *Journal of Glass Studies*, vol. 15 (1973), pp. 151–159, 172–173.

Lardner, Rev. Dionysius. *The Cabinet Cyclopedia; Useful Arts*. Philadelphia, Pennsylvania: Carey and Lea, 1832.

Lattimore, Colin R. *English 19th Century Press-Moulded Glass*. London, England: Barrie & Jenkins, Ltd., 1979.

Lechler, Doris Anderson. *Children's Glass Dishes, China, and Furniture*. Paducah, Kentucky: Collector Books, 1983.

Lechler, Doris and Virginia O'Neill. *Children's Glass Dishes*. Nashville, Tennessee, and New York, New York: Thomas Nelson, Inc., Publishers, 1976.

Lee, Ruth Webb. *Antique Fakes & Reproductions*. Wellesley Hills, Massachusetts: Lee Publications, 1966.

————. *Early American Pressed Glass*. Wellesley Hills, Massachusetts: Lee Publications, 1960.

————. *Nineteenth-Century Art Glass*. New York, New York: M. Barrows & Company, Inc., 1952.

————. *Sandwich Glass*. Wellesley Hills, Massachusetts: Lee Publications, 1939.

————. *Victorian Glass*. Wellesley Hills, Massachusetts: Lee Publications, 1944.

Lee, Ruth Webb and James H. Rose. *American Glass Cup Plates*. Wellesley Hills, Massachusetts: Lee Publications, 1948.

Lindsey, Bessie M. *American Historical Glass*. Rutland, Vermont: Charles E. Tuttle Co., 1967.

Lovell, Russell A., Jr. *The Cape Cod Story of Thornton W. Burgess*. Taunton, Massachusetts: Thornton W. Burgess Society, Inc., and William S. Sullwold Publishing, 1974.

————. *Sandwich; A Cape Cod Town*. Sandwich, Massachusetts: Town of Sandwich Massachusetts Archives and Historical Center, 1984.

Mackay, James. *Glass Paperweights*. New York, New York: The Viking Press, Inc., 1973.

Manheim, Frank J. *A Garland of Weights*. New York, New York:

Farrar, Straus and Giroux, 1967.

Manley, C. C. *British Glass*. Des Moines, Iowa: Wallace-Homestead Book Co., 1968.

Manley, Cyril. *Decorative Victorian Glass*. New York, New York: Van Nostrand Reinhold Company, 1981.

Mannoni, Edith. *Opalines*. Paris, France: Editions Ch. Massin, n.d.

Maycock, Susan E. *East Cambridge*. Cambridge, Massachusetts: Cambridge Historical Commission, 1988.

McKearin, George S. and Helen McKearin. *American Glass*. New York, New York: Crown Publishers, Inc., 1941.

McKearin, Helen and George S. McKearin. *Two Hundred Years of American Blown Glass*. New York, New York: Bonanza Books, 1949.

McKearin, Helen and Kenneth M. Wilson. *American Bottles & Flasks and Their Ancestry*. New York, New York: Crown Publishers, Inc., 1978.

Measell, James. *Greentown Glass; The Indiana Tumbler and Goblet Company*. Grand Rapids, Michigan: The Grand Rapids Public Museum with the Grand Rapids Museum Association, 1979.

Metz, Alice Hulett. *Early American Pattern Glass*. Columbus, Ohio: Spencer-Walker Press, 1965.

———. *Much More Early American Pattern Glass*. Columbus, Ohio: Spencer-Walker Press, 1970.

Millard, S. T. *Goblets II*. Holton, Kansas: Gossip Printers and Publishers, 1940.

Miller, Robert W. *Mary Gregory and Her Glass*. Des Moines, Iowa: Wallace-Homestead Book Co., 1972.

Moore, N. Hudson. *Old Glass*. New York, New York: Tudor Publishing Co., 1924.

Morris, Paul C. and Joseph F. Morin. *The Island Steamers*. Nantucket, Massachusetts: Nantucket Nautical Publishers, 1977.

Mulch, Dwight. "John D. Larkin and Company: From Factory to Family," *The Antique Trader Weekly*, June 24, 1984, pp. 92–94.

Neal, L. W. and D. B. Neal. *Pressed Glass Salt Dishes of the Lacy Period 1825–1850*. Philadelphia, Pennsylvania: L. W. and D. B. Neal, 1962.

Nelson, Kirk J. *A Century of Sandwich Glass*. Sandwich, Massachusetts: Sandwich Glass Museum, 1992.

Padgett, Leonard. *Pairpoint Glass*. Des Moines, Iowa: Wallace-Homestead Book Company, 1979.

Pearson, J. Michael and Dorothy T. Pearson. *American Cut Glass Collections*. Miami, Florida: The Franklin Press, Inc., 1969.

———. *American Cut Glass for the Discriminating Collector*. Miami, Florida: The Franklin Press, Inc., 1965.

Pellatt, Apsley. *Curiosities of Glass Making*. Newport, England: The Ceramic Book Company, reprinted in 1968.

Pepper, Adeline. *The Glass Gaffers of New Jersey*. New York, New York: Charles Scribner's Sons, 1971.

Perry, Josephine. *The Glass Industry*. New York, New York, and Toronto, Ontario: Longmans, Green and Co., 1945.

Peterson, Arthur G. *Glass Patents and Patterns*. Sanford, Florida: Celery City Printing Co., 1973.

———. *Glass Salt Shakers: 1,000 Patterns*. Des Moines, Iowa: Wallace-Homestead Book Co., 1960.

Raycraft, Don and Carol Raycraft. *Early American Lighting*. Des Moines, Iowa: Wallace-Homestead Book Co., n.d.

Raynor, Ellen M. and Emma L. Petitclerc. *History of the Town of Cheshire, Berkshire County, Massachusetts*. Holyoke, Massachusetts, and New York, New York: Clark W. Bryan & Company, 1885.

Revi, Albert Christian. *American Art Nouveau Glass*. Exton, Pennsylvania: Schiffer Publishing, Ltd., 1981.

———. *American Cut and Engraved Glass*. Nashville, Tennessee: Thomas Nelson Inc., 1972.

———. *American Pressed Glass and Figure Bottles*. Nashville, Tennessee: Thomas Nelson Inc., 1972.

———. *Nineteenth Century Glass*. Exton, Pennsylvania: Schiffer Publishing, Ltd., revised 1967.

Righter, Miriam. *Iowa City Glass*. Des Moines, Iowa: Wallace-Homestead Book Co., 1966.

Robertson, Frank E. "New Evidence from Sandwich Glass Fragments," *The Magazine ANTIQUES*, October 1982, pp. 818–823.

Robertson, R. A. *Chats on Old Glass*. New York, New York: Dover Publications, Inc., 1969. Revised and enlarged by Kenneth M. Wilson.

Rose, James H. *The Story of American Pressed Glass of the Lacy Period 1825–1850*. Corning, New York: The Corning Museum of Glass, 1954.

Rushlight Club. *Early Lighting; A Pictorial Guide*. Talcottville, Connecticut: 1972.

Sandwich Glass Museum. *The Sandwich Glass Museum Collection*. Sandwich, Massachusetts: Sandwich Glass Museum, 1969.

Sauzay, A. *Wonders of Art and Archaeology; Wonders of Glass Making*. New York, New York: Charles Scribner's Sons, 1885.

Schwartz, Marvin D. *American Glass from the Pages of Antiques; Blown and Moulded*. (Vol. I) Princeton, New Jersey: The Pyne Press, 1974.

Slack, Raymond. *English Pressed Glass 1831–1900*. London, England: Barrie & Jenkins, 1987.

Smith, Allan B. and Helen B. Smith. *One Thousand Individual Open Salts Illustrated*. Litchfield, Maine: The Country House, 1972.

———. *650 More Individual Open Salts Illustrated*. Litchfield, Maine: The Country House, 1973.

———. *The Third Book of Individual Open Salts Illustrated*. Litchfield, Maine: The Country House, 1976.

———. *Individual Open Salts Illustrated*. Litchfield, Maine: The Country House, n.d.

———. *Individual Open Salts Illustrated; 1977 Annual*. Litchfield, Maine: The Country House, 1977.

Smith, Frank R. and Ruth E. Smith. *Miniature Lamps*. New York, New York: Thomas Nelson Inc., 1968.

Smith, Ruth. *Miniature Lamps II*. Exton, Pennsylvania: Schiffer Publishing Ltd., 1982.

Spillman, Jane Shadel. *American and European Pressed Glass in The Corning Museum of Glass*. Corning, New York: The Corning Museum of Glass, 1981.

———. *Glass Bottles, Lamps & Other Objects*. New York, New York: Alfred A. Knopf, Inc., 1983.

———. *Glass Tableware, Bowls & Vases*. New York, New York: Alfred A. Knopf, Inc., 1982.

———. "Pressed-Glass Designs in the United States and Europe," *The Magazine ANTIQUES*, July 1983, pp. 130–139.

Spillman, Jane Shadel and Estelle Sinclaire Farrar. *The Cut and Engraved Glass of Corning 1868–1940*. Corning, New York: The Corning Museum of Glass, 1977.

Stanley, Mary Louise. *A Century of Glass Toys*. Manchester, Vermont: Forward's Color Productions, Inc., n.d.

Steegmuller, Francis. *The Two Lives of James Jackson Jarves*. New Haven, Connecticut: Yale University Press, 1951.

Stetson Kindred of America. *The Descendants of Cornet Robert Stetson*, Vol. 1, No. 3. Stetson Kindred of America, Inc., 1956.

Stetson, Nelson M. *Booklet No. 3; Stetson Kindred of America*. Campbello, Massachusetts: The Stetson Kindred of America, n.d.

————. *Booklet No. 6; Stetson Kindred of America*. Campbello, Massachusetts: The Stetson Kindred of America, 1923.

Stow, Charles Messer. *The Deming Jarves Book of Designs*. Yarmouth, Massachusetts: The Register Press, 1925.

Swan, Frank H. *Portland Glass*. Des Moines, Iowa: Wallace-Homestead Book Company, 1949. Revised and enlarged by Marion Dana.

————. *Portland Glass Company*. Providence, Rhode Island: The Roger Williams Press, 1939.

Taylor, Katrina V. H. "Russian Glass in the Hillwood Museum." *The Magazine ANTIQUES*, July 1983, pp. 140–145.

Teleki, Gloria Roth. *The Baskets of Rural America*. New York, New York: E. P. Dutton & Co., Inc., 1975.

The Toledo Museum of Art. *American Glass*. Toledo, Ohio: The Toledo Museum of Art, n.d.

————. *Art in Glass*. Toledo, Ohio: The Toledo Museum of Art, 1969.

————. *The New England Glass Company 1818–1888*. Toledo, Ohio: The Toledo Museum of Art, 1963.

Thuro, Catherine M. V. *Oil Lamps; The Kerosene Era in North America*. Des Moines, Iowa: Wallace-Homestead Book Co., 1976.

————. *Oil Lamps II; Glass Kerosene Lamps*. Paducah, Kentucky, and Des Moines, Iowa: Collector Books and Wallace-Homestead Book Co., 1983.

Thwing, Leroy. *Flickering Flames*. Rutland, Vermont: Charles E. Tuttle Company, 1974.

————. "Lamp Oils and Other Illuminants." *Old Time New England*, October 1932, pp. 56–69.

Towne, Sumner. "Mike Grady's Last Pot," *Yankee*, March 1968, pp. 84, 85, 136–139.

United States House Executive Documents. *Documents Relative to The Manufactures in the United States Collected and Transmitted to the House of Representatives by the Secretary of the Treasury*. Washington, 1833.

VanRensselaer, Stephen. *Early American Bottles & Flasks*. Stratford, Connecticut: J. Edmund Edwards, 1971.

Van Tassel, Valentine. *American Glass*. New York, New York: Gramercy Publishing Company, 1950.

Vuilleumier, Marion. *Cape Cod; a Pictorial History*. Norfolk, Virginia: The Donning Company/Publishers, 1982.

Walsh, Lavinia. "The Romance of Sandwich Glass," *The Cape Cod Magazine*, July 1926, pp. 9, 26.

————. "Old Boston and Sandwich Glassworks....," *Ceramic Age*, December 1950, pp. 16, 17, 34.

Warner, Oliver. *Statistical Information Relating to Certain Branches of Industry in Massachusetts for the Year Ending May 1, 1865*. Boston, Massachusetts: Wright & Potter, 1866.

Watkins, Lura Woodside. *American Glass and Glassmaking*. New York, New York: Chanticleer Press, 1950.

————. *Cambridge Glass 1818 to 1888*. New York, New York: Bramhall House, 1930.

Webber, Norman W. *Collecting Glass*. New York, New York: Arco Publishing Company, Inc., 1973.

Webster, Noah. *An American Dictionary of the English Language*. Springfield, Massachusetts: George and Charles Merriam, 1847. Revised.

————. *An American Dictionary of the English Language*. Springfield, Massachusetts: George and Charles Merriam, 1859. Revised and enlarged by Chauncey A. Goodrich.

————. *An American Dictionary of the English Language*. Springfield, Massachusetts: G. & C. Merriam, 1872. Revised and enlarged by Chauncey A. Goodrich and Noah Porter.

Wetz, Jon and Jacqueline Wetz. *The Co-operative Glass Company Sandwich, Massachusetts: 1888–1891*. Sandwich, Massachusetts: Barn Lantern Publishing, 1976.

Williams, Lenore Wheeler. *Sandwich Glass*. Bridgeport, Connecticut: The Park City Eng. Co., 1922.

Wilson, Kenneth M. *New England Glass & Glassmaking*. New York, New York: Thomas Y. Crowell Company, 1972.

Winsor, Justin. *The Memorial History of Boston; Including Suffolk County, Massachusetts 1630–1880*. (IV vols.) Boston, Massachusetts: James R. Osgood and Company, 1881.

(no author). "Cape Cod, Nantucket, and the Vineyard." *Harper's New Monthly Magazine* LI (c. 1870), pp. 52–66.

CATALOGS

A. L. Blackmer Co. Rich Cut Glass 1906–1907. Shreveport, Louisiana: The American Cut Glass Association, reprinted in 1982.

Amberina; 1884 New England Glass Works; 1917 Libbey Glass Company. Toledo, Ohio: Antique & Historical Glass Foundation, reprinted in 1970.

Averbeck Rich Cut Glass Catalog No. 104, The. Berkeley, California: Cembura & Avery Publishers, reprinted in 1973.

Boston & Sandwich Glass Co., Boston. Wellesley Hills, Massachusetts: Lee Publications, reprinted in 1968.

Boston & Sandwich Glass Co. Price List. Collection of the Sandwich Glass Museum, Sandwich Historical Society, Sandwich, Massachusetts, n.d.

Catalog of 700 Packages Flint Glass Ware Manufactured by the Cape Cod Glass Works, to be Sold at the New England Trade Sale, Wednesday, July 14, 1859 at 9½ O'clock. Collection of the Rakow Library, The Corning Museum of Glass, Corning, New York, 1859.

C. Dorflinger & Sons Cut Glass Catalog. Silver Spring, Maryland: Christian Dorflinger Glass Study Group, reprinted in 1981.

Collector's Paperweights; Price Guide and Catalog. Santa Cruz, California: Paperweight Press, 1983.

Cut Glass Produced by the Laurel Cut Glass Company. Shreveport, Louisiana: The American Cut Glass Association, reprinted, n.d.

Dietz & Company Illustrated Catalog. Watkins Glen, New York: American Life Books, reprinted in 1982.

Egginton's Celebrated Cut Glass. Shreveport, Louisiana: The American Cut Glass Association, reprinted in 1982.

Elsholz Collection of Early American Glass (III vols.) Hyannis, Massachusetts: Richard A. Bourne Co., Inc., 1986–1987.

Empire Cut Glass Company, The. Shreveport, Louisiana: American Cut Glass Association, reprinted in 1980.

F. X. Parsche & Son Co. Shreveport, Louisiana: American Cut Glass Association, reprinted in 1981.

Glassware Catalogue No. 25 Gillinder & Sons, Inc. Spring City,

Tennessee: Hillcrest Books, reprinted in 1974.

Higgins and Seiter Fine China and Cut Glass Catalog No. 13. New York, New York: Higgins and Seiter, n.d.

Illustrated Catalog of American Hardware of the Russell and Erwin Manufacturing Company 1865. Association for Preservation Technology, reprinted in 1980.

J. D. Bergen Co., The; Manufacturers of Rich Cut Glassware 1904–1905. Berkeley, California: Cembura & Avery Publishers, reprinted in 1973.

Lackawanna Cut Glass Co. Shreveport, Louisiana: The American Cut Glass Association, reprinted, n.d.

Launay Hautin & Cie. Collection de dessins representant... Collection of the Rakow Library, The Corning Museum of Glass, Corning, New York, n.d.

Launay Hautin & Cie. Des Fabriques de Baccarat, St. Louis, Choisey et Bercy. Collection of the Rakow Library, The Corning Museum of Glass, Corning, New York, n.d.

Launay Hautin & Cie. Repertoire des Articles compris dans la Collection... Collection of the Rakow Library, The Corning Museum of Glass, Corning, New York, 1844.

Launay Hautin & Cie. Usages principaux pour services de table... Collection of the Rakow Library, The Corning Museum of Glass, Corning, New York, n.d.

Libbey Glass Co., The; Cut Glass June 1st, 1896. Toledo, Ohio: Antique & Historical Glass Foundation, reprinted in 1968.

List of Glass Ware Manufactured by Cape Cod Glass Company. Collection of the Sandwich Glass Museum, Sandwich Historical Society, Sandwich, Massachusetts, n.d.

M'Kee Victorian Glass; Five Complete Glass Catalogs from 1859/60 to 1871. New York, New York: Dover Publications, Inc., reprinted in 1981.

Monroe Cut Glass. Shreveport, Louisiana: American Cut Glass Association, reprinted, n.d.

Morey, Churchill & Morey Pocket Guide to 1880 Table Settings. Watkins Glen, New York: Century House, reprinted, n.d.

Mt. Washington Glass Co. Clinton, Maryland: Leonard E. Padgett, reprinted in 1976.

Mt. Washington Glass Company (cut glassware). Collection of the Rakow Library, The Corning Museum of Glass, Corning, New York, n.d.

Mt. Washington Glass Company; Crystal Gas Fixtures. Collection of the Rakow Library, The Corning Museum of Glass, Corning, New York, n.d.

Mt. Washington Glass Works (glass prisms and beads). Collection of the Rakow Library, The Corning Museum of Glass, Corning, New York, n.d.

Mt. Washington Glass Works Price List. Collection of the Rakow Library, The Corning Museum of Glass, Corning, New York, n.d.

New England Glass Company. Collection of the Rakow Library, The Corning Museum of Glass, Corning, New York, n.d.

New England Glass Company (list of glassware). Collection of the Rakow Library, The Corning Museum of Glass, Corning, New York, n.d.

Picture Book of Authentic Mid-Victorian Gas Lighting Fixtures; A Reprint of the Historic Mitchell, Vance & Co. Catalog, ca. 1876, with Over 1000 Illustrations. Mineola, New York: Dover Publications, Inc., reprinted in 1984.

Plume & Atwood Manufacturing Company, The. Simpson, Illinois: J. W. Courter Enterprises, reprinted in 1975.

Public Auction Richard A. Bourne Company, Inc. Boston, Massachusetts: The Nimrod Press, Inc., 1970–1992.

Quaker City Cut Glass Co. Shreveport, Louisiana: American Cut Glass Association, n.d.

Rich Cut Glass Pitkin & Brooks. Berkeley, California: Cembura & Avery Publishers, reprinted in 1973.

Sandwich Glass Patterns. West Englewood, New Jersey: Bernadine Forgett, c. 1960.

Taylor Bros. & Company, Inc., Manufacturers of Cut Glass. Shreveport, Louisiana: American Cut Glass Association, n.d.

Whitall, Tatum & Co. Price List 1895. Philadelphia, Pennsylvania; New York, New York; Boston, Massachusetts: Whitall, Tatum & Co., 1895.

BUSINESS DIRECTORIES

Boston City Directories. 1789–1891.

Longworth's American Almanac, New York Register, and City Directory. 1824–1833.

Resident and Business Directory of Bourne, Falmouth and Sandwich, Massachusetts. Hopkinton, Massachusetts: A. E. Foss & Co., 1900

NEWSPAPERS AND TRADE PAPERS

Academy Breezes. 1884–1886.

Acorn, The. Sandwich, Massachusetts: The Sandwich Historical Society, 1967–1987, 1990–1992.

American Collector. New York, New York: Educational Publishing Corporation, 1933–1946.

Barnstable County Gazette. 1826.

Barnstable Patriot. 1846–1869.

Barnstable Patriot and Commercial Advertiser. 1830–1846.

Barnstable Patriot, The. 1869–1905, 1912–1916, 1918–1923.

Berkshire Evening Eagle. Pittsfield, Massachusetts: Eagle Publishing Company, 1948.

Berkshire Hills, The. Pittsfield, Massachusetts: 1904.

Boston Commercial Gazette. 1818–1828.

Bourne Pioneer, The. 1906–1907.

Brockton Searchlight, The. 1909.

Cape Cod Advocate, and Nautical Intelligencer. 1851–1864.

Cape Cod Gazette. 1870–1872.

Casino Bulletin. 1884–1885.

Chronicle of the Early American Industries Association, The. Flushing, New York: Leon S. Case, January 1938.

Crockery & Glass Journal. New York, New York: George Whittemore & Company, 1885–1890.

Crockery Journal. New York, New York: George Whittemore & Company, 1874–1884.

Cullet from the Glass Museum. Sandwich, Massachusetts: The Sandwich Historical Society, 1987–1992.

Glass Club Bulletin, The. The National Early American Glass Club, 1938–1992.

Hyannis Patriot, The. 1908–1909, 1916–1918, 1923–1925.

Illuminator, The. Toronto, Ontario, Canada: The Historical Lighting Society of Canada, 1987–1988.

Independent, The. 1895–1908.

Independent Chronicle, The. 1787.

Nautical Intelligencer, and Barnstable County Gazette. 1824.

Nautical Intelligencer and Falmouth and Holmes'-Hole Journal. 1823–1824.

Old Colony Memorial. 1827–1832.

Old Colony Memorial & Plymouth County Advertiser. 1822–1827.

Pittsburg Glass Journal. The Pittsburgh Chapter of the National Early American Glass Club, 1989–1991.

Sandwich Collector, The. East Sandwich, Massachusetts: McCue Publications, 1984–1985.

Sandwich Independent. 1920–1921.

Sandwich Independent, The. 1908–1909.

Sandwich Mechanic and Family Visitor. 1851.

Sandwich Observer. 1846–1851.

Sandwich Observer, The. 1884–1895, 1910–1911.

Sandwich Review, The. 1889–1890.

Seaside Press, The. 1873–1880.

Village Broadsider, The. 1978–1985.

Weekly Review, The. 1881–1882.

Yarmouth Register and Barnstable County Advertiser. 1836–1839.

Yarmouth Register and Barnstable County Weekly Advertiser. 1839–1846.

Yarmouth Register. 1849–1906.

BARLOW-KAISER
SANDWICH GLASS
PRICE GUIDE

for pieces in perfect condition

FOURTH EDITION

to be used with Volumes 1, 2, 3 and 4 of

THE GLASS INDUSTRY IN SANDWICH
and
A GUIDE TO SANDWICH GLASS

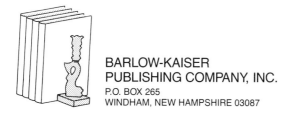

**BARLOW-KAISER
PUBLISHING COMPANY, INC.**
P.O. BOX 265
WINDHAM, NEW HAMPSHIRE 03087

INTRODUCTION TO PRICE GUIDE

It is most important to determine the condition of a glass item before you purchase it. We are often so fascinated by a good "find" that we miss its obvious condition. The prices in this guide are for items that are in perfect, or *mint*, condition. *Mint condition* is an article of glass that is pristine. It has no defects. If there is roughage only in places where there are mold marks, it is still considered to be mint, because if the item was good enough to pass inspection at the time of production, it is good enough to be called mint today. Shear marks (often called "straw marks"), caused by cutting through a glob of glass while it was hot, do not detract from value. They are a fact of construction procedure. Manufacturing errors, such as annealing marks, bent or twisted pieces, off-center pieces, underfilled or overfilled molds, and overheating, add character to a piece of glass. However, the mint condition status of the glass is not affected. Rapid reductions in pricing are caused by damage after the time of manufacture in the following order, using the 100 percent value of a mint item as a base.

An unusually rare article, even though broken, must be considered for purchase regardless of price, if the serious collector is to have an example of that article.

Glass cannot be repaired without removing additional glass to smooth out or eliminate a chip. The "repair" rarely adds to value because the form of the article is altered. A goblet that has been machined down to eliminate a rim chip will not match its undamaged counterparts.

CONDITION	MAXIMUM VALUE OF MINT
CHIPPED Damage serious enough to penetrate into the body of an article, but small or shallow enough so that it cannot be glued back or replaced.	80%
BRUISED When an article has been struck with enough force to send cracks in several directions, penetrating the surface at the center.	60%
CRACKED When the glass is split through one or more layers, caused by a blow, a change in temperature, or stress in the glass at the time of manufacture. This is the first stage of deterioration, leading to eventual destruction. Value is seriously affected.	50%
BROKEN An article is broken when it is in two pieces, even though one of the pieces may only be the tip of a scallop, or the corner of a base, or the peg of a lamp font. If one piece must be glued back in order to make the article whole, the article is broken and its value must be reduced accordingly.	25%

PRESSED TABLEWARE

Most glass produced in Sandwich factories was clear, so expect the price of colored articles to be high. Reproductions issued by museum gift shops have contaminated the antiques market. Learn where the "repros" were signed. Inspect for damage that may indicate the removal of a museum "logo".

Photo No.	Clear	Clambroth (Alabaster)	Opaque White	Canary	Amber	Blue	Amethyst	Green	Unusual Color
1001 a	100								
b	100								
1002 a	100					350			
b	100					350			
c	125					475			
1003	450								
1004	100								
1005	45								
1006 a	45								
b	285								
1007	550								
1008	300								
1009	200								
1010	475								
1011 a	400								
b	—								
1012	900								
1013	4000								
1014 a	125								
b	60								
1015	45					175			
1016	60					350			
1017 a	125								
b	80								
1018 a	550								
b	80								
1019	700								
1020	38								
1021	125						625 pale		
1022	210								
1023	225								
1024	325								
1025	45								
1026 a	900								
b	40								
1027	900								
1028	2500					4500			
1029	3800					6500			
1030 a	1000								
b	—								
1031	1500			11,000		14,000	11,000		
1032	1400								
1033 a	40			200		200	275	200	
b	40			200		200	275	200	
1034	40			200		200	275	200	
1035	175								
1036	1800								
1037 a	45								
b	38								

Photo No.	Clear	Clambroth (Alabaster)	Opaque White	Canary	Amber	Blue	Amethyst	Green	Unusual Color
1038	38					175	200	300	
1039 a	550								
b	75	350 fiery opalescent					350		
1040	500			1200		3000	3000		15,000+
1041	450	2750 fiery opalescent							
1042	500		1200			1750 opaque	2000		
1043	500					4800			6000
1044	650								
1045	90								
1046	300	700 fiery opalescent							
1047	4000								
1048	1200								
1049	1500					5500			
1050	375	1600	500			2000	2800	6500	
1051	5200			15,000		12,000			
1052	6500			20,000					
1053	700			3200		3600			
1054	650								
1055	90					800			
1056	235	1400 fiery opalescent	525			1600			
1057	38	110	110	210	450	375	375	450	550
1058 a	38	110	110	210	450	375	375	450	550
b	500			900		1100		2400	
1059 a	38			210		375		450	
b	450			1100		1200			
1060	42								
1061 a	900								
b	250								
1062	7500								
1063	7500								
1064	650					6000			
1065	750								
1066	475								
1067	45			250 pale					
1068 a	750								
b	85								
1069	110								
1070	85 / 1100 silver nitrate								
1071	135			1800		2500			
1072	185								
1073	—								

Photo No.	Clear	Clambroth (Alabaster)	Opaque White	Canary	Amber	Blue	Amethyst	Green	Unusual Color
1074	125								
1075 a	550								
b	600								
1076	135								
1077	1100								
1078	2400								
1079	375					4000			
1080	525								
1081	4800								
1082	625								
1083	525					2100			
1084	235	1000	900	1200		1400	1800		
1085	35			250		300	325		
1086 a	185					875			
b	—								
1087	375			2000		3200			
1088	210						500 pale		
1089	210								
1090	285								
1091	140								
1092	120								
1093	900								
1094	130								
1095	185								
1096	875								
1097	140					300			
1098	35								
1099	175								
1100	1250								
1101	110 1800 silver nitrate								
1102	225							750	
1103	575								
1104	150								
1105	150								
1106 a	250								
b	195								
1107	80	450 fiery opalescent							
1108	80								
1109	65	150 fiery opalescent				300	400		
1110 a	80	210 fiery opalescent				400	500		
b	35	125 fiery opalescent						100 pale	
1111 a	1100								

Photo No.	Clear	Clambroth (Alabaster)	Opaque White	Canary	Amber	Blue	Amethyst	Green	Unusual Color
b	90	250 fiery opalescent							
1112	55					400			
1113 a	125			900					
b	50			875					
1114	140								
1115 a	185								
b	110								
1116	65 85 gilded								
1117	110			1100		1500			
1118	110								
1119 a	95			400		500			
b	65								
1120	150			450					
1121	500								
1122	150								
1123	150								
1124	235								
1125	1600								
1126	1600	10,000 fiery opalescent					12,000	20,000	16,000+
1127	25			95		135			
1128	25					125			
1129 a	28					75			
b	25					125			
1130	110				450	375			
1131	65								
1132 a	65								
b	20					120			
1133	1750			4200		6500			
1134	40			650		725		850 peacock	
1135	110			900		1400			
1136 a	45			625	1050	850	950	1050	
b	45			625	1050	850	950	1050	
1137	60			625					
1138	55								
1139	65								
1140	35						185		
1141	235			3200		7500	7500		
1142 a	35			275		450			
b	—								
1143	95	575 fiery opalescent		2200		2400 peacock			
1144	185			2000		2500			
1145	15			85					
1146	235					2500			
1147	185			2000			3000		
1148	265						3000		

Photo No.	Clear	Clambroth (Alabaster)	Opaque White	Canary	Amber	Blue	Amethyst	Green	Unusual Color
1149	265			2000					
1150	95			600					
1151	375	6500 fiery opalescent		4000			6500		
1152 a	250			1600					
b	—								
1153	235			3200		7500	8000		
1154	35 ea.								
1155	110			1200					
1156	95	375 fiery opalescent							
1157	150	600 fiery opalescent							
1158	75	350 fiery opalescent					350		
1159	50 ea.			875 ea.					
1160	300 pr.								
1161	165								
1162	195								
1163 a	55			350			750		
b	60			350			750		
1164	60 ea.			350 ea.			750 ea.		
1165 a	95								
b	50								
1166	95		250	400		600			
1167	85			1400					
1168	225			1400					
1169	285			3200					
1170	100			900					
1171	475								
1172	600								
1173	110			1050					
1174	650								
1175	525			5400		6500	7500		
1176	1500			10,000		15,000	18,000		25,000+
1177	85								
1178	110			1200					
1179	85 ea.	1100 ea. fiery opalescent	775 ea.	1400 ea.		1500 ea.			
1180	95			700			750		
1181 a	110			850			1400		
b	85					900			
1182 a	110								
b	55								
1183	28								
1184	165		400						
1185	135	1200 fiery opalescent							

Photo No.	Clear	Clambroth (Alabaster)	Opaque White	Canary	Amber	Blue	Amethyst	Green	Unusual Color
1186 a	75								
b	75								
1187 a	125	900 fiery opalescent				1500			
b	400								
1188	165			650		1000			
1189	325						1200 light		
1190 a	—								
b	18								
1191 a	235								
b	285								
1192	55								
1193	55								
1194	50	400 fiery opalescent							
1195	95		185			525			
1196 a	110								
b	110								
1197	75					325			
1198 a	55								
b	—								
1199	—								
1200 a	65 / 80 engraved								
b	15 ea. / 18 ea. engraved								
1201	30 / 40 engraved								
1202 a	40								
b	—								
1203 a	70								
b	75								
c	55								
d	125								
1204 a	125								
b	60 without cover	225 without cover	300 without cover	550 without cover		550 without cover		750 without cover	
c	75								
1205	100								
1206 a	75								
b	70								
c	75								
1207	35 ea. without cover	235 ea. without cover fiery opalescent							

Photo No.	Clear	Clambroth (Alabaster)	Opaque White	Canary	Amber	Blue	Amethyst	Green	Unusual Color
1208 a	40					140			
b	—								
1209	—								
1210	85 engraved								
1211 a	18			100	160	120	120	175	
b	28			125	175	150	150	200	
c	185						575		
1212 a	150								
b	185								
1213	55								
1214	550		750						
1215	45					1800			
1216 a	55								
b	195		575						
1217	—								
1218	275								
1219	55								
1220	45								
1221	325								
1222 a	65								
b	375		575						
1223 a	95								
b	185								
1224 a	35								
b	95								
1225 a	95								
b	145								
1226	75								
1227	50								
1228	95								
1229	55	325 / 375 gilded				1100 / 1250 gilded		1300 / 1450 gilded	
1230	225								
1231 a	125								
b	160								
1232 a	50								
b	40								
1233	325 pr. / 500 pr. engraved								
1234 a	135								
b	160								
1235	95								
1236	115 / 265 decorated		300					575	
1237 a	525								
b	475								
1238	525								
1239	110								
1240 a	85								
b	—								

Photo No.	Clear	Clambroth (Alabaster)	Opaque White	Canary	Amber	Blue	Amethyst	Green	Unusual Color
1241	18								
1242	55								
1243 a	90								
b	115								
1244	295 the set								
1245	40								
1246	40								
1247	65								
1248	30								
1249	35								
1250 a	12 / 15 gilded								
b	28 / 35 gilded								
1251	135 / 165 gilded								
1252 a			115						
b			65						

FREE-BLOWN AND BLOWN MOLDED TABLEWARE

Most glass produced in Sandwich factories was clear, so expect the price of colored articles to be high. Blown objects have been heavily reproduced. It is difficult to find originals on the open market. Pieces accompanied by family documentation are worth up to three times more.

Photo No.	Clear	Clambroth (Alabaster)	Opaque White	Canary	Amber	Blue	Amethyst	Green	Unusual Color
1253	400								
1254	125					525	525		
1255	180 with stopper								
1256 a	140			750		900	900		
b	80			700		850	850		
1257	400								
1258	18								120
1259	18 ea.			25 ea.	45 ea.	30 ea.			
1260	18 ea.			25 ea.	45 ea.	30 ea.			
1261		45 opal decorated							
1262	225								
1263	325								
1264	125								
1265	390					1500			
1266	750								
1267	700								
1268	4800								
1269	4600								

Photo No.	Clear	Clambroth (Alabaster)	Opaque White	Canary	Amber	Blue	Amethyst	Green	Unusual Color
1270	—								
1271	3200								
1272	3800								
1273	110					325			
1274 a	45 with stopper								
b	—								
c	45 with cap								
1275	180					450	475		
1276	35					235	250		
1277	70								
1278 a	235								
b	—								
1279	180 ea.					450 ea.	475 ea.		
1280 a	180					450	475		
b	180					450	475		
1281 a	235								
b	110								
c	100								
1282 a	70								
b	70								
1283	—								
1284	475 the set								
1285	—								
1286	235 with cap								
1287	—								
1288	90					325			
1289	125								
1290	125							150 pale	
1291	250								
1292	150					375			
1293 a	150					375			
b	185					750			
1294	275								
1295	425								
1296	200								
1297	175								
1298	165								
1299	600								
1300	1500					2200			
1301	600								
1302	900								
1303	235								
1304	325								
1305 a	150								
b	25								
1306 a	225								
b	225								
1307	275								
1308	325								

Photo No.	Clear	Clambroth (Alabaster)	Opaque White	Canary	Amber	Blue	Amethyst	Green	Unusual Color
1309	4200					6000			
1310	235								
1311	875								
1312	325								
1313	275								
1314	400								
1315	125								
1316 a	220								
b	275								
1317	325								
1318	275								
1319 a	275								
b	25								
1320 a	190								
b	225								
1321	600								
1322	275								
1323 a	150					600			
b	1200								
1324	800								
1325	575					2200	3000		
1326	600					3200			
1327	235								
1328	115								
1329	275								
1330	300								
1331	235 ea.								
1332	1200 the set								
1333	775					4000	3800		
1334 a	235					900			
b	250					1000	1200		
1335	875					4000			
1336	550								
1337	140 without stopper								
1338 a	250								
b	550								
1339 a	2100								
b	900								

PRESSED CUP PLATES

A cup plate with a pontil mark is a base that was broken away from a lamp or a candlestick. It should not be highly valued. The invention of the cap ring allowed the number and shape of rim scallops to vary on the same pattern cup plate. This variation does not indicate a rare example and does not affect value of a given cup plate pattern. Value is not affected by slight changes in pattern due to handwork by the mold maker. Prices given for unrecorded colors may be for variants.

Photo No.	Clear	Clambroth (Alabaster)	Fiery Opalescent	Opaque White	Amber	Blue	Amethyst	Green	Unusual Color
1340 a	52								
b	—								

Photo No.	Clear	Clambroth (Alabaster)	Fiery Opalescent	Opaque White	Amber	Blue	Amethyst	Green	Unusual Color
c	35					400			
d	35								
1341	55								175 pale pink
1342 a	32					900			
b	35								
1343 a	110								
b	35								
c	38					750			
d	32					900			
1344 a	35								
b	40								
c	48								
1345	45				225				
1346	42								
1347	48		175					235 pale	
1348	60		235						
1349	75						650		850 black
1350	30								
1351	1600								
1352	60		250 blue						
1353	50								
1354	90					1500 silver-blue			
1355	40			175		1500 silver-blue			
1356	55					1500 silver-blue			
1357	75					1600 silver-blue			
1358	—								
1359	25								
1360	45								
1361	75								
1362	75								
1363	75								
1364	35							395	
1365	40		135			180 opalescent			
1366	100					450		650	
1367	110								
1368	38								
1369	32 ea.	150 ea.							
1370	60								
1371	32					235 / 235 pale	235 / 235 pale		
1372	38					350 peacock			
1373	38								
1374	35	90		90					
1375	250								

Photo No.	Clear	Clambroth (Alabaster)	Fiery Opalescent	Opaque White	Amber	Blue	Amethyst	Green	Unusual Color
1376	—								
1377	50			110					
1378	50					390		650	
1379	65		175			600		850	
1380	32	90		110		375	375	450	
1381	35			110				275 pale	
1382	25	90					135 pale		
1383	20								
1384	35								
1385	28		90		500		375		
1386	35					175 pale			
1387	40								
1388	32								400 canary
1389	35					195			
1390	20								
1391	20								
1392	25	85						375	
1393	18								
1394	22								400 canary
1395	60					1000	450 light	1000	
1396	48					250		1000	
1397	55					350	650		
1398	22					400		875	875 canary
1399 a	32						550		
b	28	190				250		350	
1400	28								1000 opaque green
1401	28						500	850	
1402	25	110							
1403	22								
1404	35					500			
1405	22				275	375 / 325 peacock	175 light	375 / 325 peacock	
1406	22	90		90	400 red-amber		250		
1407	30					300 / 250 pale		450 / 425 pale	375 yellow-green
1408	22	250							
1409	40								
1410	35					500			
1411	30		175						
1412	350								
1413	35					225		375 pale	

Photo No.	Clear	Clambroth (Alabaster)	Fiery Opalescent	Opaque White	Amber	Blue	Amethyst	Green	Unusual Color
1414	50		325						
1415	50				400	425			1000 citron
1416	100								
1417	75				450				
1418	100	90				375 / 400 peacock		210 pale	
1419	75	250				325			
1420 a	800 silver nitrate center								
b	2000 silver nitrate border								
1421	2000 silver nitrate								
1422	100					325		1400	
1423	100					1200			
1424	40					500			750 canary
1425	50							2500	
1426	100					1000		3500	
1427	55								
1428	80								

OPEN AND SHAKER SALTS

Plain, heavy open salts made during the first decade of production do not command the prices of intricately molded Lacy pieces. An intense color is worth more than a pale color. Expect to pay more for shakers with patented devices that break up the salt. A slight variation in a mold due to handwork by a mold maker does not affect value. Prices given for unrecorded colors may be for variants.

Photo No.	Clear	Clambroth (Alabaster)	Fiery Opalescent	Canary	Amber	Blue	Amethyst	Green	Unusual Color
1429	35						750		
1430	350								
1431	125					600			
1432	400					600			
1433	400 without cover					600 without cover			
1434 a	400 without cover					600 without cover			
b	400					600			
1435	150					600			
1436	60							375	
1437 a	40								
b	—								

Photo No.	Clear	Clambroth (Alabaster)	Fiery Opalescent	Canary	Amber	Blue	Amethyst	Green	Unusual Color
1438 a	30								
b	—								
1439	85				450	450		550 yellow-green	700
1440	85					450		550	700
1441	85					450			700
1442 a	60								
b						750			
1443	150	300	300			500 900 silver-blue			
1444	80	450	450			700			875
1445	60					750 1000 silver-blue			
1446	40							350 light	
1447	125	225	225		600	500		875	1000
1448	150 without cover	225 without cover				350 without cover	450 without cover		600 without cover
1449	900	1200				1400	1600		
1450	135					575			700
1451 a	900		900			1400	1600		
b	—								
1452	175								
1453	200		750		875			1000	
1454	375							450 pale	
1455		225							
1456	35				150	175	200		200
1457	110				300	275			
1458	150								
1459	100				400	250		375	400
1460 a	185					900 silver-blue			
b	150					500			
1461	75					1000 silver-blue			400 opaque white
1462	75					375 pale			
1463	300	575				900			
1464 a	300					1100 silver-blue 1100 opalescent			
b			1500			900			
1465	125	575	575			575		650	750
1466	110					475		575	
1467	150					900			
1468	150					900			
1469 a	300					1500			
b	300		1100			1500			

Photo No.	Clear	Clambroth (Alabaster)	Fiery Opalescent	Canary	Amber	Blue	Amethyst	Green	Unusual Color
1470 a	300								
b	—								
1471	125				300			575	2000
					750				black
					red-amber				
1472	25				150	140	185		
1473	25				150	140	185		
1474 a	35								
b	—								
1475 a	25								
b	—								
1476	35 ea.					185 ea.			
1477	60								
1478 a	28					500			
b	225								
1479 a	28					500			
b	60								
1480	32			125		225			
1481	175								
1482	65								
	85								
	frosted								
1483	75								
1484	110								
1485	75 ea.		150 ea.	235 ea.		425 ea.			
1486	2 ea.	8 ea.			8 ea.	8 ea.			
	1000								
	twelve								
	with box								
1487 a	35					90	110		
b	—								
1488 a	35	60				90	110		
		opaque							
b	—								
1489	32					90	110		
1490 a	—								
b	3	8				8			
		opaque							
1491	65 ea.								
1492	65								
1493	90								
	silvered								
	engraved								
1494	90								
	silvered								
	engraved								
1495 a	15	35		90	140	200	275	250	400
		opal							ruby
b	15	35		90	140	200	275	250	400
		opal				250			ruby
						peacock			
c	150								
	stand								

Photo No.	Clear	Clambroth (Alabaster)	Fiery Opalescent	Canary	Amber	Blue	Amethyst	Green	Unusual Color
1496	180 the set	200 opal the set		300 the set	450 the set	500 the set	650 the set	600 the set	1000 ruby the set
1497	40	60		115	165	225 / 275 peacock	300	275	425 ruby
1498		110 ea. opal decorated							
1499 a	35				175	175	325	325	
b	55				200	200	375	375	
1500 a		85 opal decorated							
b		40 opal decorated							
1501		90 ea. opal decorated							
1502		450 opal decorated the set							
1503		235 pr. opal decorated							
1504						150 spangle			